Modern Protestantism
and Positive Law

Modern Protestantism and Positive Law

The Contours of a Continental Theological Tradition

BRADLEY SHINGLETON

☙PICKWICK *Publications* · Eugene, Oregon

MODERN PROTESTANTISM AND POSITIVE LAW
The Contours of a Continental Theological Tradition

Copyright © 2019 Bradley Shingleton. All rights reserved. Except for brief quotations in critical publications or reviews, no part of this book may be reproduced in any manner without prior written permission from the publisher. Write: Permissions, Wipf and Stock Publishers, 199 W. 8th Ave., Suite 3, Eugene, OR 97401.

Pickwick Publications
An Imprint of Wipf and Stock Publishers
199 W. 8th Ave., Suite 3
Eugene, OR 97401

www.wipfandstock.com

PAPERBACK ISBN: 978-1-5326-1902-1
HARDCOVER ISBN: 978-1-4982-4503-6
EBOOK ISBN: 978-1-4982-4502-9

Cataloguing-in-Publication data:

Names: Shingleton, Bradley, author.

Title: Modern protestantism and positive law : the contours of a continental theological tradition / by Bradley Shingleton.

Description: Eugene, OR : Pickwick Publications, 2019 | Includes bibliographical references.

Identifiers: ISBN 978-1-5326-1902-1 (paperback) | ISBN 978-1-4982-4503-6 (hardcover) | ISBN 978-1-4982-4502-9 (ebook)

Subjects: LCSH: Religion and law—Germany—History. | Reformation—Germany. | Law and ethics. | Church and state. | Religion and state.

Classification: KK381 .S56 2019 (print) | KK381 .S56 (ebook)

Manufactured in the U.S.A.   MARCH 30, 2021

In Memory of My Parents
and
Dedicated to Sherburne, Bill, and Matt

Contents

Preface | ix
Acknowledgments | xi
Abbreviations | xii

I Introduction | 1

II Karl Barth—The Christocentric Premise of Law | 28

III Emil Brunner—The Orders of Creation and Law | 63

IV Jacques Ellul—The Foundation of Law | 91

V Erik Wolf—The Law of the Neighbor | 124

VI Helmut Thielicke—Law as Provisional Compromise | 144

VII Wolfhart Pannenberg—Law as Mutuality and Reciprocity | 169

VIII Wolfgang Huber—Law as an Instrument of Preferential Justice | 196

IX Postscript: Hartmut Kreβ—The Ethics of the Legal Order | 225

X Toward a Conclusion | 233

Bibliography | 251

Preface

This book presents a critical exposition and assessment of the thought about positive law of several major figures in modern continental Protestantism. In large part, it aims to define and introduce a tradition of theological and ethical reflection on human law that has not been accessible to a North American audience because a number of their writings are unavailable in English. And although several of the thinkers here, such as Barth and Brunner, are well known in the Anglophone world, their reflections on positive law have received little critical attention. Hopefully, this book will prompt greater interest in and appreciation of their insights about a vital social institution.

A further aim of the book is to contribute, however modestly, to the multi-disciplinary study of law, religion, theology, and ethics. Although the cultural, legal and theological contexts of the theologies and ethics of law discussed here vary from those of contemporary America, many of the themes and problems with which these authors grapple are relevant for us as well.

I wrote this book after a career as a practicing attorney. My view of the law has been deeply affected by my professional experience over several decades. I have come to see that law shapes all kinds of personal and collective activity—for better and for worse. Law can be oppressive and inhumane, but it can also be deeply humanizing and civilizing. Even for those who have no daily involvement with it, it serves an indispensable social and political role. Its improvement should be a concern of everyone who benefits from it, that is to say, all of us.

Portions of chapters 5, 6, and 7 are drawn from my previous publications in the *Journal of Law and Religion* and the *Oxford Journal of Law and Religion* (see Bibliography). That material has been considerably expanded and revised for these pages.

Acknowledgments

I would like to express my appreciation to the following people who helped make this book a reality. Kenneth Glazer, Bruce Russell, Mary Lou Savage, and Timothy Fort read portions of the manuscript and offered valuable comments. I thank Professor Dr. Harmut Kreß of Bonn for his interest in this project and for his comments on various parts of the text. I would also like to acknowledge Ilonka Osvald for her terrific assistance with preparation of the manuscript and Wesley Seminary Library for research assistance. Of course, remaining errors are my own. The editors and staff at Wipf and Stock provided expert guidance through the publication process. Above all, I would like to thank my wife, Sherburne Laughlin, for her patience during the long hours I spent researching and writing. For this, I am more grateful than I can say.

—Bradley Shingleton
April 2019

Abbreviations

CD   Barth, Karl. *Church Dogmatics*. Translated by G. T. Thomson et al. 13 vols. Edinburgh: T. & T. Clark, 1936–77.

RPP   *Religion Past and Present: Encyclopedia of Theology and Religion*. Edited by Hans Dieter Betz et al. 14 vols. Leiden: Brill, 2007–2013.

TRE   *Theologische Realenzyklopädie*. Edited by Gerhard Müller et al. 36 vols. Berlin: de Gruyter, 1977–2004.

I

Introduction

Law bears deeply on a broad range of individual and social activity, from the routine to the profound. It expresses the highest aspirations of a society as well as its most basic rules of interaction. "Law," asserts Ronald Dworkin, "is our most structured and revealing social institution."[1] Yet contemporary Protestant theology and social ethics has had relatively little to say about positive law. Wolfgang Huber speaks of the "marginal interest" of theological ethics in law and refers to positive law as a neglected area in Protestant theology.[2] Other writers have expressed similar opinions.[3] Why is this?

From a theological perspective, this situation is somewhat surprising. Law is an essential theological category in western religion.[4] It is a

1. Dworkin, *Law's Empire*, 11.

2. Huber, *Gerechtigkeit*, 14. All translations from German sources throughout are mine, except as otherwise indicated.

3. The adjective "marginal" recurs in this connection. For example, Kerstin Gäfgen refers to the "unjustified marginalization of law" in theology (Gäfgen, *Recht*, 1); Hartmut Kreβ observes that legal themes have been dealt with only "marginally" (Kreβ, "Sonne der Gerechtigkeit," 235); Hans-Richard Reuter observes that the number of twentieth-century theological authors with a developed concept of law is quite limited (Reuter, *Rechtsethik*, 92); and Christian Starck alludes to the "uncertain restraint" with which Protestant dogmatic theology has approached positive law (Starck, "Law and Legislation," 373).

4. Conceptually, law has various usages and meanings, depending on context: theological, philosophical, scientific and jurisprudential. The focus here is on positive law (*ius positivum*), and is alternately referred in this book as "mundane" or "human" law. A legal dictionary defines positive law as "law actually and specifically enacted or adopted by proper authority for the government of an organized jural societies" (Black, *Black's Law Dictionary*, 1324). Unless otherwise specified, references in the text relate to law as positive law.

constitutive element of Jewish faith and tradition, comprising a comprehensive body of interpretation and learning relevant for individual and social life.[5] Christian tradition is also deeply concerned with law. The Protestant reformers viewed human law as an indispensable element of social theology and ethics.[6] Their treatment of law was epochal for jurisprudence and legal philosophy. John Witte Jr. describes the effect of the Protestant Reformation as one of the watershed events in the Western legal tradition.[7]

Some of the reasons for the estrangement of theology and law are theological in nature. Ernst Wolf contends that the alienation between the two domains in German Protestantism began in the seventeenth century with "its rejection of the catholic notion of *ius divinum*, its discarding of divine law, and ultimately law itself from the realm of faith, its juxtaposition of both divine and human justice and love and law."[8] Further, Wolf claims that Luther's doctrine of two kingdoms was often interpreted such that the two realms became bifurcated, with individual Christians having dual citizenship in separate realms. As a result, law as an institution of the wordly kingdom became emptied of theological significance.[9] These tendencies led to Rudolph Sohm's influential opposition of secular law and the law of love (*Liebesrecht*) on the other, a view that has continued to color later theological thinking about law in German legal and theological cultures.[10] The result is what Ralf Dreier terms "a certain alienation from law" in Lutheran thought that contrasts with notions of communal democracy in the Reformed traditions that accord law a more affirmative role in social life.[11]

Certain cultural circumstances have also disfavored theological engagement with positive law. To the extent that theological reflection on law is seen as a kind of public theology, it is viewed by some as outmoded and problematical. When understood as a discipline that belongs in religious communities, theology is often considered to have little to say about matters in the public square.[12] While this view is not universally held, it complicates

---

5. See generally Novak, "Law and Religion in Judaism." Wolfhart Pannenberg notes that "the God of Israel is in a particular way a God of law" (Pannenberg, "Christliche Rechtsbegründung," 327).

6. See Robbers, "Grundsatzfragen der heutigen Rechtstheologie," 230.

7. Witte, "Protestantism and Legal Thought," 222.

8. Wolf, "Protestanischen Rechtsdenken."

9. Pannenberg argues in a similar manner; see Pannenberg, "Luther's Doctrine of the Two Kingdoms," 112–31. For Calvin's view of positive law and its relation to natural and divine law, see Little, *Religion, Law and Order*, 33.

10. On Sohm's theory of law, see Adams, "Law and the Religious Spirit," 188–206.

11. Dreier, "Recht," 1454.

12. See generally Tracy, *Analogical Imagination*, on the diminished status of public theology.

theological engagement with public institutions such as law. It requires justification.[13]

Another factor contributing to law's tangential situation in theology and ethics is the character of contemporary legal cultures in western societies. In general, those cultures tend to be considerably secularized.[14] Prevailing jurisprudential understandings emphasize the autonomy of law and its independence from ethical norms considered external to it. Theoretical analysis and interpretation of law have been largely dominated by philosophers, often of an analytic orientation, and legal academicians, who often have little professional interest in religion. (Of course, there are exceptions.) Some influential sociological theories, such as that of Niklaus Luhmann, also conceive of law in terms of an autonomous social sphere.[15] The specialization of legal knowledge and technique, along with the professionalization of legal practitioners have helped create what Judith Shklar calls an ideology of legalism that emphasizes the distinctiveness of law in comparison with other political institutions.[16] This emphasis has been counterbalanced somewhat by an increasing number of interdisciplinary studies relating law to fields such as economics, anthropology, literature and religion. In interdisciplinary studies of these kinds one or the other of the disciplines tends to have the upper hand, and sets the terms of engagement. Much activity under the rubric of law and religion concerns the legal, especially constitutional, status of religious organizations and practices rather than engagement with law from a theological or ethical perspective.

The relation between law and theology/ethics has not always been seen in this way. There have been periods of more active engagement, beginning with the Reformers themselves. Luther and Calvin were both students of the law, and were convinced of its importance for questions of social ethics. Luther was deeply concerned with the role of law in the worldly kingdom, and considered law to be 'dear' in the sense of being politically and socially indispensable. Calvin's thinking about law was deeply wedded to legal categories and modes of reasoning. As Bruce Gordon writes: "The enduring legacy of Calvin's legal training on his theology was enormous. His positive account of the law, by which believers are taught the will of God, his attachment to order and discipline in the church, and his emphasis on the majesty

---

13. For a recent effort to do so, see generally Mathewes, *Theology of Public Life*.

14. Harold Berman refers to an "almost completely secularized legal culture" (Berman, "Law and Logos," 155).

15. See, e.g., Niklas Luhmann's notion of law as an autopoetic sphere in Baxter, "Luhmann's Theory," 16–84.

16. Shklar, *Legalism*, 1–2 (defining legalism as an ideology).

of God all flow from his training in the law."[17] Law figured significantly in Calvin's social thought: his notion of the three uses of law—the political, theological and spiritual—exemplify his appreciation for the mundane as well as the theological dimensions of secular law[18]. For him, and indeed for the Reformers collectively, law was a shared social good, a vital institution with social, political and ethical dimensions. Calvin described law as "the strongest sinews of the commonwealth."[19] Its rationality and capacity to constrain and correct human misdeeds rendered law an indispensable element in the social vision of early Protestantism.

The primary concern of the Reformers was with the theological use of law.[20] This is not surprising, but they also considered the civil uses of it by emphasizing its social and ethical importance in the functioning of society. In its civil use, law serves the interest of order and therefore also of love.[21] If nothing else, this understanding of the usefulness of law shows a recognition of its importance for organized social life in its own right, and not simply from being analogous to religious law.

Law necessarily reflects assumptions about human capabilities and frailties, and it is precisely this anthropological reference that is often overlooked in contemporary jurisprudential theory. Understood in this context, law has an important therapeutic function. It prescribes, and in so doing guides conduct in beneficial directions. These convictions on the part of Luther and Calvin were not merely abstract; they were borne out of the nature of law itself. Both contemplated the character of civil law: its relation to natural law and Roman law, its need for equity and its dependence on a well-functioning judicial system. The Reformers' appreciation of law was an informed appreciation.

Protestantism's initial engagement with human law was followed by an era of progressive disengagement partially prompted by Enlightenment-era trends in jurisprudence. Already contained in the Reformers' views of secular law were the seeds of a future recognition of the independence of law from supernatural deference.[22] This reflected both the rationalization of natural law and the anthropological grounding of law in sociability or other characteristics. The legal and ethical were increasingly distinguished

---

17. Gordon, *Calvin*, 28.

18. See generally Alexander, "Validity and Function of Law"; Søe, "Three Uses of Law," 297–323.

19. Calvin, *Institutes* 4.20.14.

20. Alexander, "Validity and Function of Law," 515.

21. See Hesselink, *Calvin's Concept of Law*, 242.

22. Wolf, "Recht," 1960.

from each other, and Protestant theology progressively had less and less to say about the former.[23] Efforts to maintain the unity of law on the basis of a humanistically oriented jurisprudence were defeated by the uncoupling of divine law and natural law by Thomasius and Grotius and promotion of a rationalized foundation of natural law reflected in a *sensus communis*. To the extent this represented a re-conception of natural law on an anthropological basis in human sociality, positive law became increasingly autonomous, leaving theologians with a considerably reduced basis for engagement with positive law.[24]

The lengthy alienation of theology and law gave way in the twentieth century to renewed interest in law from a theological perspective. Germany, with its experience of totalitarianism, was the primary forum. In the decades flanking World War II, theologians such as Barth and Brunner (though both were Swiss) were forced to wrestle with questions about law; the Nazi regime had undermined and co-opted the administrative and legal structures of the Protestant Church in Germany, and promoted the German Christian movement as more in line with Nazi ideology than the established churches.[25] Though the church struggle was primarily an ecclesial conflict, it nevertheless raised pressing questions about law: When does law forfeit its status as law because of its unjustness? Is power the basis of law? How should the church react to legally sanctioned repression? These and other questions, as well as the pressure of historical circumstances that prompted them, provoked renewed engagement with law. While the focus was largely on ecclesiastical matters and canon law, it was not limited to them. Barth questioned the status of human law broadly in an essay of 1934 entitled "Rechtfertigung und Recht": "Is there an inward and vital connection by means of which in any sense human justice (or law), as well as divine justification, becomes a concern of Christian faith and Christian responsibility, and therefore also a matter that concerns the Christian Church?"[26]

---

23. Wolf, "Recht," 1960. Wolf, writing in 1957, noted that Protestantism in the seventeenth century had prepared the way for its increasing distance from secular law that has not been subsequently overcome, at least not in German Protestantism.

24. Wolf, "Recht," 1960. See also Reuter, "Rechtsethik in der Neuzeit," 230–31.

25. Brunner was in Switzerland, but nevertheless closely observed the events in Germany. See McGrath, *Brunner*. On Barth's confrontations with the Nazi regime, see Jehle, *Politics of Karl Barth's Theology*. See also Haddorff, *Barth's Ethics*; Barnett, *Protestant Resistance to Hitler*; Scholder, *Churches and the Third Reich*, 8–10.

26. Barth, "Rechtfertigung und Recht," 101. The title of this significant essay is rather misleadingly translated in that volume as "Church and State," which is far from a literal translation. The text of the essay makes it clear that Barth was considering law itself, and not only justice.

The post-World War II era with its tasks of political and legal reconstruction saw continuing involvement by Protestant theologians and ethicists in Germany with the foundation of law and its social and ethical dimensions.[27] The drafting of the quasi-constitutional Basic Law and efforts to rehabilitate the German legal system spurred reflection and debate on fundamental questions of jurisprudence and legal philosophy. In 1949 and 1950, the Protestant Church convened several symposia involving theologians and jurists to ponder these questions. Several theologically minded jurists in Germany, among them Erik Wolf and Hans Dombois, sought to work out the connections between law and specific theological themes. Wolf's *Recht des Nächsten* (1958) attempted to develop a vision of law based on personalism and neighborly solidarity, while Dombois's *Recht der Gnade* (1961) sought to place law within a horizon of divine grace.[28] In succeeding decades, theologians such as Helmut Thielicke and Wolfhart Pannenberg produced theological critiques of positivist and natural law theories of law in an effort to find an alternative to them.

This revival of concern with law endured into the 1960s when it was displaced by new concerns. In the course of that decade, theological interest shifted to political theology and other directions, and law received little notice.[29] After the millennial turn, theological interest in law has again revived in Germany, evidenced by an increasing number of publications on theology, ethics and law.[30] It is not clear what prompted this recent uptick in interest, but possibly it involved a renewed awareness of the social and political significance of law.

Though most of the writers involved with these activities were German or Swiss, noteworthy theological reflections on law appeared elsewhere in Europe. Jacques Ellul's *Theological Foundation of Law* appeared in France in 1947 and was almost immediately translated into German.[31] The Swedish theologian Gustav Aulen's *Law, Church, and Society* was published in the same year.[32] In Ellul's case, his interpretation of law was strongly influenced

---

27. Regarding this period, see Marsch, "Evangelische Theologie," 481–510.

28. Unfortunately, little of their work has been translated into English, and consequently, little has been written about them outside of the Germanophone realm. For brief descriptions in English of their work, see Hollerbach, "Erik Wolf," 523–24; Dreier, "Hans Dombois," 156. For comprehensive expositions of both writers, see Steinmüller, *Evangelische Rechtstheologie*, 1, 259–445 (on Wolf), 457–778 (on Dombois).

29. Huber, "Rechtsethik," 137.

30. For example, Huber, *Gerechtigkeit*. See also Kreβ, *Ethik der Rechtsordnung*.

31. Ellul, *Theological Foundation of Law*. The English translation was published twenty years later.

32. Aulen, *Law, Church, and Society*.

by Barth.³³ Aulen's book reflected views of social ethics associated with the Scandinavian school of Lutheran thought and its affinities with the social ethics of the two kingdoms. Both were received as attempts to emphasize the importance of secular law in the spiritual, economic and political reconstruction of Europe. At the same time, they were also seen as as arguments for religiously and ethically informed notions of law in light of the failure of law to provide a stronger bulwark against totalitarianism.

These mid-century theologies/ethics of law represent a more sustained tradition in continental, and especially German, Protestantism than in Anglophone Protestantism. This is not only the result of the relationship between the state and organized religion in Germany, in which the legal status of state churches entailed extensive engagement with law.³⁴ It is also a consequence of modern German history. According to Wilhelm Steinmüller, the strongest modern impetus for theological engagement with law in German Protestantism was the historical experience of the Nazi dictatorship.³⁵ English-speaking countries present a different legal-cultural landscape. Individual works by British and American authors on theology/ethics and law have appeared from time to time.³⁶ The constitutional separation of church and state in the United States has undoubtedly contributed to the hesitation on the part of theologians and ethicists to engage positive law.

Prior to the groundbreaking work of Harold Berman in the United States, little attention was devoted to theology and law by the legal academy. There has been, however, a recent increase in interest in Anglophone circles in the interdisciplinary field of law and religion.³⁷ An increasing number of publications, journals, organizations and symposia have appeared that are dedicated to this rather broadly defined field.³⁸ While the level of interest

33. See generally, Bromiley, "Barth's Influence on Ellul," 32–51.

34. Monsma and Soper, *Challenge of Pluralism*, 155–99. See also Robbers, *Law and Religion in Germany*.

35. Steinmüller, *Evangelische Rechtstheologie*, 6.

36. For example, see Nathaniel Micklem and Norman St. J. Stevas in Britain and Harold Berman and Milner Ball in the United States.

37. Berman's *Interaction of Law and Religion* was one of his early works on the subject, and it was followed by numerous other books and articles. Recent British publications in law and theology include McIlroy, *Trinitarian Theology of Law*; Beaumont, *Christian Perspectives on the Limits of Law*.

38. See, for example, recent symposia entitled, "Theological Argument in Law"; "Competing Claims of Law and Religion." The recently established journal, *Oxford Journal of Law and Religion*, holds annual conferences; another recently established research consortium is International Consortium of Law and Religion Studies (ICLRS). Academic centers include the Center for the Study of Law and Religion at Emory University.

has experienced ebbs and flows, according to John Witte, Jr. the growth in interest in the U.S. has been explosive in recent years.[39]

In the United States, most of this recent activity has occurred within the legal academy and primarily concerns the interdisciplinary field of law and religion, with more modest activities on the theological side. The analyses of legal writers tend to view religion in its legal, anthropological, comparative, sociological or political dimensions, rather than its normative and theological ones. Religion is framed as primarily a social and anthropological phenomenon. Its interactions with law are viewed in terms of certain established legal categories of rights (such as freedom of belief), constitutional constraints (such as questions of state support for religious institutions), and international conventions. This is not so much a criticism as a recognition that the conceptualization of law and religion and their interaction presents a knotty challenge. This gives a certain quixotic quality to some interdisciplinary studies in law and religion. As the editors of a recently established journal on law and religion put it, "The study of both law and religion has been making an ever more marked impact upon a number of well established fields within the humanities and social sciences, but it has been difficult to determine to what extent these different disciplines have been able to build bridges and to initiate conversations about each other's findings."[40] The journal editors go on to conclude that "the most pressing need is to pursue legal and religious perspectives on trends in the interaction between law and religion themselves."[41] These and other methodological challenges also bear on much of the contemporary work in law and theology.

The historical background of law and religion as a discipline suggests that the relation between modern Protestant theology and secular law is historically one of alternating distance and engagement, characterized by hesitation and uncertainty, but also a certain curiosity and engagement, at least from the side of theology. On the one hand, law has been rather uninviting terrain for Protestant thinkers; on the other, there is growing interest in exploring how the domains of law and theology interact.

The conviction behind this study is that, to the extent the relation between theology and law is seen as tentative and sporadic, it is unsatisfying. Law is too significant a social and political institution in contemporary societies to be ignored theologically and ethically. Consequently, this book has two fundamental aims. First, it seeks to describe, both objectively and

---

39. Witte, "Study of Law and Religion," 327.
40. Durham et al., "Editorial," 1.
41. Durham et al., "Editorial," 1.

critically, a modern tradition of Protestant reflection on law expressed in the views of several prominent Protestant thinkers about the nature and significance of positive law. It interprets those understandings of law as constituting a diverse and diffuse yet nevertheless coherent mode of interpretation that explores the ethical dimensions of law, its claims of autonomy, its status as a social institution. As such, it necessarily addresses some of the classic themes of jurisprudence such as the nature of justice and its relation to law. It also engages with other jurisprudential topics, such as the role of coercion in law, the character of legal validity, normativity and legitimacy and the historical provenance of certain key legal concepts.

Second, and within the context of this delineation of the theological tradition, this study presents a justification for contemporary theological and ethical reflection on law, and suggests some themes for future consideration. These ethical contentions, suggestive rather than comprehensive, must relate the insights of tradition to the pluralistic circumstances of contemporary society and come to terms with the predominantly secular sensibility of modern jurisprudence.

The theologians and jurists considered here represent a considerable diversity in method and substance in their reflections on law. They proceed from different theological orientations. Since they were active in different historical contexts with different theological approaches, their efforts reflect different understandings of law and its theological import. In some cases, the theology and ethics of law resembles a kind of applied ethics; in others, a more fundamental theological enterprise. Yet they share a conviction of the relevance of theological insights as deepening and leavening resources for reflection on law.

The remainder of this introduction provides an overview of the major themes and approaches of the following chapters. The exposition is organized typologically into contrasting theological and ethical understandings of law.[42] These include approaches reflecting foundational, ethical and anthropological perspectives. Each approach draws upon a distinctive combination of elements: theological, ethical, phenomenological, historical and sociological. One purpose here is to demonstrate the consequences of the distinctive blending of these perspectival elements in a given interpretation of law with differing strengths and liabilities. For example, Barth's Christological notion of law is theologically profound but politically dubious;

---

42. Another use of a typology to present varying theological attitudes to law is developed by Robert Cochran. See Cochran, "Christian Traditions, Culture, and Law," 242-52. Cochran's typology is organized thematically, as here, but without reference to specific writers.

Pannenberg's anthropological interpretation of law has secular appeal but seems to understate the relation of justice and law.

Various concepts and terms appear and reappear in the writings considered in the following chapters. At the outset, some introductory remarks about them may be useful.

Some Preliminary Delineations

A basic distinction exists between the broad interdisciplinary field of law and religion, and the more specific discipline of the theology of law, understood as theological/ethical reflection on law. These categories require some elaboration.

Law and Religion

Law and religion each are complex phenomenon. Sellers and Yelle observe that each term is fact in curiously amorphous, and their individual ambiguities are compounded when they are linked together.[43] Both relate to fields such as anthropology, ethnography, sociology, and philosophy. As an interdisciplinary field, law and religion deals with diverse themes of church and state relations, freedom of belief, civil resistance, the relation of civil and religious law, the law of religious organizations and the historical and cultural origins of law.[44] The character of these interdisciplinary studies depends particularly on how religion is conceptualized. Is it an objectively cognizable collection of practices or beliefs? Is it a set of institutional arrangements or beliefs? Within the law and religion rubric, religion tends frequently to be conceptualized in social/cultural terms. Typically, this means that it is equated with social institutions and groups, and externally observed, empirical practices. The functionalist understanding of religion tends to draw on the schemata of the social sciences. While it generates useful insights, it also risks resulting in an reductionist understanding of religion in all its multi-dimensional complexity.

Various theories seek to describe the interaction of religion and law. In one view of their interaction, they are viewed as bounded, relatively autonomous social systems and normative domains. They share certain structural similarities: their social function as protective, ordering institutions,

---

43. See Sullivan and Yelle, "Law and Religion," 5325.

44. Regarding the tendency of church-state topics to overshadow other ones, Fort states: "It is too easy, and too deceiving, to simply understand the interaction of law and religion as the relationship of church and state" (Fort, *Law and Religion*, 10).

their reliance on canonical sources, their performative aspects, their value orientations and their dependence on historical and interpretive traditions. Alternatively, each may be interpreted in terms of the problems it presents to the other. For example, religion may be seen primarily as a source of disputes and challenges for a legal order: freedom of belief, the rights and duties of religious organizations, conscientious objection, civil resistance and the relation of religious law to civil law are some of these legal problemata. Underlying this view is an assumption that the relation between law and religion as essentially one of conflict. Conversely, law may be interpreted from a religious perspective as an ordering myth sanctioned by divine directive or priestly consecration, leading to legalism, or worse, an ersatz religion.[45]

According to Wolfgang Huber, explanations of the interaction of law and religion in German Protestantism typically concern three basic categories: (1) the theological foundation or grounding of law, (2) the relation of law and ethics, and (3) church-state relations, including church law (*Kirchenrecht*).[46] The first two categories involve, at least for Anglo-American sensibilities, normative theologies and ethics of law, while the third corresponds to more conventional legal issues, such as the relation of church and state.

In Germany, the topic of church/state has long received attention. This focus is not surprising. While Germany does not have state-established churches, an outsider would not, on first glance, guess that this is the case. State and the church are much more legally intertwined than in the United States. Stephen Monsma and Christopher Soper refer to a principle of partnership to describe German church-state relations: "Germans typically see church and state, not as mutually exclusive, separate spheres of human endeavor, but as cooperative partners, both of whom have a role to play in contributing to a prosperous, stable German society."[47] As a result, an extensive body of state-church law has developed, governing state collection of church taxes, religious instruction in public school, ecclesiastical administration and discipline, display of religious symbols in public spaces and other topics.[48] This broad field lacks a direct counterpart in American

---

45. Sullivan and Yelle write, "Increasingly, it appears that law is, for us moderns, 'our religion,' not merely in the sense of having inherited part of religion's role as an arbiter of values and guide to conduct, but also in the sense of being historically or genealogically related to older modes of religiosity" (Sullivan and Yelle, "Law and Religion," 5326).

46. Huber, *Gerechtigkeit*, 15.

47. Monsma and Soper, *Pluralism*, 155.

48. A German legal dictionary defines *Kirchenrecht* as "the entirety of legal norms that regulate the relation between the state and religion and religious communities (*Staatskirchenrecht*), or the internal relations within churches (*Kirchenrecht*)" (Weber, "Kirchenrecht," 753).

law, which tends to address such topics in discrete legal contexts, such as constitutional law, education law and tax law, and for the most part without specialized statutory law dealing with churches and religious institutions.

The Theology of Law

In contrast to the general field of law and religion, the discipline of law and theology has a more circumscribed ambit that is concerned with the application of theological concepts in scrutiny of the basis of law, law's role in the maintenance of human societies, and law's normative status. Its concern is with the religious/ethical aspects of law rather than with religion as a source of problems for a legal order. In a German context, the field of law and theology includes the theology of law (*Rechtstheologie*) and the ethics of law (*Rechtsethik*). These sub-disciplines represent more systematic and constructive efforts to theorize the theological and ethical dimensions of law. One definition of the genre of law and theology speaks of it as "the discipline that seeks to bring the conceptual categories of theology (for example, God, creation, fall, covenant), or the insights of particular theologians (for example, Karl Barth, Dietrich Bonhoeffer), to bear on the theory and practice of law."[49] Similarly, Gerhard Robbers speaks of *Rechtstheologie* as having as its task "theological reflection on law in its totality."[50]

In German Protestant thought, the theology of law, carried out under that name, is a fairly recent undertaking. Steinmüller attributes the first use of the term *Rechtstheologie* to M.W. Rapaport in 1913, and notes that, as of 1933, it had become a *terminus technicus*.[51] Generally, it is taken to refer to the theological interpretation of law, its characteristics, historicity and normativity. Further, it relates law to specific theological/ethical themes such as covenant and promise. Traditionally, the theology of law in German Protestant usage is closely linked to canon or ecclesiastical law, which deals with ecclesiastical and church-state matters.[52]

A telling difference in scope between the Anglo-American and Germanic notions of theology and law is evident in the contrast between the linking of two separate domains (law and theology) compared to a single, integrated term: *Rechtstheologie* in Germanophone usage. Both the theology of law and *Rechtstheologie* are traditionally understood as challenges to

49. Chase, "Law and Theology," 421–35.
50. Robbers, "Grundsatzfragen der heutigen Rechtstheologie," 230.
51. Steinmüller, *Evangelische Rechtstheologie*, 1:3.
52. See generally Honecker, "Kirchenrecht II," 724–49; Landau, "Canon Law-Protestantism," 357–71.

positivism either with or without resort to natural law. They seek to provide a basis for positive law in a social/ethical framework, often converging on an emphasis on biblical authority as a basis for the legitimation of law.

The theology of law encompasses historical studies of the influence of religion and theology on law as well as systematic-constructive efforts to relate human and divine law to each other, typically in terms of the dependence of the former on the latter. These include attempts to establish a basis for grounding human law by relating it to theological categories and doctrines; examples are Pannenberg's essays on the Christian foundation of law[53] and Jacques Ellul's volume on the theological foundation of law.[54] In the Germanophone sphere, the writings of jurists such as Erik Wolf and Hans Dombois attracted attention in the postwar era. They combined historical, juridical, theological and philosophical perspectives in attempts to develop a superpositivist concept of law that would provide a new foundation for law in reconstruction-era Germany. For Wolf and Dombois, law is ontologically framed such that it draws upon categories such as personhood, solidarity and the neighbor. This perspective yielded relatively abstract conceptual schemes that, in the view of their critics, threaten to theologize law. While Huber contends that the efforts of these jurists have had little continuing influence, they did figure prominently in discussions about law and theology in Germany in the postwar period, culminating in several conferences organized by the Protestant Church in Germany in 1949–50 at Treysa and Göttingen.[55] Though largely neglected nowadays, they are not completely forgotten.

The category of the ethics of law (*Rechtsethik*) essentially is concerned with the relations of law, morality and justice. According to Huber, this is a relatively underdeveloped topic in German Protestant thinking. His own work is an effort to address this situation; he has produced a substantial volume developing a Christian ethics of law.[56] In essence, an ethics of law is concerned with the relation of justice and law, and often takes the form of a critique of positive law that manifests a strong concern with social justice and the social ramifications of legal systems. Unlike the theology of law, the ethics of law has engaged both the theologically minded as well as the secularly minded.[57]

53. Pannenberg, "Christliche Rechtsüberzeugungen"; "Recht und Religion."
54. Ellul, *Theological Foundation of Law*.
55. Regarding these conferences, see generally Wolf, "Recht," 1954.
56. Huber, *Gerechtigkeit*.
57. Huber and Kreß belong to the first group, and Dietmar von der Pforten to the second. See von der Pforten, "Rechtsethik." Robin West has proposed a normative jurisprudence of law that has certain affinities with an ethics of law. See West, *Normative Jurisprudence*.

Understood in these ways, the theology of law is narrower in scope than law and religion: it is explicitly theological in that it is concerned with the conceptualization and critique of the noetic contents of a belief tradition, rather than with its social practices, behaviors and institutions. The difference between law and religion and the theology of law is nicely illustrated by two essays of Pannenberg, who devoted much attention to the social sciences, especially anthropology.[58] In an early essay entitled "On the Theology of Law" (1961), he engages with theological interpretations of law, primarily those of Barth and Brunner. Anthropological elements are also introduced, but he moves quickly to discussion of theological doctrines. Law's theological significance derives from its status in Jewish religion, which carries over, with modification, into Christian notions of law. In a later essay, "Recht und Religion" (1985), Pannenberg proposes essentially an anthropological theory of law. He refers extensively to the work of anthropologists such as Bronislaw Malinowski and others to relate the development of law to primordial social practices. In this context, religion and law are correlated in their functional and constitutive roles in societies. According to Pannenberg, the relationship between law and religion has continuously evolved from a primordial association to one more distanced and not infrequently contentious.

Theologies and ethics of law tend to draw upon certain theological doctrines: Luther's notion of two kingdoms, the three uses of law, and the theological categories of law and gospel. Some writers embrace these doctrines, others reject them or find them inapplicable to law. Thielicke's theology of law is largely premised on a modified version of Luther's notion of the two kingdoms. Barth, on the other hand, blames that doctrine for contributing to the subversion of law in the Third Reich. Theological commitments have both methodological and substantive consequences for theologies/ethics of law. In foundational approaches to law, doctrines appear explicitly and prominently. In the ethics of law, doctrines may be implied in some manner but are not directly asserted. In anthropologically oriented versions, doctrine is implied through categories of theological anthropology, and is less explicit than in the grounding of law.

As noted, the modern theology of law has had a more modest profile in the Anglophone realm than in Continental theology. Harold Berman is a pioneer in the field, and his work remains widely influential and often cited, also by German writers.[59] In the United States, relatively few theo-

---

58. Pannenberg, *Anthropology*, 448.

59. For a helpful overview of Berman's writings on law, theology and religion, see Witte, "Concordance of Discordant Canons"; Witte and Alexander, *Weightier Matters of the Law*. See also the writings of Milner Ball and Frank Alexander.

logical works on theology and law have appeared during the past few decades.⁶⁰ In Britain, several practicing barristers and solicitors have produced noteworthy publications on the subject.⁶¹ One distinctive subgenre within Anglo-American contributions to law and theology is Christian jurisprudence. It has been defined in various ways; one is "the analysis of the contributions of modern Catholic, Protestant, and Orthodox figures to fundamental questions of law, politics, and society."⁶² David Skeel speaks in terms of "Christian legal scholarship," which he identifies as either "a normative theory derived from Christian scripture or tradition or a descriptive theory that explains some aspect of the influence of Christianity on law, or of law on Christianity."⁶³ Significant effort in this area is devoted to explicating the historical Christian influences on jurisprudential questions and on the development of secular law.

In the hands of some, the interdisciplinary field of law and religion often presents an objectivized view of religion. The focus is on the interaction between law and religion, understood through a variety of encounters viewed externally.⁶⁴ Further, there is a tendency to see religion as a source of problems in need of legal resolution. resolution. To point this out is not to deny that religions create legal problems and present legal challenges; they certainly do. The issue is rather of the proportion of attention devoted to them. The theology of law is less concerned with the encounter of religious institutions and practices with legal regimes and more with the scriptural and theological elements that impinge on the methodological assumptions and substantive provisions of positive law. It would seem that a more adequate way of studying the interaction of law, religion, theology, and ethics would be to appropriate elements of each of a law and religion approach, the theology of law, and the ethics of law. The field of law and religion quite properly points out the importance of the social aspects of religion and its practices in addressing the practical problems related to religious freedom, rights, and practices. A theology/ethics of law attests to the significance of

60. An exception are several essays of Martin Marty—see, e.g., Marty, "Religious Foundations of Law"; Alexander, "Beyond Positivism."

61. For example, see McIlroy, *Trinitarian Theology of Law*; Beaumont, *Perspectives on Limits of Law*.

62. Center for the Study of Law and Religion, "Christian Jurisprudence II."

63. Skeel, "Christian Legal Scholarship," 1504. Skeel identifies four areas of writing and research that qualify as Christian legal scholarship under these criteria: natural law theory, Christian lawyering and legal ethics, First Amendment and church-state issues, and Christian legal history.

64. For example, see Richardson, "Religion and the Law," 418, which treats religion and law prospectively as "independent variables" in the equation relating law and religion.

situating positive law within a theological-ethical frame that contextualizes it and points out the ethical dimensions of law in its related activities: legislation, enforcement, adjudication, administration. Neither law and religion nor the theology/ethics of law necessarily excludes the other.

The focus of this book is on the theology and ethics of law rather than on the broader field of law and religion. That said, several of the authors considered below also deal with the kinds of problems with which contemporary studies in law and religion are concerned. The interpretation advanced here is that modern theological/ethical reflection on positive law in Continental Protestantism forms a reasonably coherent tradition. Further, that tradition displays a trajectory from foundational views of law anchored in theological categories to ethical critiques of law in which theological elements, though still influential, are subdued in the context of the increasingly pluralistic and secularized character of Continental societies, particularly Germany. This study seeks to contribute to an understanding of a tradition that has received little attention in North America, and suggests how it may be relevant to that context.

A Plurality of Approaches

One common thread that pervades Protestant reflection on law is its embrace of a critical, as opposed to dogmatic, stance.[65] This attitude combines dissatisfaction with prevailing ideas of law and justice expressed more through the scrutiny of existing law than in constructive theories of its own, with an impulse toward more theologically and ethically satisfying ones. It affirms a fundamental connection between human existence and law, and between law and justice as a divine predicate of law. As Martin Honecker expresses these connections, "Christian love and faith in God, in whose kingdom law is cherished and respected (Psalm 99:4), can provide motivation for commitment to seek just law, and justice in law."[66]

Protestant thinking about law is often characterized as a search for an alternative to positivist and natural law theories. While there is some truth to this, it is too categorical. Positivism and natural law as legal theories each encompass a spectrum of variations. Outright dismissals of either is simplistic and overlooks contributions each makes to better, more adequate understandings of law in its complexity. Some have contended that there is an affirmative affinity between Protestant attitudes toward law and

---

65. Richardson, "Religion and the Law," 365. See also Wolf, "Protestantischen Rechtsdenken."

66. Honecker, "Recht, Ethos, Glaube," 405.

positivism, based in part on Protestant understandings of the state and politics, and particularly reflecting Luther's two kingdoms doctrine.[67] Others have opposed positivism as inimical to maintaining an ethical dimension in law. For example, Pannenberg warns against what he discerns to be the implicit amorality and relativism of positivism in law.[68] These admonitions are connected with a debate in German jurisprudence and history during the postwar era about positivism's role in the subversion of the German legal system in the Third Reich.[69]

As for natural law, the attitude of most Protestant writers regarding it in the early part of last century largely ranged from guarded skepticism to outright dismissal. Brunner stands as an exception in being a qualified proponent of natural law. Others incorporated natural law elements in their thinking about law while maintaining a critical distance; Thielicke allows some room for the validity of natural law despite a fundamental aversion to it; Pannenberg also is willing to grant a limited role to natural law, though in a revised, eschatological form.[70]

These themes—the roles of positivism and natural law and the critical character of Protestant attitudes toward law—recur throughout the following typology. It identifies three fundamental approaches to relating theology and law. These are not the only alternatives nor are they exclusive of each other; they instead serve to show the diversity of approaches that exist. The concepts of positive law of the Protestant thinkers treated here often do not fall neatly into a single category. More often, they combine elements of different types. The distinctive characteristic of each writer lies in his blending of themes.

Foundational Approaches

Foundational approaches to law proceed from first-order theological premises to envision law as a social institution with specific provisional functions such as the preservation of social order, the protection of individual freedom and preservation of institutional authority, limitation of state power and protection of individual rights. The theological premises of these approaches assess the nature and social function of law and integrate it into a comprehensive theological economy of divine action and salvation.

---

67. Wolf quotes a remark of Veit: "The positivist is an eternal Lutheran. The moral claim of natural law seems to be presumptuousness toward God" (Wolf, "Recht," 1960).

68. Pannenberg, "Theology of Law," 23–57.

69. See generally Wolf, "Protestantischen Rechtsdenken."

70. See Woon, "Pannenberg's Understanding on Natural Law," 346–66.

The major exponents of foundational approaches are Barth, Brunner, Thielicke, and, to a large extent, Ellul. Their theologies of law are typically grouped into two broad categories: those based on the orders of creation in Brunner's case, and those grounding law in the kingly rule of Christ, associated with Barth and Ellul. Their interpretations of law share an emphasis on a Christocentric notion of atonement and justification as the central and relativizing salvific event.

In contrast to natural law theories, foundational accounts emphasize the interplay of divine authority with law and justice in light of the corrosive effects human sinfulness has on them. Further, they affirm positive law's role as a defense against disorder, which is the first use of law (*usus politicus legis*), and the second, theological, use of the law that prompts recognition of the pervasiveness of human sin. These uses figure more prominently in theories of orders of creation and preservation in Lutheran ethics, less so in those based on the kingly rule of Christ. Reformed understandings of law further envision a third, didactical use of law, a *usus tertius legis*, that sees a more affirmative role for law. As Calvin describes it, the third use of the law gives believers a realization that "the best instrument for enabling them to daily learn with greater truth and certainty what that will of the Lord is which they aspire to follow, and to confirm them in this knowledge."[71] It also expands the functional understanding of law as essentially coercive to include its facilitative capacity as well. This use is particularly reflected in Barth's thought about positive law, as well as in that of Erik Wolf.

Barth and the Kingship of Christ

Barth's early writings on law date from the 1930s and as such are marked by the experience of the Nazi dictatorship.[72] His first treatment of law was produced in the waning years of the Weimar Republic; later writings appeared in the era of Nazi totalitarianism and in the period of postwar reconstruction. Barth's principal concern is not with jurisprudential questions but with the relationship of human law to the reconciling law of Christ—it is the fundamental question for him. It led Barth to further questions about the role of the church in society, the church's support of state neutrality in matters of belief, the connection between human rights and democracy, and

---

71. Calvin, *Institutes* 2.7.12. Regarding the third use of the law, see generally Aus Der Au, "*Tertius Usus Legis*."

72. Heinrich Bedford-Strohm notes that "Barth's Christological approach is strongly contextual and very specifically shaped by historical experiences" (Bedford-Strohm, "Public Theology," 280).

the necessity of law is as a means of enabling human social existence. It also implied for him an understanding of the dependence of human law on a divine law as its true, justificatory ground, with ecclesiastical law having exemplary significance for positive law.[73] Applying an analogical method, Barth proposes certain correspondences between the human legal order and divine law. While Barth's analogical correlations have drawn criticism, they show that he affirms a positive connection between divine and human law.

For Barth, law is properly seen monistically through the lens of the kingly rule of Christ. In several essays written in the years immediately before and after World War II, Barth poses the question of the relation of human law to the Christological center of history.[74] In one of these essays, "Rechtfertigung und Recht" (1938), Barth asks about the relationship between "the reality of justification of the sinner through God in Jesus Christ through faith alone and the problem of human law."[75] This question pressed itself upon Barth in the midst of intense controversy between the Confessing Church and the Nazi regime, and reflects his urgent concern with the survival of an ecclesial community in the face of state repression and the existential threat posed by the state-supported German Christian movement.

While Barth's thinking about positive law has jurisprudential implications, it is characterized by its vigorously theological character. Nevertheless, it exerted a certain public influence in the postwar era.[76] His approach to law was taken up by Erik Wolf, Jacques Ellul and others. In essence, each seeks, like Barth, to correlate specific theological themes with aspects of law. For Wolf, the primary themes are personality and solidarity, which he develops in his essay *Recht des Nächsten*.[77] For Ellul it is the concept of covenant, worked out in his *The Theological Foundation of Law*.[78] These efforts aim at integrating law, in all its complexity, into an ethically salient yet essentially theological framework. This vision of law rejects more compartmentalized notions of it as an autonomous institution subject to its own ethos and legitimization.[79] At the same time, the foundational vision acknowledges the limits of law, its ideological character, and potential for idolatry. Theologically,

---

73. Barth, CD 4/1 §61.

74. For example, see Barth, "Rechtfertigung und Recht."

75. Barth, "Rechtfertigung und Recht," 101–148.

76. For example, see the essay by Helmut Simon, a justice on the German Federal Constitutional Court, on Barth's theology of law in Simon, "Rechtstheologie."

77. Wolf, *Recht des Nächsten*.

78. Ellul, *Theological Foundation of Law*, 23.

79. See Wannewetsch, "Kingly Reign," 198.

the dependence of human law on divine law reflects the human need of reconciliation. Ernst Wolf identifies this theological orientation, along with a critical, non-dogmatic attitude, as characteristic of Protestant attitudes towards positive law.[80]

Brunner and Orders of Creation

The notion of law as an order of creation, along with its variations, appears in the thinking of several German and Swiss Protestant theologians of the early twentieth century, among them, Brunner. Besides Brunner, Thielicke and Dietrich Bonhoeffer developed variations of it in the form of mandates (Bonhoeffer) or orders of preservation (Thielicke). Other writers also developed concepts of orders of creation. Theologians such as Paul Althaus, Walter Künneth and Emmanuel Hirsch also employed the notion of created orders in some form, relating it to *völkisch* racial ideas.[81]

For Brunner, the doctrine of creation and its implications for the concept of justice plays a key role in his view of law. His writings are much concerned with law's dependence on justice for its legitimacy as well as its ability to achieve proximate justice. In contrast to Barth's monist understanding of law that roots mundane law in divine grace and reconciliation, Brunner's approach is more receptive to secular notions of law and justice and is more accommodating of prudential concerns. This was not a static conception: Brunner's notion of law as a divinely authorized, creational order, alongside property, marriage, state and church, developed markedly as his thinking on the subject evolved.

Brunner's earliest thinking on law is contained is his treatise on ethics: *The Divine Command* (1932).[82] Law is understood fundamentally as the order of human communal relations.[83] An order, for Brunner, is a supra-individual, constant structure manifested in and through encounters with neighbors.[84] Though part of this creational order, law exists in sinful circumstances. It is a function of the state, and shares the state's ambiguous moral status and dependence on coercion. Yet law remains ethically significant. Its creational dimension helps to secure and order human community, and community is a divinely sanctioned command of human existence.

---

80. Wolf, "Protestantischen Rechtsdenken," 200.

81. See Ericksen, *Theologians under Hitler*, 79–119, regarding Althaus.

82. The title of the German original edition is, literally translated, *The Command and the Orders*.

83. Brunner, *Divine Command*, 96.

84. Brunner, *Divine Command*, 194.

Law's ethical potential derives from its dependence on justice, which is its regulative principle. Justice is manifested in law through three basic characteristics: its legality, understood as stability and reliability; its reciprocal character manifested in its compensation of performances rendered and its remedying of detriments inflicted; its concern for the individual, regardless of the needs or demands of community.[85] This is an affirmative conception of law's capabilities that goes beyond an understanding of law as basically prophylactic and disciplinary. It provides for indirect yet efficacious divine guidance of human law. As Robin Lovin notes, "There is an inseparable link between the commandment of God and the concrete historical circumstances and natural limitations in which we are set."[86]

Whether conceived as an order, command or a mandate, the creational orders with their affirmation of universal, permanent structures bear some parallels to natural law. Many of the critiques leveled at natural law were also aimed at order-based ethics, especially its ahistorical character on one hand, and its time-bound content on the other. Further, critics questioned the normativity of the orders. As Reinhold Niebuhr contended in critiquing Brunner's idea of the orders of creation, it is difficult to identify a normative element in the orders "because man is a historical creature and there are no purely "natural" forms in his life which have not been subjected to both the freedom and the corruption of history."[87] Orders-based ethical notions have also been criticized for their susceptibility to ideological distortion, a danger demonstrated by the thought of Althaus, Hirsch and others.

Though it had been tarnished by right-wing ideologues, the concept of orders was revived and refashioned in the postwar era by Thielicke as orders of preservation. For his part, Brunner gradually placed less emphasis on the concept of orders in his later volume on justice (*Justice and the Social Order*) and his Gifford lectures, *Christianity and Civilization*.[88] But given the prominence of the idea of law as creational order in *The Divine Command*, it remains associated with his name.

The Eclipse of Foundational Views

The first postwar decades saw the high-water mark of foundational theologies of law in continental theology. In the following decades, they came to be overshadowed by more ethically oriented approaches. Concern with

85. Reuter, *Rechtsethik*, 96.
86. Lovin, *Christian Faith and Public Choices*, 49.
87. Niebuhr, "Concept of the 'Order of Creation,'" 266.
88. Brunner, *Civilization*.

the ethical potential of law seemed more promising for advancing social justice. For example, attention shifted to human rights.[89] At the same time, a renewed focus was directed to ecclesiastical law and perennial questions about its theological basis and relationship to secular law.

Notwithstanding this ebb in interest, foundational interpretations of law remain instructive. They serve to illustrate the advantages and disadvantages of forging unmediated connections between law and theological doctrine. They forcefully articulate the theological and ethical implications of law for the realization of community, as symbolized in the motif of the kingdom. They order law within a comprehensive economy of reconciliation. A weakness of some foundational theologies of law is their reliance on what Pannenberg describes as the 'supranatural positivism" implicit in the theological categories used to interpret law.[90] Further, Barth's (and others') understanding of law in particular has been criticized as out of step with contemporary cultural understandings. Kreβ contends that "In contemporary pluralistic society, a religious grounding of mundane law is no longer capable of achieving consensus."[91] He cites Barth's essay "Christian Society and Civil Society" as an example of this kind of outmoded approach to law.

Similarly, orders-based notions of law fell out of favor fairly quickly in the postwar years despite a reawakening of interest in natural law. In addition to its vulnerability to ideological distortion, the concept of the orders were seen by some as inadequately acknowledging the historical and cultural character of law despite its universalistic aspirations. Further, the orders purportedly underappreciate the autonomy of law and refuse to acknowledge the historical process of its secularization. Dissatisfaction with both foundational approaches led to a focus on the ethical dimension of law.

Ethical Understandings

Given the limitations of foundational interpretations of law, some theologians have come to favor ethical interpretation of law, or more precisely, an ethics of law. Ralf Dreier contends that "the most important desiderata of a Protestant theology of law is the systematic working out of a Protestant

---

89. On this shift, see generally Robbers, "Grundsatzfragen der heutigen Rechtstheologie," 234, who states, "One of the most essential changes in directions during the last two decades is the redirection of Protestant legal thought toward common human rights and political praxis."

90. Pannenberg, "Review," 439–41.

91. Kreβ, *Ethik der Rechtsordnung*, 212.

ethic of law, for which important beginnings already exist."[92] Contemporarily, Huber and Kreß are prominent proponents of this view; von der Pforten has argued for its recognition as a sub-discipline within the philosophy of law. For both Huber and Kreß, a primary theological focus should be on the ethical critique of law. An ethics of law commends itself in Huber's view for its modesty and social relevance. He writes: "A theological ethic of law today does not claim the ability to provide a theological foundation of law. It understands law is a part of mundane reality and as a task for human structuring."[93]

What, exactly, is an ethics of law? Kreß states that the task of an ethics of law consists in the "systematic, critical, and constructive thinking through of the law, statutes and constitution of a state with the help of ethical principles and norms."[94] Reuter defines it as that part of ethics that inquires about just law, and therefore about the criteria for the moral validity of positive law.[95] An ethics of law does not dispense altogether with theological themes. Huber places his ethical analysis in a theological context in which the significance of the world is interpreted within the horizon of the universality of God. He concludes that "the interaction of mundane law in the horizon of God is the theme of an ethic of law as understood in a Christian sense."[96]

For Huber, an ethics of law takes the form of a critical theory that continuously inquires about the validity of law, and critiques it for the sake of its improvement. The relevant ethical criterion for him is a biblically grounded preference for the disadvantaged, informed by eschatological realism about the deficiencies of any given realization of justice. Such an understanding of justice values legal norms and principles for the purpose of the constant reform of law.[97] As such, it corrects notions of negative freedom that emphasize the absence of individual constraint to the detriment of richer and deeper community.

Huber's ethics of law identifies and seeks to analyze law's subjective and objective dimensions of validity, meaning its relation to both individual and collective rights and obligations. Legal validity, for him, is conceived not only in terms of legality but also social and ethical plausibility.[98] The

---

92. Dreier, "Recht," 1454.
93. Huber, "Rechtsethik," 137. See also Kreß, *Ethik der Rechtsordnung*, 15.
94. Kreß, *Ethik der Rechtsordnung*, 11.
95. Reuter, "Rechtstheologie/Rechtsphilosophie," 227.
96. Huber, "Rechtsethik," 128.
97. See Reuter, "Rechtsethik," 242.
98. Huber, "Rechtsethik," 128.

basic interplay in law between its individual and social aspects is expressed through the ethical imperative of mutual recognition: "Law in the ethical sense is a system of enforceable rules and duties that permit mutual recognition and thus also reciprocity and cooperation."[99] Further, law should not be assessed from the perspective of either the individual or society alone, but from the perspectives of both. As such, Huber's ethics of law distances itself from ahistorical principles found in varieties of natural law, as well as from a hard positivistic rejection of an ethical dimensionality of law. An ethics of law must also account for the limits of law. When law's ethical validity is radically compromised, there is a right of legitimate resistance to law. Huber's project combines an openly confessional perspective, conceived and expressed in a rationally explicable terms, with engagement with contemporary jurisprudential inquiries about law's normativity and validity.[100]

In Kreß's ethics of law, the ethical integrity of legal systems depends upon their ability to protect the pluralistic diversity of contemporary societies in the name of a fuller recognition of legal rights. Among other things, this means that law must overcome religiously sanctioned privileges and protections. His approach combines a notion of the ethical potential of law with vigorous respect for the secular nature of the contemporary public arena. As such, it relates to contemporary debates in the United States about the balance between religious freedom and a right of non-discrimination. Overcoming entrenched and unwarranted deference to, for example, religious institutions promotes progress toward more just law. For Kreß, the relation between religious practice and civil rights will continue to be contested, and a critical ethics of law can and should participate in such debates.

Anthropological/Cultural Interpretations

Another kind of theological/ethical approach to law grew out of dissatisfaction with existing foundational interpretations of law and involves a turn to the anthropological and cultural character of law. Among its principal advocates are Wolfhart Pannenberg and Martin Honecker.[101] Their anthropological view of law is grounded in the cultural and anthropological origins of law as a mediating social institution whose function is to regulate and ameliorate social conflict. From these anthropological premises, ethical themes are inductively developed.

99. Huber, "Law and Jurisprudence," 367.
100. Also see Shingleton, "Motifs."
101. For an overview of Pannenberg's theology of law, see Shingleton, "Recognition and Mutuality," 225–52.

Pannenberg and Honecker both express dissatisfaction with interpretations of law based on the theological premises of Brunner and Barth. Brunner's orders are ahistorical and fail to account adequately for the historical development of law. In Pannenberg's view, "the main difficulty remains that of how to abstract from the social process specific basic structures that can remain unaffected by all historical activity."[102] In Barth's case, his focus on the revelation of reconciliation and grace says more about law's place in the economy of salvation than about its social role and normativity. Honecker criticizes Barth's reliance on theological abstractions that are inapposite to law due to their failure to acknowledge its secular character. He is also disturbed by the vagueness of the concepts Barth employs: "If one takes the term 'Christological' in a very general sense as a synonym for 'Christian,' then one can ask what place law is consigned to within the comprehensive understanding of God, world, and humanity."[103] Both orders-based and Christological notions of law, in their view, involve theological repristinations of law, and are insufficiently attentive to the social and secular nature of law.

In contrast, an anthropological point of departure entails interaction between theological insight and social knowledge. This is necessary in order to avoid a theologized view of law that fails to recognize its contemporary character as secularized, technical and relatively autonomous. Overly theological notions of law inhibit interdisciplinary dialogue. They may also lack a sense of history and eschatology. In Pannenberg's view, law's historicity is critical and the failure to account for it is a major reason for the appeal of positivist notions of law. For him, positivism leads to relativism. A theological or ethical theory of law must confront positivism's relativistic consequences.

An anthropological perspective relates law to basic practices of societies such as reciprocity and recognition. How are they associated with religion? For Pannenberg, they require legitimation that religion has provided as societies became more complex. In its genesis, law fundamentally consists of social practices which cannot be sustained without normative backing. The coercive effect of force and sanction is insufficient; rather, the linkage of practice and value—of individuals and groups—provides a religious valorization that validates law.

---

102. Pannenberg, "Theology of Law," 28.
103. Honecker, *Grundriß der Sozialethik*, 402.

Some Preliminaries

These writers discussed in this book were selected on the basis of two considerations. First, each produced a substantial enough body of writing on positive law to provide a meaningful basis for analysis and critique.[104] Second, each engaged to some extent with at least one of the other writers, creating something of a dialogue. Of course, other figures could have been chosen in addition to or instead of those that appear here. A certain degree of arbitrariness in selection is unavoidable. Nevertheless, the reflections of these thinkers constitute at least somewhat of a representative sampling of reflections on positive law in modern Protestant thought on the continent.

The figures treated in this book share both similarities and differences. Most are theologians, while two, Ellul and Wolf, are jurists. All (except Ellul) are German or Swiss. Theologically and historically, the writers span different epochs, with Barth and Brunner's earliest writings on law dating from before the Second World War during the era of dialectical theology, those of Wolf and Thielicke appearing in the postwar decades, Pannenberg's in the 1960s and continuing for several decades in which much attention was devoted to eschatology and the future, and the publications of Huber and Kreß have appeared within the last two decades in an era of post-modern theology. Some of these thinkers are widely read today, others unfortunately receive little attention.

In engaging with the work of each writer, I apply two analytic criteria. First, I view it from the perspective of what might be called a pluralistic premise. This inquires whether the writer privileges a single religion or non-religious perspective to the disadvantage of other religions or worldviews. This goes beyond Rawls's duty of civility to take account of pluralism as a contemporary religious phenomenon. Second, I apply a criterion of accessibility. It seeks to determine whether, and to what extent, a writer's conception of positive law depends on a specific theological understanding of law that excludes or marginalizes alternative ways of understanding. As with the pluralistic premise, the accessibility criterion seeks to avoid privileging any particular mode of discourse or set of theological presuppositions. It inquires about the degree of dependence a set of reflections have on a specific context of interpretation and understanding. Some of the writers here self-consciously and intentionally address a faith community;

---

104. Most of the writers concentrate on domestic law, rather than on international law. Brunner and Huber are two exceptions; they devote significant attention to international law. But given that most of the others do not address it, the focus below is on domestic law. For a recent volume on the theological dimensions of international law, see Reed, *Theology for International Law*.

others use approaches and conceptualizations more accessible to secular jurisprudence.

These criteria seek to gauge the contemporary viability of a given theology/ethics of law. Obviously, they are not the only relevant criteria. But they relate to an important consideration—the ability of a theology/ethics of law to engage positive law in its capacity as an institution of the public and political realm. Beyond these criteria, each chapter considers the writer's thoughts about the nature of law itself—its characteristics, distinctiveness, and normative dimension. Much more could be said about each writer's thinking about law; hopefully these studies will spur further interest.

II

Karl Barth

The Christocentric Premise of Law

One of the most influential interpretations of positive law in modern Protestantism is that of Karl Barth. This partly reflects Barth's stature in contemporary theology. But it is also a consequence of his particular contribution to modern Protestant reflections on law, one that moves beyond natural law and positivism to ground law Christocentrically. Despite its influence, contemporary appraisals of it are divided. Some, such as Hans-Richard Reuter, find Barth's theology of law superior to those of Emil Brunner and Wolfhart Pannenberg.[1] Others dismiss it as flawed and outdated. For example, in a recent book on the ethics of the legal order, Hartmut Kreβ contends that Barth's interpretation of human law is based on religious patterns of thought that are no longer tenable in secularized societies.[2]

Curiously, while Barth's ethics have recently received considerable attention, his theology of law is largely overlooked, at least outside of the continent. This reflects the marginal status of positive law as a topic in contemporary theological ethics, as described in the introduction. There are other reasons as well: historical, methodological, and practical. Barth's discussions of positive law are colored by the historical period in which he wrote, which extended from the latter years of the Weimar Republic through the Nazi era of the 1930s and 1940s into the postwar years of reconstruction. As this tumultuous era recedes into the past, his reflections on positive law seem increasingly remote. They also reflect a social context that is no longer our own.

---

1. See Reuter, *Rechtsethik*, 120. In her study of the theology of law, Gäfgen selects Barth alone for special, extended attention. See Gäfgen, *Recht*.

2. Kreβ, *Ethik der Rechtsordnung*, 18.

Another hindrance to the Anglophone reception of Barth's theology of law is practical—the difficulty of its translation into English. Although most of Barth's major writings on law have appeared in English (unlike those of many of the writers discussed in the following chapters), frequently those translations make terminological choices that obscure the significance of positive law. This is largely a result of differences in technical legal vocabulary between German and English. An example is the existence of alternate meanings of the word "*Recht*" in German. Unsurprisingly, Barth uses *Recht* often in dealing with law and the state. English translations of these writings alternately render "*Recht*" as "justice" or "right" and even as "state." While law is obviously associated with these concepts, they are not synonyms for it. Law is different from justice, and is other than the state. "*Recht*" would in most cases be more appropriately translated simply as "law."[3] The Germanophone secondary literature on Barth's texts also provides guidance for translation and interpretation. That literature frequently analyzes his discussions of "Recht" in jurisprudential terms and as dealing with jurisprudential and legal matters.[4]

Beyond this linguistic problem, there are elements in Barth's theology that complicate thematic study of his ethics. Barth's ethics constitute an integrated whole inseparable from his theology in its entirety. Barth is insistent that dogmatics and ethics belong together.[5] Each ethical theme implicates his theology as a whole. Obviously, it is impossible to accomplish that in a single chapter. A few comments about the theological and ethical context of Barth's analysis of positive law will have to suffice.[6]

---

3. The word *Recht* has two distinguishable aspects. Objectively, *Recht* refers to the system of law and the legal system. Subjectively, *Recht* primarily means right or entitlement; see the definitions of *Recht* in an authoritative German legal dictionary, Creifeld's *Rechtswörterbuch*. Which aspect is intended in a given usage is context-dependent. Is the writer referring to law as an individual right or as an aggregation of legal norms? Barth's references are most often to the latter. This is consistent with German-language theological usage. In a widely cited German theological reference work, *Theologische Realencyclopedia* (TRE), Reuter writes, "In the following, law (*Recht*) is understood subjectively as a justified interpersonal claim; objectively as the entirety of norms for external coordination of actions, the compliance with which is expected, and whose validation is based on the fact that it is socially effective, appropriately established and (at least minimally) just" (Reuter, "Rechtsethik," 227). Further, law and justice are distinct, so again the proper word choice depends on context. Barth uses the word "*Gerechtigkeit*" in a way that references an ethical/theological concept rather than a legal system. See Reuter, "Fiat iustitia!," for an analysis of Barth's understanding of justice suggesting that "*Recht*" is a means to an end: justice. See also Reuter, *Rechtsethik im Perspektive*, 44–70. *Recht* is rendered throughout this volume as "law."

4. See, e.g., Reuter, *Rechtsethik*; Gäfgen, *Recht*; Huber, *Gerechtigkeit*.

5. See, e.g., Honecker, *Einführung*, 26–28.

6. Fortunately, several excellent studies of Barth's ethics have recently appeared;

The Theological Context

Two initial contextual observations about Barth's reflections on law deserve mention. First, Barth's approach is unabashedly theological. He rarely cites or discusses legal philosophers or jurists. Unlike Brunner, he spends little time on classic jurisprudential themes, such as the normative validity of law, the nature of legality, positive law's relation to ethics, and the role of justice in positive law. This gives his theology of law a distinctly theological orientation. Second, Barth sees law as Christologically grounded. The Christological center is, for him, the *terminus ad quo* for human law. In his view, to ask about the basis of law is to inquire about the meaning of Christ for a human institution. From this perspective, and from nowhere else, Barth proceeds to develop his notion of what law is and how it should function in modern societies.

In a programmatic sense, Barth states that he is intent on counteracting the "sterile and dangerous separation" between human and divine law, church and state, the kingdom of Christ, and the kingdom of the world.[7] But how are they related? In modern understanding, they are incommensurate and discontinuous. The state and positive law are bound by neutrality in matters of ultimate truth, while the Christian community attests to the reality of God in Christ. Barth insists, however, that there is a connection, and it is rooted in divine grace and action. Divine law is an expression of divine justice and justification, accomplished through Christ, and it reaches out to encompass human law.

In his essay "Gospel and Law" (1935), Barth presents the relation between gospel and law in terms of form and content. In essence, Barth's contention is that law is not an alien, oppressive institution fashioned by human beings to preserve life and property, but is a mode of the divine/human interaction. Famously, Barth revised the traditional opposition of gospel and law in order to assert a positive relation between them: the law is the form of the gospel, and the gospel is the content of the law. This eliminates the kind of differentiation between them that leads to different realms of spiritual and political activity.

In this theological sense, law is the form of the gospel. Ethically, law serves the purpose of ordering human society so that the gospel can be

---

unfortunately, few of them much to say about his views on positive law. See Biggar, *Hastening*; Webster, *Barth*; Haddorff, "Introduction." An exception, limited to natural law, is VanDrunen, *Natural Law*, 331–47.

7. Barth, "Church and State," 105. (The translated title of this essay is rather misleading as explained in footnote 3 above. In order to avoid confusion, however, the title of the published English translation is used here.)

proclaimed. This is the ordering function of law, serving both divine and human purposes. As an institution, law reflects the reality of divinely initiated reconciliation. In addressing the human situation marked by sin but not exhausted by it, Christ defines the human through reconciliation. As an affirmative, ordering institution promoting the kingdom of God with the reconciled world, law has a teleological-eschatological function. It also has an affirmative vocation in that it supports the human status of created being, destined for relationship with God; it has a protective vocation in that it confronts and contains human sin.

The Evolution of Barth's Theology of Law

Barth's treatment of positive law falls into three phases: the early lectures on ethics, the essays of the war and postwar years, and the volumes of the *Church Dogmatics* that appeared in the 1950s. These writings take various forms: lectures, occasional writings, letters, newspaper articles, and theological texts. They address various forms of human law, including church law (*Kirchenrecht*), criminal law, civil law, and constitutional law. The focus here is on the following writings: (i) the posthumously published *Ethics* dating from 1929–30; (ii) the lectures/essays entitled "Church and State" (1938) and "The Christian Community and the Civil Community" (1946), and (iii) the section of volume 4/2 of the *Church Dogmatics*, which appeared in 1956. Barth deals with human law in other writings as well, but these four writings contain the essential part of his output treating law. Each dates from different decades: the turbulent years of the Weimar Republic, the ascent of National Socialism, war, the devastation of postwar Europe. These historical settings significantly impacted Barth's attitudes toward positive law.

Barth's lectures on ethics of 1929–30 reflect his break with liberal theology early in his career. The lectures were preceded by several essays and lectures on ethical topics written during and after Barth's pastorate in Safenwil from 1911 to 1912. Among the most prominent of them was the Tambach lecture of 1919, a text that reflects Barth's growing dissatisfaction, at the time, with the ethical program of liberal Protestantism. In the lecture, Barth rejects strenuous social action as a means of satisfying the ideal of the Kingdom of God and urges instead that "neither our rest nor our unrest in this world, necessary though both of them be, can be final."[8] He concludes by asking: "What can the Christian in society do but follow attentively what is done by *God*?"[9]

8. Barth, *Word of God*, 282.
9. Barth, *Word of God*, 327.

The *Ethics* lectures comprise two sets of lectures, the first delivered in Münster in 1929 and the latter, a reworking of the first set, delivered in Bonn in 1930. One of the topics he treated in the lectures was the concept of the orders of creation (*Schöpfungsordnungen*). Considerable theological debate surrounded it at the time. Several prominent theologians advocated different versions of the idea, among them Paul Althaus in Germany and Emil Brunner in Switzerland. Brunner's influential work on ethics, *The Divine Command*, which applied the idea of the orders of creation to various spheres of social life, appeared in 1932, shortly after Barth's lectures were delivered. It is evident from contemporary correspondence between Barth and Brunner that the concept of orders of creation and mandates was a major point of discussion between them.[10] Barth initially found the idea to have some limited theological validity, for he discusses it briefly in the *Ethics*. But he was wary of its susceptibility to ideological distortion, and he devoted little attention to it.

Shortly after Barth delivered the ethics lectures, the Nazis came to power in Germany, and the Protestant churches in Germany (among other groups) found themselves in an intense struggle with the regime. The *Kirchenkampf* of the 1930s led to Barth's involvement in the drafting of the Barmen Declaration of 1934. These events formed the context for two of his most important writings on law—"Church and State" (1938) and "The Christian Community and the Civil Community" (1946). Barth's activities during this period have been described in detail elsewhere.[11] Three consequences bear mention.

First, the church struggle required him to grapple with fundamental theological questions about ethical existence in a secularized and even paganized political environment. It prompted urgent questions for him about the nature of sin and idolatry, the limits of politics, the meaning of the church, and the role of the state and the legal order.

Second, the experiences forced Barth to engage law and legality. They primarily arose in an ecclesial context. As Wolfgang Huber observes, the central debates in the *Kirchenkampf* concerned the nature of the church, but also involved its role and relation to the state and politics. The ensuing struggle between the Confessing Church and the regime raised questions about the autonomy of various spheres of social life—the question of *Eigengesetzlichkeit*. At issue was the autonomy of social and political institutions, including the legal order. These questions bore on church governance,

---

10. On this point, see Hart, *Barth vs. Brunner*, 116–19.

11. For example, see Busch, *Unter den Bogen*, 199–214; Jehle, *Against the Stream*, 46–56.

leadership, and authority, as well as its relation to the state. The Nazi-aligned German Christians appealed to Aryan-inspired theology to justify their usurpation of the German church, but these were also questions about law. How do the other social and political domains relate to it and to each other? Are politics, economy, law and technology subject to their own norms and controls, detached from religion and from each other? Or not? These were not merely matters for abstract and theoretical speculation.

Third, the war led Barth to challenge, and later to blame, the Lutheran notion of two kingdoms for its role in contributing to the rise of Nazi totalitarianism. He wrote in a letter in December 1939 that "The German people are suffering from the heritage of the greatest German Christian, from the error of Martin Luther concerning the relationship between the law and the gospel, the secular and the spiritual order and authority: as a result natural paganism has not been so much limited and restricted as transfigured, confirmed and strengthened."[12] The Lutheran idea of independent state authority "provided a certain space for German paganism."[13] These criticisms reflected Barth's conviction that the separate spheres of church, society, and state are subject to overarching Christological authority. Barth felt that history sadly confirmed the theological failures of a fractured and segmented vision of autonomous realms implicit in the two kingdoms notion—or distortions of it. Historical experience forced him to acknowledge the reality and the necessity of law, as well as its limits.

Theology and Ethics

Barth's view of law reflects his conception of ethics in general. He believes that theology precedes and frames ethics. Ethics is based on theological presuppositions. Ethical analysis is ultimately theological analysis, and before it is ethical, it is theological. As Barth proclaims in the *Church Dogmatics*, "Dogmatics is ethics."[14] Ethical scrutiny of law therefore takes place within a theological frame; it is grounded in, and informed by, a theological hermeneutic.

For Barth, ethics involves response to divine grace. It does not consist of casuistical guidelines or principles. It is not conventionally classifiable as teleological or deontological; it does not presuppose a specific metaethical theory. Barth describes ethics as a "helping science" (*Hilfswissenschaft*). The word of God is the source of ethics. Ethics does not provide direct moral

---

12. Barth, *Eine Schweizer Stimme*, 113.
13. Barth, *Eine Schweizer Stimme*, 121.
14. Barth, *CD* 1/2:782.

guidance but assists in interpreting the divine word for a given time and place. The keystone of Barth's ethics is the will of God as known through the word of God. The word of God, for Barth, is known through revelation, and its revelatory content is grace.[15] This is encountered as divine command, and Barth conceives of the command in a trinitarian manner, comprising the divine actions of creation, reconciliation, and redemption.[16] Barth emphasizes the command of God as Reconciler, but emphasizes that reconciliation anticipates, and is completed in, redemption. The divine command defines the good and encounter with that command entails obedience to it. For Barth, as David Haddorff remarks, "ethics is responsible action in relation to God's command of grace."[17] That responsible action has the character of what Barth called "filial engagement in absolute trust."[18]

This conception of ethics relates to law in that all ethical activity, including activity within the domains of politics and law, takes place within the economy of divine command and reconciliation. Law derives its ethical significance in being related, however indirectly and proximately, to the divine commands implicit in the divine word. The relation orients human law to divine law. Divine law is the objective basis (*Realgrund*) of human law. As a consequence, Barth understands law primarily in its theological dimension and in relation to its third use (*tertius usus legi*).[19] He tends to downplay the first two uses of the law (*usus politicus* and *usus elenchticus*), and distances himself from Luther's embrace of those two uses of law on the grounds that it implies a kind of natural theology.[20]

As Barth developed his theology of law, it came to stand in contrast to other understandings of law current at the time, particularly those current in Lutheran ethics. Barth's view amounted to, as Huber puts it, "a declaration of war" on Lutheran understandings of law and the state.[21] This softened somewhat over time, but Barth's critique illustrates early on how different the foundations for his thinking were from that of the Lutheran social ethics of the first decades of the twentieth century.

It is important to note that Barth distinguishes between law and politics as well as between law and the state. The relationship between Christianity

---

15. Barth, "Gospel and Law," 72.
16. See Biggar, "Barth's Trinitarian Ethics," 216–20.
17. Haddorff, "Introduction," 4.
18. Barth, *Christian Life*, 49–105.
19. See Honecker, *Einführung*, 71, who refers to the "closeness" of Barth to Melanchthon and Calvin in this regard.
20. See Gäfgen, *Recht*, 224–25.
21. Huber, *Gerechtigkeit*, 120.

and law is different from that between Christianity and the state or politics. Law and state are relatively different domains. Positive law differs from the theological understanding of law. Readings of Barth that fail to note this difference tend to subsume questions of law under questions of state and politics, including church-state relations. Law then recedes into the background, along with its relation to justice.

Certain elements of Barth's theology particularly impinge on his notion of positive law. They include covenant, reconciliation, and above all, a Christological orientation, as expressed in the notion of the kingly Lordship of Christ. Each of these doctrines and motifs is treated extensively by Barth in his *Church Dogmatics*. The first two are only mentioned briefly here, the third is detailed below, given its special relevance for Barth's views on positive law.

Barth affirms a *covenant* between God and humanity established through the redemptive work of Jesus Christ. Christ both elects and is elected. Humanity is elected by God as a covenant partner. Through this divine initiative, gospel, law and justification are inextricably linked. This divine action precedes and underlies any distinctions among them. The concept of covenant is one of the architectonic elements in the structure of Barth's theology.[22]

Similarly, the doctrine of *reconciliation* is foundational for Barth's theology. It treats the fundamental theme of the divine economy of grace through the atoning work of Christ. This expresses God's justification of himself through establishing divine justice in the face of human sinfulness.[23]

A Christological Concentration: The Kingly Lordship of Christ

Central for Barth's theology of law is the motif of the kingly lordship of Christ.[24] Following Schleiermacher, Barth believed that theology should have an organizing principle. In Barth's case, this principle is a trinitarian Christocentrism.[25] Heinz Zahrnt speaks of Barth's Christocentrism as

22. Covenant is discussed in the first book of volume 3 of the *Church Dogmatics*.

23. Barth treats reconciliation in the books comprising volume 4 of the *Church Dogmatics*.

24. It is often referred to in German original as the "*Königherrschaft Christi*" or translated as the "kingly lordship of Christ"; it is alternatively used here in the abbreviated form of "lordship of Christ."

25. Obviously, "Christological" and "Christocentric" do not have the same meaning. In much of the secondary literature on Barth, "Christological" appears more frequently. For present purposes, "Christocentric" is used in the sense of a central emphasis on the theological role of Christ in the divine economy of salvation.

"unparalleled."[26] In Barth's thought, "the whole of theology becomes Christology," and "there exists no independent theme in theology other than Christology—neither directly or indirectly."[27]

But the concept of Christocentrism is not self-explanatory. It is often taken to mean that Barth's basic orientation to positive law is framed by a basic conviction of the central significance of reconciliation in and through Christ. What does it mean within the context of Christian ethics? What does it imply for human law? Martin Honecker observes that, with reference to law, "Christological" can have various meanings: dogmatic; soteriological; or simply "Christian."[28]

Interestingly, Barth does not often use the adjective "Christological" in connection with human law. Instead, he presents theological positions from which Christological implications follow for law. This can be seen in Barth's relating of law to the doctrine of reconciliation and sanctification. These theological affirmations identify the actual basis of law on which human law rests. In an interview conducted in his later years, Barth was asked about the basis of human law. He responded: "If there are traces of genuine law contributing to and mixed in with so-called law and so-called natural law, they are not traces of human goodness and capabilities, but are traces of the kingly rule of Christ, who is lord overall, also over those who don't know him, and those who don't want to know anything about Christianity, also those who want to attack Christianity."[29]

Barth's Christological orientation is crystallized in his notion of the kingly lordship of Christ. This is a foundational motif in his ethics, serving as a theological affirmation of the preeminence of divine grace. It voices the claim that Christ is fundamental for all aspects of social existence, including the state and law.

Christ's rule anticipates the triumph over sin and death through humiliation and resurrection, signifying that Christ's lordship is not immanent and mundane but spiritual and transcendent, though with mundane consequences. It is a harbinger of the coming Kingdom of God. Eberhard Busch interprets the kingly lordship motif in terms of "the dawning of the kingdom of God in the crucifixion and resurrection of Christ, in which he has given our all powers." Through the motif, Barth insists on the uncompromising

---

26. Zahrnt, *Question of God*, 94.

27. Zahrnt, *Question of God*, 94.

28. Honecker, *Grundriß*, 582. Honecker believes that all of these meanings presuppose, and aspire to, a theological grounding of mundane law, something he largely rejects.

29. Barth, *Gespräche*, 106.

centrality of Christ and his soteriological significance for all realms of human existence and activity.

The lordship motif has a lengthy history dating from early Christian times. In the early years of the Reformation, it was understood as one of the three spiritual offices of Christ (prophet, priest, king), through which he has dominion over the church through grace. This follows from the saving power of the cross, not from any form of mundane sovereignty. In later Reformed thought, the kingly reign of Christ connected the kingdom of Jesus Christ with the Kingdom of God, emphasizing the centrality of Christ and the proclamation of divine authority over all areas of life. This dominion was understood in spiritual rather than in worldly terms, and as latent rather than patent. Modern interpretations of the kingly rule tend to stress specific aspects of it, such as the soteriological, eschatological, or ethical. In each of these conceptions, the motif introduces an eschatological dimension. Barth expanded these original understandings to incorporate the political and legal realms. Among the implications of the kingly lordship motif was a rejection of the alleged autonomy orders of society, economy and state. Increasingly, it also came to stand for rejection of a compartmentalized, privatized notion of faith.[30]

Barth's embrace of the kingly rule of Christ is evident in the Barmen Declaration of 1934, which he principally authored. The second thesis of the Declaration states that Jesus Christ is God's "vigorous announcement of his claim on our whole life," and it rejects "the false doctrine that there could be areas of our life in which we would belong not to Jesus Christ but to other lords."[31] This essentially affirms what he considered to be the non-negotiable convictions of the Confessing Church in its confrontation with the German Christians. According to Huber, the thesis was aimed at the "provincialism" of Protestant thinking, which reduced the reality of faith to the status of one special reality alongside others."[32]

The Declaration's fifth thesis declares that the state, by divine appointment (*Anordnung*), has the task of maintaining law (*Recht*) and peace, so far as human discernment and human ability make this possible. The Church "draws attention to God's Kingdom, God's commandment and justice (*Gerechtigkeit*), and with these the responsibility of those who rule and those who are ruled."[33] This understanding of the relation of the church and state is consistent with two kingdoms thinking in that it assumes a difference

---

30. Walther, "Königherrschaft," 311–23.
31. Quoted in Jüngel, *Christ, Justice, and Peace*, xxiv.
32. Huber, "Barmen Theological Declaration," 31.
33. Quoted in Jüngel, *Christ, Justice, and Peace*, xxvii.

between religious and non-religious realms. But it also transcends it by asserting that the church has responsibilities for the state and law.

Within the kingly lordship motif are two sets of polarities. First, there is a tension between the present and the unrealized character of the kingly reign. Second, a polarity exists between the absolute character of the kingship and its application to mundane circumstances. To what extent has the kingly reign already been realized, and to what extent does it require compromise with existing human structures?

Barth is forced to confront these questions in relating the kingly rule to positive law. In the *Ethics*, law is an interactive social process for regulating conflict. That interpretation culminates in the *Church Dogmatics*, where law consciously looks to divine law for guidance, though without surrendering its commitment to neutrality and toleration of the worldviews of fellow citizens. Perhaps his most widely noted and renowned attempts to answer them are contained in the essays "Church and State" and "The Christian Community and the Civil Community."

In "Church and State," Barth asks, "Is there an inward and vital connection by means of which in any sense human law, as well as divine justification, becomes a concern of Christian faith and Christian responsibility, and therefore also a matter which concerns the Christian Church?"[34] This is the central question Barth's theology of law seeks to answer. He grapples with it in a manner that is both hermeneutical and analogical. Barth's approach is hermeneutical in that the kingly lordship motif supplies the ultimate interpretive frame for social reality. That reality is not self-constituting or self-defining; it does not supply its own interpretive context. That is provided solely through the action of Christ, who decisively establishes the electing, covenanting, reconciling and sanctifying nature of God.[35] For law, this implies that Christ is sovereign over it, not manifestly but implicitly by means of its supramundane character and its eschatological anticipation. Further, his method is analogical in that he believes there are parables and correspondences between the mundane world of law and politics in the divine reality of covenant and reconciliation.

---

34. Barth, "Church and State," 101.

35. Regarding the history of the two kingdoms concept, see Steinmüller, *Rechtstheologie*, 55–68.

Beyond the Two Kingdoms and *Eigengesetzlichkeit* (Autonomous Orders)

The two kingdoms doctrine—under that name—dates from the early twentieth century, although in substance it is traceable to Luther and beyond.[36] Some attribute its modern formulation to Barth, who purportedly coined the phrase "two kingdoms."[37] Barth rejected the doctrine in principle fairly early on (at least as early as 1922), and his opposition to it intensified during the Nazi era. Indeed, his biographer speaks of Barth's "repulsion" to the two kingdoms idea.[38] He leveled sharp criticisms against it, particularly in the 1930s.

Barth's rejection of the doctrine is not surprising, given that it seems to distinguish the realms, while he seeks their alignment. He is interested not in differentiation but in association. To the extent one can speak of separate spheres, realms or kingdoms, the question for him is not what separates them but "first and foremost, to what extent they are connected."[39] And even the state, even when it perpetrates acts of deep injustice, retains a positive relation to the order of redemption.[40] Since divine justification is the "true and only real source and norm of all human law" there can be no question for Barth of a fundamental separation of the kingdoms.[41] Of course, connection does not mean similarity. The realms are different in character, so that it is more appropriate to speak of similarity in difference.

Barth's view of law proceeds from different premises than the bifurcated relation of the two kingdoms. He locates law within the doctrine of reconciliation; indeed, it forms the basis of law. Law is divinely established as an antidote for human sin. The authority of law is grounded in the kingship of Christ. Though not readily acknowledged by sinful humans, natural law provides some access to this truth, although its contents are limited and vulnerable to distortion.

As noted, Barth's Christologically based understanding of the relation of divine sovereignty is a response to the notion of the autonomy of social spheres. This concept has been attributed to Max Weber, who analyzed the increasing independence, separation, and moral autonomy of various

---

36. Wright, *Understanding*, 32.

37. Huber, "Barmen Theological Doctrine," 35. Others ascribe it to different authors. Wright, *Understanding*, 31, traces its first use to Reinhold Seeberg in 1917.

38. Busch, *Barth*, 379.

39. Barth, "Church and State," 102.

40. Barth, "Church and State," 114.

41. Barth, "Church and State," 126.

spheres of social activity, such as economy, politics, and law. The notion of autonomous orders implies a rejection of any comprehensive ordering principle, leading to a segmentation of social reality to discrete and potentially conflicting spheres. It stands in contrast if not in opposition to an ethic of brotherliness that Weber identified with a religious outlook.[42] The autonomous orders were also a polemical concept that underwrote increasing secularization in favor of the critical rationality of modern positivism. As Weber asserted, "As economic and political actions follow laws of their own, so every other rational action within the world remains inescapably bound to worldly conditions. These conditions are remote from brotherliness and must serve as a means or as ends of rational action."[43] Barth was likely familiar with Weber's thesis of autonomous orders.[44] His response to it takes the form of a Christocentric affirmation against a pluralism of autonomous orders. This comes to the fore in the Barmen Declaration and is subsequently developed by Barth in his war-era essays.

At the time, the two kingdoms and the lordship of Christ symbolized contrasting if not competing visions of social ethics. Writing in the 1960s, Heinz Zahrnt contends that the two watchwords "the kingly rule of Christ" and the "two kingdoms" represent a "fundamental division of theological opinion."[45] "This point, and not as in the past in the Eucharist, is the dividing line between the two Protestant confessions has to be sought."[46] Yet, as Ernst Wolf argues, both presuppose divine sovereignty over all social orders and activity. While the Lutheran doctrine implies a certain deference to the secular world, it does so on the basis of ultimate subordination to God. This raises the question of how mundane structures differ when seen in the light of Christ's Lordship. Barth became increasingly convinced that such sovereignty was not to be based on any order of creation.

The Orders of Creation

As already noted, the orders of creation was a common theme in continental Protestant ethics in the 1930s. It was especially prominent in Lutheran

42. Martin Honecker defines *Eigengesetzlichkeit* as expressing "a separation between religion and life-world, an emancipation of society, economy and science from theology and church" (Honecker, "Autonomous Right," 209).

43. Weber, "Religious Rejection," 339.

44. Lienemann, "Gewalt," 55.

45. Zahrnt, *Question*, 175.

46. Zahrnt, *Question*, 175. Huber speaks of both concepts having a "foundational, interpretative or legitimating role and significance for the political action of church bodies" (Huber, "Barmen Declaration," 29).

thought, but it also attracted the interest of reformed thinkers such as Emil Brunner. Law was often viewed as one of the creational orders itself, or as a part of the state and serving as an important support for the orders of marriage, work, and economy. Barth's attitude towards the concept evolved over time, moving from a distant reserve to open criticism.[47] His ultimate rejection was based on a conviction that the orders of creation were a form of natural theology, which he rejected. Although Barth incorporated the idea of the command of creation in the *Church Dogmatics*, he uses it in the singular, and expressly derives its material content from Christ.[48]

This rejection led Barth to oppose many prominent Lutheran theologians of the pre-war years, especially those sympathetic to *völkisch* values. Conservative theologians such as Althaus and Elert discerned theological significance in the institutions and history of distinct cultures (particularly in Germanic traditions). But for Barth, law and creation were not a source of revelation. To hold otherwise was to imply a subversive plurality of competing revelations. Barmen expressly rejects this.[49] Barth's refusal to base law on any kind of order or natural capability reflects his essentially negative attitude toward natural law.

Natural Law: A "Dark Groping"

By and large, Barth is skeptical, and at times dismissive, of natural law. His rejection, however, was not absolute. One commentator has argued that Barth proposes an eschatological ontology that is functionally similar to traditional understandings of natural law.[50] But how does Barth understand natural law? In the "Christian Community" he defines it as "the embodiment of what man is alleged to regard as universally right and wrong as necessary, permissible, and forbidden "by nature," that is, on any conceivable premise."[51] Barth's resistance to it is theological in nature, for it suggests a competitive source of revelatory truth. In the "Christian Community," Barth

---

47. Nimmo, "Orders of Creation," 28–31.

48. Barth, *CD* 3/4:35.

49. Eberhard Jüngel, *Christ, Justice, and Peace*, 51. See also Hunsinger, *How to Read Karl Barth*, 246, referring to the "impossibility of revelational pluralism."

50. See Couvenhoven, who contends that Barth was not actually opposed to natural law because of its dependence on natural theology, but because most conceptions of it lacks an eschatological dimension, which he integrated into his conception of the divine command (Couenhoven, "Barth's Rejection," 36). Also see Schüller, who contends that Barth, despite his protestations, in effect affirms a version of natural law understood as the capacity of human rationality to discern law (Schüller, *Herrschaft Christi*, 52).

51. Barth, "Christian Community," 163.

warns against basing "Christian decisions" on natural law.[52] He claims that natural law fails to provide a "firmer and clearer motivation for political decisions than the word of God."[53] Barth detects an affinity between natural law and natural theology, which he dismisses as not based on the knowledge of God in Jesus Christ manifested in proclamation, scripture, and revelation.[54] Natural law relies on human reason rather than on the Word of God in its three modes of proclamation, scripture, and revelation. It suffers from a noetic deficiency in that its contents are only haphazardly discernible. Nevertheless, he concedes the necessity of "so-called natural law" for the state, which is concerned with externalities and lacks knowledge of the Word.[55]

For its part, the state is dependent on natural law, though it is consigned to guessing and groping for its contents.[56] It is a "porous well,"[57] based on diffuse and indistinct notions of good and evil. It labors under illusions of its own authority, and in fact amounts to a "more or less refined positivism."[58] The state's embrace of natural law is subject to the requirement of religious neutrality. If natural law were considered a valid source of law, the church could claim to be a privileged interpreter of it, and this would create the danger of ecclesial interference in political and legal matters.

The fundamental deficiency of natural law is that it lacks the guidance of a Christological fixed point, a norm that "is anything but natural."[59] As George Hunsinger remarks, "What natural law theory would ascribe to nature, Barth critically relocated in a context of grace."[60] Grace alone could overcome what Barth sees as the misguided separation of nature and grace. His Christological orientation effectively excludes natural law as a separate and independent source of law. Whatever substance it has is ultimately attributable to Christologically informed law, which is the true natural law. As Barth writes in the *Church Dogmatics*, "In human history, and beyond all history, human or otherwise, there is no other or higher law than the law of

52. Barth, "Christian Community," 163.
53. Barth, "Christian Community," 163.
54. Barth, *CD* 1/1:187–98. While VanDrunen notes at natural law is not the same as natural theology, he argues that Barth's critique of natural law was simply one aspect of his more general critique of the idea of the natural knowledge of God. See VanDrunen, *Natural Law*, 333.
55. Barth, "Christian Community," 163.
56. Barth, "Christian Community," 163–64.
57. Barth, "Christian Community," 169–70.
58. Barth, "Christian Community," 164.
59. Barth, "Christian Community," 165.
60. Hunsinger, "Barth," 178.

divine mercy, now revealed, established and applied in the oblation of the Lamb of God.... There is no place from which it can be relativized. It is the true "natural law" which necessarily limits and relativizes all positive law."[61]

Anthropological Interactions with Law

Barth's anthropology shapes his understanding of law in two ways. First, Barth sees law as a necessary response to the ubiquity of human sin, serving prophylactic and preservative purposes.[62] At the same time, law is grounded Christologically, transforming human life and its structures and giving them a promise of future fulfilment. To the extent law responds to human sinfulness, it challenges the self-centeredness, untruthfulness, lassitude and mendacity of human beings—all characteristics of sin as Barth conceives it.[63] In this context, law is primarily penal and deterrence-oriented. But since law is also soteriological, it reflects true humanity in Christ achieved through reconciliation. Barth refuses to root sin in anthropological pessimism. Rather, it is the result of an irruption of nothingness, to which God responds on the basis of his covenant. Sin is preceded by reconciliation, and it is understood fully only in relation to it.[64]

Political and social orders are therefore to be judged by the criterion of humanity, configured through Christ's reconciliation into a principle of co-humanity (*Mitmenschlichkeit*). This perspective envisions Jesus as the human for other humans, whose humanity corresponds to his divinity, in his devotion (*Zuwendung*) to fellow humans. For Barth, an understanding of humanity in light of the imperative of co-humanity measures and judges human reality.[65]

The interaction of sin and creatureliness is reflected in law. Law is Christologically based yet simultaneously shaped by human sin. Because of sin, law is an expression of both divine patience and providence. But because of its Christological foundation, it is at the same time an instrument of reconciliation. While law is necessitated by sin, it is also grounded in divine, reconciling activity.

The deeply theological character of Barth's theology of law is evident from how Barth relates law and justification. For him, justification follows from the primary act of divine self-justification exercised in divine

61. Barth, *CD* 3/2:484.
62. Barth, *CD* 4/2:491–92.
63. See Gäfgen, *Recht*, 210–11.
64. Barth, *Ethics*, 376.
65. Barth, *CD* 3/2:203.

freedom.⁶⁶ Divine self-justification leads to the establishment of divine law. That law condemns human law and justice.⁶⁷ Divine law is the source, norm and boundary of human law. Barth speaks of a "legal continuum" existing in divine justification, constituted by divine law and human law in which both are related, affirmatively yet critically.⁶⁸

Also of fundamental importance, as mentioned above, is reconciliation. This is evident early on in the ethics lectures, where Barth asserts: "It is intrinsic to law that society plans and prepares for the worst in any of us. Wittingly or unwittingly it accepts thereby a highly theological presupposition."⁶⁹ This double grounding leads Barth, for example, to view criminal law as a "protective measure" in light of human sin, but to deny that it is, in light of reconciliation, a punitive system of sanctions.⁷⁰ Interpretation of law in terms of reconciliation endows it with an affirmative vocation that contrasts in emphasis on the containment of human sinfulness, such as one encounters in Thielicke. Barth rejects a sin-centered understanding of human beings in favor of an acknowledgment of sinfulness contextualized by reconciliation. In helping to organize and maintain social life, human law reflects a coinherence of the negative and the positive, of sinful actuality and divine redemption.

Barth sees the character of law as dependent on its communal context, whether in the Christian or the civil community. Both are communities, and both require law. The church exists in a political continuum with the state, but they are not of equal dignity, for the Christian community is closer to the Christological center than the state. Within the Christian community, law is liturgical, sacrificial, and conciliatory; within the civil community, it is conflictual, contentious, and corrigible.

These basic theological convictions inform Barth's theology of law; closer consideration of his principal writings on law will illustrate their importance.

---

66. Barth, *CD* 4/1:563–68.

67. Barth, *CD* 4/1:529. Also see "Church and State," in which Barth asserts that it is the preaching of the justification of the Kingdom of God that founds, here and now, the true system of law (Barth, "Church and State," 120).

68. Barth, "Church and State," 141.

69. Barth, *Ethics*, 378.

70. Barth, *CD* 3/4:437–50. Barth rejects the concept of general deterrence in favor of specific deterrence in criminal law, on the grounds that is implies a refusal of election and reconciliation. See Barth, *CD* 3/4:440–42.

Barth's Principal Writings on Positive Law

The Ethics of 1929–1930

The ethics lectures of 1929–1930 were delivered in the waning years of the Weimar Republic, during which the relative stability of the mid-1920s was giving way to increasing political and social turmoil. They were not published until after Barth's death, reportedly out of concern about his use of the concept of the orders of creation.

Barth organized the lectures in a nontraditional, thematic manner under headings such as order, authority, humility, gratitude, conscience and hope. Law appears in the section dealing with authority, not order. There, Barth defines law: "By law, we understand the order of human life in society that is publicly known and recognized and protected by public force, made known and recognized by the decree of society and protected by its power."[71] This order of life serves as the framework for the assertion of the interests of individuals. The assertion of interests is often obstructed by conflicting interests asserted by others, and law must regulate these collisions. For Barth, the function of law is the regulation of conflict: "The problem of law begins where the collision of my own activity with the social order begins; where this collision cannot be eliminated; where the neighbor and not I has right; where he claims publicly acknowledged and protected right for himself and against me."[72] In this view, law is a social and anthropological set of practices before it is a political institution. Through reason and order, conflicts may be resolved. Barth's approach here is informed by a Kantian idea of law as the coordination of individual action by means of rules based on reason and freedom.[73]

The validity of this view of law ultimately depends on recognition of the rights of the other, whether voluntary or coerced. But if validity depends on recognition, what is recognition's content? In a fundamental sense, it is the obligation of observance of the rights of others that serves to secure their observance of my rights.[74] Reciprocity requires the adjustment of self-interest in the encounter with the self-interests of others. Law is therefore

---

71. Barth, *Ethics*, 376 (translation altered). The translation uses "right" instead of "law." It is unclear what an "order of right" would be.

72. Barth, *Ethics*, 377 (translation altered).

73. On the early Kantian influences on Barth's interpretation of law, see Lienemann, "Gewalt," 157.

74. Recognition is also important for Pannenberg, who proposes a notion of it based on the personhood of others. See below chapter 6, as well as Shingleton, "Pannenberg's Theology of Law."

both an expressive as well as a receptive form of social interaction. "Law is not in us, but encounters us."[75]

Barth's notion of law as based on rights and conflicts renders it a human enterprise, not an order of creation. Its *telos* is co-humanity (*Mitmenschlichkeit*), which evidences divine election and covenant.[76] The state serves this end by creating order and preventing chaos, and it does so in furtherance of a God-willed community, not because of divine anger. To view law primarily in terms of a creational order obscures its role as a command of reconciliation, expressing divine freedom and initiative.

This notion of law as an institutional system of ordering rights, understood broadly, had been previously proposed by Barth in a lecture delivered during his Safenwil years entitled "Menschenrecht und Burgerpflicht." There, Barth contends that law is concerned with the coordination of activities of self-determining agents with each other, and it accomplishes that through rules regulating the encounter of actors with each other. Such rules must take the form of universalizable directives. This anticipates a principal theme of *Ethics*: the relationship with the neighbor is an arena of encounter. They involve not only the neighbor but also Christ. Through them the primary relationship to Christ becomes concrete. "Thus the saving command of God contradicts us by placing a Thou over against the I and in opposition to it."[77]

Instead of a state-centric notion of law, Barth proposes an individualist-interactionist one, although one in which the individual is not atomistic, but other-related. It also involves a functional/transactional understanding of law in keeping with Barth's aversion to generalized, abstract conceptualizations. Essentially, it is concerned with the regulation of conflict. Again, Barth contends that "The problem of law begins where the collision of my own activity with social order begins; where he [the other] claims publicly acknowledged and protected right for himself and against me."[78] Barth's language here is significant: law is not a matter of personal rights, but the encounter in the conflict of rights, manifested in and through the person of the neighbor.

What is particularly theological about this? Seeing law as imposing limits on individual self-assertion reflects, for Barth, "a highly theological" presupposition.[79] Barth finds theological/anthropological presuppositions

---

75. Barth, *Ethics*, 214, 377.
76. Marsch, "Christliche Begründung I," 209.
77. Barth, *Ethics*, 349.
78. Barth, *Ethics*, 377 (translation altered).
79. Barth, *Ethics*, 378.

reflected in jurisprudential debates about the historical origins of law. He scrutinizes the positions of two nineteenth-century German jurists, von Ihering and Kohler, who advanced contrasting views of law in relation to human capability and frailty. Is law grounded in *ius* (v. Jhering), which equates to conventional positive law, or in *fas* (divine law) (Kohler)? Barth agrees with von Jhering that law is a human institution, involving the containment of conflict. At the same time, he also affirms Kohler's position: "I have to obey, not because this is right for a vast majority of other people, but because this vast majority is the mouth which expresses, and means to express what is right in itself."[80] This act of acknowledgment, Barth contends, is ultimately tenable only on a religious basis.

Barth frames law theologically by asserting that law belongs under the doctrine of reconciliation rather than of creation. Law relates to human deficiency but more significantly to reconciliation. Barth's view of the function of law does not adequately account for its moral validity. He believes that such validity is necessary, but that it is to be derived from Christianity. Only on a Christian basis, rather than a religious one, can law be free of ideological distortion by revealing law's capacity for unjust consequences without rejecting law altogether.[81] For Barth, Christianity accomplishes this by envisioning the law-enforcing neighbor as a sinful yet divinely appointed counterpart. To the extent that law sanctions the assertion of others' legal rights in a way that constrains me, it not only corrects but illuminates. As Barth puts it, "law opens my eyes to the neighbor."[82]

Law's religious aspect derives from this ability to reveal persons to each other. In this sense, it supports a neighbor-oriented ethics, in which the interactions of persons are fundamental to social existence. Admittedly, these encounters can be disagreeable, for they may involve "irksome and dubious" claims to rights.[83] But conflict can culminate in acknowledgement: not only of the existence of the neighbor, but also of the reality of reconciliation with God.

The church as the body that remembers and celebrates the ultimate divine event parallels, in a sense, the state with its encounters among citizens. Anticipating, inversely, the metaphor of the concentric circles of church and state in "Church and State" and "The Christian Community and the Civil Community," Barth proposes in the *Ethics* that the state is the center with the church as its circumference: "The church does not simply have the state

---

80. Barth, *Ethics*, 379.
81. Barth, *Ethics*, 222.
82. Barth, *Ethics*, 382.
83. Barth, *Ethics*, 382.

somewhere alongside it, but essentially has it in itself, acknowledging its function as necessary within the earthly and temporal city of God, which can only be one."[84] The fundamental dynamic dealt with by law—the encounter of right with right—is present within both church and state. The church sees that the significance of human encounters is defined by the divine-human encounter. For the state, encounter is also the interactive basis of law, and law in turn forms a part of the foundation of the state. This gives law a certain universality, though its specific norms vary from one political community to another. Law as interactionist encounter with neighbors: this is the core understanding of law in the *Ethics*.

Though Barth's presentation of law in the *Ethics* deals minimally with jurisprudential concerns, he puts forward a theological view of law as an arena of confrontation, limitation, and reconciliation. Yet it is theological in a particular way, less in terms of specific, substantive content and more as theological reflection on ethics itself. He sees ethics as a questioning, situational activity that requires the acknowledgment and preservation of each individual's autonomy as hearers of divine commands. This means that in his early views of law, Barth is not interested in advancing ethical theories of the good and right so much as in the basic ethical act of attending to the divine word in the face of human idolatries. As Thies Gundlach remarks, "Barth's *Ethics* unfolds the difference between God and human beings (and theologians!) as a questioning and relativizing of all ethical positions and it does this not because it occupies an absolute position, but because its particular competence is in preserving the difference between relative, human positions and the indisposible, absolute position of God."[85] This leads Barth to portray law as a social institution stripped of theocratic pretension that cannot be divinized or consecrated by religious authority. It is not something that is "fallen from heaven, but is honestly and actually human law."[86] Indeed, "All law is essentially human law."[87]

The Essays of the War/Postwar Years

Barth's two essays "Church and State" and "The Christian Community and the Civil Community," both originally delivered as lectures, were written before and immediately after the Second World War, respectively. The earlier essay was drafted during the church struggle and the ascendance of the

84. Barth, *Ethics*, 383.
85. Gundlach, "Theologische Ethik," 218.
86. Barth, *Ethics*, 220 (translation altered).
87. Barth, *Ethics*, 380 (translation altered).

Nazi regime; the latter one following the regime's demise and amidst the resulting destruction and chaos. While these writings have been closely studied for their political and church-state implications, their references to, and implications for, positive law have drawn less attention. This is partly a result of Barth's tendency in "Church and State" to speak interchangeably of law and the state. Barth frames the basic theme of the essay in terms of human law (evident from its German title and opening paragraphs), although he proceeds to devote most of his attention to the state. One commentator, Bruno Schüller, contends that Barth's references to the state apply to law as well because the state is both particularly concerned with law and is a subject of law itself.[88]

Certain themes prominent in *Ethics* recede into the background in these essays. For example, the collision-based understanding of law and the role of recognition is superseded by a more Christologically oriented notion of law. This echoes the Barmen Declaration's emphasis on the kingly rule of Christ. "Church and State" reflects this evolution in its increasingly explicit affirmation of a theological basis for human law. In the beginning of the essay, Barth poses the question of a link between justification and law: "Is there a connection between justification of the sinner through faith alone, completed once for all by God through Jesus Christ, and the problem of justice, the problem of human law?"[89] By framing the question in this way, Barth emphasizes the theological centrality of justification, understood in terms of a Reformed concern for mundane structures rather than a Lutheran differentiation between sacred and secular. Barth's concern is to reaffirm the relation between law in justification in the face of contemporary pressures forcing them in opposite directions: towards either pietistic individualism or rationalistic secularism. The question also implies that human law requires a theological connection if it is not to be overwhelmed by relativism and political manipulation.

Barth's concern with establishing a relation between divine and human law was anticipated in the essay "Gospel and Law" (1935). Barth primarily deals there with the theological concept of law, but it has relevance for human law as well. There, he argues that if Christ is not the goal of law, then law vacillates unsteadily between nomianism and antinomianism. By nomianism, Barth has in mind natural law and abstract reason; he refers to the Nazi notion of a *Volksnomos*. In contrast, an antinomian attitude is marked by an inwardness "averse to every concrete command and tie." By

---

88. Schüller, *Herrschaft Christi*, 19

89. Barth, "Church and State," 101–2. The translation here has been altered to reflect Barth's reference here to law (*Recht*) and not justice (*Gerechtigkeit*). Barth uses the word "*Gerechtigkeit*" elsewhere in the text.

this juxtaposition, Barth seems to suggest that law is reducible neither to individual rights nor social function, but is connected with questions of teleological import encompassing both dimensions.

"Church and State" consists in large part of scriptural exegesis, informed by the centrality of the Christ event. That is definitive for human life in all its aspects, individual and social. It is attested by election, command, and covenant and drives toward eschatological consummation. Barth proceeds to examine certain Biblical texts that appear to imply a diastasis between church and state. He rejects the view that there is no relation between the two, for that leads to "sterile and dangerous separations." Behind the pursuit of a relation is Barth's conviction that the salvific activity of Christ is definitive and absolute for human law and justice.

Much of "Church and State" is focused on the scriptural accounts of Jesus's trial before Pontius Pilate. For Barth, they show an integral connection exists between law and the state, yet one vulnerable to distortion and perversion. This may take the form of the suppression of the proclamation of justification; it may also appear as subversion of law and its procedures. Ironically, in Jesus's trial, both occur yet nevertheless serve the gospel. In his exegesis, Barth seeks to define a proper relationship between the theological and the political/legal. The state is not, and should not be, concerned with the significance and veracity of justification.[90] But this does not render the state neutral to the reality of justification. Barth's reading of the scriptural texts leads him to contend that the state "in its relative independence has a substance, dignity, function and purpose as serving the person and work of Jesus Christ."[91] Interpreting Romans 13:1–7, Barth declares that, through the intercession and ministrations of the angelic orders, the state belongs originally and ultimately to Jesus Christ.[92] It serves divine purposes through its independence rather than through subservience. Its independence is exemplified in its administration of justice and protection of law.[93] Further, the state—not the church—is the primary eschatological symbol of fulfillment.

As activities of the state, the rule of law and the administration of justice therefore have abiding significance. The eschatological order is a

---

90. In the essay, there is a drift in Barth's argument away from his original question of the relation of law and justification to that of church and state. This seems to be prompted by his focus on the Biblical texts he discusses. One consequence of this drift is that Barth tends to link state and law in a way that overshadows his distinction between them in *Ethics* and elsewhere.

91. Barth, "Church and State," 118.

92. Barth, "Church and State," 118. Kreß criticizes Barth's interpretation as based on a misinterpretation of the word "*exousia*" (Kreß, *Staat*, 43).

93. Barth, "Church and State," 119.

political order.[94] It is a justified community. The true, eternal law of the ideal state is based on the preaching of justification of the Kingdom of God.[95] The church's duty is to proclaim justification. The state's protection of the ability of the church to proclaim this is a vital service it renders. Its responsibility for the administration of justice requires the state to maintain neutrality in matters of truth and belief. Otherwise, the state would deny its existence.[96]

Barth's emphasis on law's responsibility for the freedom to proclaim justification makes one pause. Is this really a responsibility of the law? The state protects all exercise of religion, regardless of content. Perhaps Barth's allocation of this specific task to the state reflects the circumstances under which he was writing, in the throes of the *Kirchenkampf*. He was understandably sensitive to the necessity of state protection for the church's freedom.

Ultimately, "Church and State" is more concerned with church/state relations than with the connection between human and divine law. But Barth is clear in his affirmation that the state (in the sense of the governmental apparatus within the civil community) is an "instrument of divine grace."[97] This acknowledges the role positive law plays in securing the freedom of the Christian community for its work of proclamation. It is not, without more, concerned in the first place with the intrinsic integrity of the law and its capacity for justice.

"Church and State" is an endorsement of law as one of the core functions of the state, one that serves to protect the church in the exercise of its activities through preserving order. Law is placed in service of the church in the pursuit of its spiritual ends. As Müller-Simon argues, the essay "provides a theory of human law only to the extent that its momentarily presupposed human character is again negated."[98] Barth's vigorous insistence on the neutrality of the state, the limits of citizens' obligation to it, and the integrity of the individual conscience are all important attributes of any tenable idea of law. But law has other concerns as well, such as justice and the preservation of order. The essay is helpful in distinguishing between the activities of the church and its proclamation of justification from the activities of the state and the maintenance of the political and social circumstances for that proclamation. But on the whole, it gives short shrift to the mundane functions of positive law.

---

94. Barth, "Church and State," 124.
95. Barth, "Church and State," 126.
96. Barth, "Church and State," 132.
97. Barth, "Church and State," 156.
98. Müller-Simon, *Rechtstheologie*, 123.

The later essay, "The Christian Community and the Civil Community," takes a somewhat different approach to law. In it, Barth introduces an analogical method of identifying the theological import of the characteristics of the state and law. The essay is known for its metaphor of two concentric circles representing the Christian and civil communities (rather than of the institutions of church and state). This shift from church and state to community implies a precedence of individuals and associations over institutions.[99] Again, connection between the two communities—Christian and civil—is Barth's primary concern. The connection is accomplished through a common relation to the Christocentric center common to both communities. "The civil community shares both a common origin and a common center with the Christian community."[100]

The communities remain distinct; their relationship is neither one of identity nor of heterogeneity. The essence of the Christian community, the assembly (*ekklesia*), is "the common life of those people in one Spirit, the Holy Spirit, that is, in obedience to the Word of God in Jesus Christ."[101] The civil community is concerned with law: it is the "commonality of all the people in one place, region or country insofar as they belong together under a constitutional system of government that is equally valid for and binding on them all, and which is defended and maintained by force."[102] It stands in contrast to the love that marks the Christian community. Yet the Christian community depends on institutions of the civil community, especially law, for its own freedom.

Barth posits a mutual dependence of the Christian and civil communities. The Christian community serves God through proclamation, and the civil community serves to enable this activity. Barth writes: "The deepest ultimate divine purpose of the civil community consists in creating opportunities for the preaching in hearing of the Word."[103] It achieves this by means of the "rational, secular and profane way of the establishment of law."[104] This view of law, simultaneously functionalist and positivist, forgoes any substantive notion of the normativity and legitimacy of positive law. While Barth later addresses these aspects in the *Church Dogmatics*, they are absent here.

---

99. Haddorff contends that the essay is "arguably Barth's most important essay in theological politics" (Haddorff, "Introduction," 12).

100. Barth, "Church and State," 156.

101. Barth, "Church and State," 150.

102. Barth, "Church and State," 150.

103. Barth, "Church and State," 166.

104. Barth, "Church and State," 166.

The relation between the spiritual and political realms in this essay is more subtly affirmative than it is in "Church and State." There, state and church primarily inhabit their own realms and interact, as it were, on their peripheries. In "The Christian Community," the spiritual community serves as a directive and guideline (*Richtschnur*) for political decisions, as well as for the structure and role of the political community. Barth remarks that these two communities are porous and overlapping; persons belong simultaneously to both. But they are different in grounding and ethos: the Christian community is conscious of the central significance of Christ while the civil community is not. It nevertheless carries out a divinely ordained purpose of maintaining order so that the gospel may be proclaimed. Here, Barth continues to see law as prior to and, to an extent, independent of the state. It is not derived from the state, but in a sense anticipates it. As Wolfgang Lienemann observes, "Barth judges statehood from law, namely from the perspective of whether and how people place demands on law, how it is challenged, protected, defended and promoted, but he will never consider law to be subordinate to the facticity of the state."[105]

Barth now describes the state largely in terms of its legal activities: it legislates, carries out laws, and administers justice.[106] The civil community and its activities are spiritually and metaphysically agnostic, and its members share no common awareness of their relation to God. Divine appeals have no place in the activities of the civil community.[107] Its activities are provisional, external and relative. But Barth again seeks a positive relation between the two communities. He finds it in a combination of commonality and difference, expressed in the image of two concentric circles. The Christian community is the center and the civil community is the circum. The center is shared by the two groups; this establishes the commonality. The peripheries of the two circles are distinguishable, one inclusive of the other, one exceeding the other. This illustrates difference. The nexus is the Christological center. Both circles are grounded in reconciliation, meaning that each community is knowable *ex post facto* as reconciled, redeemed, and restored reality.[108] But for the center, neither one is knowable or comprehensible. The capacity for reflection of Christological illumination is the capacity for analogy; "analogical capability is the ability to reflect [the Christian community] indirectly in a mirror."[109]

---

105. Lienemann, "Gewalt," 154.
106. Barth, "Christian Community," 151.
107. Barth, "Christian Community," 151.
108. Gäfgen, *Recht*, 254.
109. Barth, "Christian Community," 169.

The Christian community articulates the rationale for the state that it itself does not and cannot comprehend. The state is "dependent on a message being delivered to it."[110] Barth develops the essential attributes of the state Christologically; they reflect certain qualities of the divine kingdom, but they do so by analogy, not identity.

In "The Christian Community," Barth devotes attention to the role of law in the church community. Law in this context is exemplary for secular law, a thesis he later develops at some length in the section in the *Church Dogmatics* entitled "The Order of the Community." The exemplary character of communal law (as Barth calls the law of the Christian community) emphasizes its analogical suggestiveness. It communicates both directly and indirectly. The community of faith possesses direct knowledge of reconciliation reflected in its proclamation within the civil community, which has only indirect knowledge of it. In the Christian community, the ontic and the actual are united; the civil realm lacks any comparable foundation.

As in his earlier writings, Barth emphasizes the legal order as the constitutive element of the civil community: "This external, relative, and provisional, but not on that account invalid or ineffective, form of legal order is the civil community."[111] The state's primary legal responsibility lies in the preservation (*Wahrung*) of law. He affirms the importance of the civil community as a divine ordinance, an *exousia* sharing a common origin and center with the Christian community. As such, Christians are obligated to participate in the affairs of the civil community. Yet, as before, Barth dismisses any repristination of the state or law in Christian terms: "In the political sphere Christians can only bring in their Christianity anonymously."[112]

Barth stresses the provisional and relative nature of the political structures in the civil community, including law. In light of the common center of both the Christian and civil communities, the differentiation of the two kingdoms is transcended. As Lindenlauf remarks, "In that the rule of God in Jesus Christ is determined by the common center of the two circles of sovereignty—Church and State—that brings them together, the two kingdoms doctrine is overcome, while at the same time it unmistakably fixes the obligation of Christians to participate in the civil community."[113] Obviously, civil citizens must also commit themselves to the support of the state and its legal system, and in doing so, they support, indirectly, the *telos* of the Christian community.

110. Barth, "Christian Community," 158.
111. Barth, "Christian Community," 154.
112. Barth, "Christian Community," 184.
113. Lindenlauf, *Königherrschaft*, 221.

The relation of the civil and Christian communities is analogous to that of the relation of creation and covenant. The former is the exterior basis of the latter, yet without openly acknowledging that relation. The relation involves distinct yet complementary roles. The Christian community, primarily concerned with the gospel, is both vertically and horizontally oriented; the state, concerned with proximate ends, has horizontal responsibilities flowing from its obligation to assist in the humanization of creation. Its concern is with relations among human beings.

Barth proposes twelve analogies in "The Christian Community." In each analogy, the analogans is the witness of the Christian community to the divine justification of human beings, and the analogata is the commitment to the rule of law and opposition to anarchy and tyranny. The analogon, the *tertium comparationes*, is law.[114] Yet in this analogical context, law remains abstract. Only one of the analogies deals with law with any specificity. In that analogy, Barth asserts that, to the extent the church witnesses to divine justification, the church "will always be found where the order of the State is based on a commonly acknowledged law, from submission to which no one is exempt and which also provides equal protection for all."[115] While this analogy affirms the dependence of law on recognition and its implicit equality, it does not address law's proximate nature or normativity. To be sure, other analogies proposed by Barth have legal dimensions, but they do not alter the basic vision of law as an instrument for equitably securing and protecting order. Further, the analogies flow from the theological to the legal, never in the other direction.

The controlling principle of the analogies relating to law also remains vague. Barth states that the Kingship of Christ is the *Realgrund* of mundane law, but it is not quite clear what this means. In one sense, it suggests a derivative relationship; Gäfgen interprets it as suggesting that "human law can correspond to divine law, as it is visible in divine justification."[116] But this does not identify the analogon, the common element between the two. Barth relates, for example, the church's witness of Christ's salvific mission to the lost with the imperative that the church stand for social justice in the political sphere.[117] Another example is the fellowship of believers in one Lord and baptism, which is analogous to a principle of equality.[118]

---

114. Lindenlauf, *Königherrschaft*, 239.
115. Barth, "Christian Community," 172.
116. Gäfgen, *Recht*, 258.
117. Barth, "Christian Community," 171–72.
118. Barth, "Christian Community," 175.

Barth's use of analogy in "The Christian Community" has been criticized by several commentators. For example, Brunner contends that Barth's analogies are arbitrary, while Pannenberg finds them to be ahistorical.[119] Honecker suggests that Barth demands too much of analogy: "Analogies can perhaps decode, illustrate, interpret, communicate insight, clarify, but cannot ground actions and legitimate them."[120] Thielicke proposes a series of counter-analogies that he argues could also be derived by Barth's analogical reasoning.[121] There is a somewhat strained, gratuitous quality to Barth's analogies.[122]

Late in his career Barth expressed reservations about the use of analogy in connection with law. In a conversation, he confessed: "I don't know if the concept of analogy I used in "Christian Community and Civil Community" is indispensable (it created a lot of confusion and discussion). One can also say in German "correspondence" instead of "analogy"—it is namely the same."[123] He went on to insist on the necessity of some correspondence between divine law and positive law.[124]

From a contemporary perspective, this understanding of the two communities seems rather presumptuous and dated. Its presumptuousness stems from Barth's location of law in the ecclesiastical community, specifically the Christian community. While Barth eschews theocratic thinking, it is hard to see how the emphasis on the Christian community can be plausible to those outside of that community. It appears to reflect a privileged position and social influence that is no longer accurate. The cultural relativity of Barth's vision of law in the Christian community limits its contemporary relevance.

Barth's view of the relation of the Christian and civil communities also prompts questions. It tends to understate the autonomy of the civil community. He emphasizes the positive relation between the two communities, but one searches in vain for acknowledgment of their potential for conflict,

---

119. Brunner, *Christian Doctrine of Creation*, 319.

120. Honecker, *Einführung*, 30,

121. For example, he suggests that the scriptural passages enjoining that the Messianic status of Jesus should be kept secret would justify secret diplomacy—the opposite of what Barth proposes. See Thielicke, *Theologische Ethik*, 2:717; Lindenlauf, *Könighterrschaft*, 250.

122. John Webster refers to the "conscripted" use of theological material in Barth's analogies (Webster, "Ethics," 153).

123. Barth, *Gespräche*, 103.

124. In the same conversation just quoted, Barth proceeded to state that "In the realm of law, the Christian will always affirm correspondences with divinely established law, as they are realized in Christ. He cannot wish to introduce the Kingdom of God into state law. But he can promote that state law is a reflex of God's law" (Barth, *Gespräche*, 103-4).

an omission that is curious given Barth's own experience with the Nazi dictatorship.

What does "The Christian Community" mean for positive law? Law is protective and defensive, preserving freedom for the Christian community by establishing order and preventing chaos. The norms and procedures of law, its prescriptive, adjudicative and penal aspects are of secondary interest. Law essentially serves liturgical ends. But Barth leaves a seeming contradiction unresolved. For the Christian community, positive law does not rest on natural law foundations. If it did, it would not "take its bearings from the Christian center," but would be adopting the methods of the "pagan state."[125] But the state can "only draw from the porous wells of the so-called natural law."[126] This underestimates the resources of the state and the civil community for the improvement of law and the advancement of justice. A more affirmative case for improvement of the internal law of the state is necessary.

Church Dogmatics

Barth's primary treatment of human law appears in the second half of the fourth volume of the *Church Dogmatics*, which was published in 1955 as one of the four books dealing with the doctrine of reconciliation. Although law is addressed elsewhere in the work, this is the most extensive discussion. Barth places the section on law under the heading "The Order of the Community." There, he develops the relation between the Christologically oriented law of the church community and mundane law by means of a series of correspondences and oppositions between the two.

Barth relies primarily on juxtaposition—comparing and contrasting church law, or perhaps better, law in the church with secular law. In contrast to "The Christian Community," the emphasis is on identification of similarity and difference rather than on analogy. Church law comes more explicitly to serve as the measure and ideal for positive law. Echoes of the *Ethics* are discernible in that law is presented as a normative implication of the order of specific social relations.[127] Law reflects the nature of its communal context, and it is antecedent to the state.[128]

Barth again makes a forceful argument for the necessity of law in its ordering and preservative functions. In a word, law is indispensable for community. Barth is arguing here against Sohm and Brunner, both of

125. Barth, *Gespräche*, 163.
126. Barth, *Gespräche*, 169–70.
127. Reuter, *Rechtsethik in Perspektive*, 109.
128. See Marsch, "Christologische Begründung II," 209.

whom he sees as harboring antinomian tendencies, or worse, promoting misunderstandings about the nature of community itself. When Sohm contrasts love and law, positing the church as a community of love that only requires law for those weak in faith, Barth sees an unjustified denigration of law that denies its affirmative possibilities. Barth prefers Erik Wolf's notion of the Christian community as a "Christocratic brotherhood" in which law reinforces the ethos of a reconciled community.[129]

In *Church Dogmatics*, Barth continues to rework the content of the concepts of church, community, and law. The church is largely synonymous with community, and order with law. Each of these pairs combine difference and continuity. The communal character of the church manifests itself both visibly and invisibly. It is constituted by order, which Barth interprets as relational in form and structure; this is, as the "basic law," according to which Christ is the head and the community is the body. Order comprises an essential part of law, especially church law: "If it is the case that the Christian community is the human fellowship in which Jesus Christ as the Head is the primary Subject, and the acting communion of saints as his body is the secondary, to say "community" is at once to say "law and order."[130] This means that just as the Christian community is distinctive, so is its law distinctive.

Church law is, Barth proclaims, "clearly and sharply differentiated from every other kind of law."[131] In emphasizing the special qualities of church law and mundane law, Barth is proposing a somewhat dualistic differentiation between church law and positive law. Positive law is not grounded in the basic law and order of the Christian community; church law is not based on positive law. This is positive law's loss, leading Barth to say that "The world and its law are evil."[132] He hastens to add that they are not wholly evil. At the same time, both kinds of law relate to humanity, though this commonality is only discernible from the perspective of divine law.[133] The special qualities of church law that stand in prophetic contrast to positive law are evident in several characteristics: as a law of service (*Dienstrecht*) of members of the community to each other, as liturgical law, facilitating worship by the community, and as exemplary law, guiding and correcting mundane law. Church law is in no sense superior to human law, rather its function is one of "clarifying and deepening, of simplifying and

---

129. Barth, *CD* 4/2:677–80.
130. Barth, *CD* 4/2:682.
131. Barth, *CD* 4/2:682.
132. Barth, *CD* 4/2:724.
133. Barth, *CD* 4/2:724.

differentiating, of loosening and strengthening, in short, of correcting the law which obtains in the world."[134]

How persuasive is this notion of an exemplary form of church law? Its exemplary significance seems increasingly questionable as the influence of institutional religion declines. Apart from this, how is the exemplary nature of church law demonstrated and communicated? Barth does not address this question. He appears to assume that the influence of church law is secured through the basic vocational activity of Christian communities in society—proclamation. Is this plausible? Church law, even as broadly conceived as Barth would have it, is largely unknown in some legal systems (such as that of the United States) that have deeply rooted ideas regarding the separation of church and state. It is difficult to envision church law as possessing secular influence in a North American context. Faith communities are models of intergenerational care and outreach, not of legal structures. The prospects for the exemplary influence of faith communities in their secular settings would seem to lie in acts of engagement with law. This may take the form of legal advocacy, litigation, and legislation. The possibilities for influence are real, but they must be realized in accord with positive law, and this requires a modicum of generally accessible concepts and expression, but Barth seemingly did not consider this important or appropriate.[135]

Concluding Observations

Sociologically, analogically, and comparatively: Barth approaches positive law from each of these perspectives. They illuminate aspects of law theologically. In particular, Barth's view of law as the regulation of social interaction opens up a broader perspective on law. His analogical affirmations seek to connect theological and secular understandings of law, avoiding sterile separation. But one misses an elaborated concept of legal justice, one that legitimates and corrects positive law through the application of criteria of justice apposite to law and the legal system. Law establishes order and prevents chaos, but it does so with legitimacy and a modicum of justice. While Barth sees law as essential for state and society, he provides few criteria for strengthening the justness of law. His understanding of law is more thoroughly Christological in character than is the case with Brunner, Ellul or

---

134. Barth, *CD* 4/2:725.

135. See Laubscher, "Barth's Public Theology," 245, who writes, "[Barth] has no intention to make his language and point of departure open and accessible for others who were not part of it. It is difficult to see from this how he actually takes other non-Christians seriously in what they have to say with regard to public life."

Thielicke. Barth conceptualizes positive law theologically; his emphasis is on law's participation in the economy of reconciliation and sanctification.

This poses two difficulties that limit the contemporary appeal of his notion of positive law. First, his lack of attention to the internal nature and functioning of law and legal authority or to the basis of legal norms and their relations to ethics provides limited ground for interaction with other conceptions of law. Reflecting on Barth's rejection of traditional natural law theories and his disinterest in secular jurisprudence, one commentator concludes: "An evangelical ethics that wishes to say anything in the contemporary world, and hopes to be taken seriously, must treat both with a great deal more respect than Barth managed."[136] Further, Barth's understanding of positive law suffers from a remoteness from the practical reality of how law functions in contemporary society.

A further problem in Barth's view of law is his relative inattention to institutional and substantive aspects of law. His approach to law is often fundamentally functional (law as an antidote to chaos), ethical/theological (law as enabler of salvific proclamation) and analogical (law as egalitarian in spirit). But little is said about the substantive nature of law, its rationality, its procedural character, and its concern with fairness. Admittedly, theologians do not often address these jurisprudential matters. But in making broad claims about law, Barth awakens expectations that they will be considered in some way.

Theological criticism of Barth's theology of law reflects similar concerns. Pannenberg criticizes his approach for its failure to consider the "actual data of the structures of legal procedures."[137] He contends that Barth's Christological concentration leads him to disregard the *contexts* in which that concentration is expressed.[138] Further, Pannenberg suggests that Barth's emphasis on a Christological orientation restricts his ability to grasp concrete historical manifestations of law and to engage critically with law. This threatens to open a gap between the theory and actuality of law. Underlying these criticisms is a dissatisfaction with the Christocentric basis of Barth's ethics due to its ahistorical tendencies.[139]

---

136. Rae, "Barth's Ethics," 419.

137. Pannenberg, "On the Theology of Law," 33.

138. Pannenberg, *Grundlagen*, 98.

139. On this point, see Lindenlauf, who speaks of a paradoxical "Christological deficit" in Barth's political ethics resulting from an inadequate differentiation between the event of the Lordship of Christ and the Christological starting point (*Ansatz*) (Lindenlauf, *Königsherrschaft*, 262).

Others echo Pannenberg's critique. Zahrnt criticizes Barth for inattention to the structure of the world.[140] Jacques Ellul disapprovingly notes Barth's remoteness from legal reality.[141] Brunner contends that an exclusively Christological interpretation of law stands in overt opposition to reformed doctrine, and rejects Barth's attempts to deduce the order of law and state from the Christ event as "fantastic."[142] From a Catholic perspective, Schüller concludes that Barth's Christological concentration, combined with his disavowal of natural law, results in inconsistency. Though Barth acknowledges that mundane law can and does exist, since Christ is the *Realgrund* of law for him, he does not adequately explain how such law can exist without admitting a basis for it in human capability. Barth, Schüller contends, approaches law as a theologian proceeding from theological affirmations rather than with the actual reality of law.[143] It is a theologically facing understanding of law. As a result, law tends toward being subsumed in ethics, with little or no effort to distinguish between them.[144] Barth's reflections on positive law ask to be expanded.

Of course, Barth resists mediation of his theological premises out of concern that it would dilute their integrity. This stance may have its virtues under contemporary circumstances, as Jeffrey Stout suggests.[145] But theological presuppositions permeate his reflections on law to an extent that one cannot easily imagine them to be particularly accessible in secular circles. This is not to dismiss Barth's insights, only to judge the breadth of their appeal. When Barth states that setting "that which is human, worldly and rational alongside that which is Christian is inevitably to expel that latter," this does not promote interdisciplinary interaction.[146] This does not have to be the case. Interpretations of his insights can render them available for interaction with legal principles. For example, Hans Michael Heinig has argued that Barth's understanding of democracy, church and state helpfully illuminates aspects of German constitutional law.[147] There is no reason that such insights cannot be productively applied to other areas of law.

---

140. Zahrnt, *Question of God*, 182.

141. Ellul, *Theological Foundation of Law*.

142. Brunner, *Justice*, 272.

143. Schüller, *Herrschaft Christi*, 248.

144. See Gägfgen, *Recht*, 275.

145. Stout, *Democracy*, 109–111.

146. Barth, *CD* 3/1:414.

147. Heinig, "Gerechtigkeit in Recht." Barth's views of the intrinsic autonomy of human law, its rational methodology and its dependence on state-facilitated compliance resemble in certain respects the "interior view of law" proposed by H. L. A. Hart.

One can pose a question about Barth's theology of law similar to the one he asks in "Church and State": What is the inner, vital connection between his conception of law and other understandings of law—whether philosophical, political, or jurisprudential? Christ is, for Barth, both the ontological and epistemological basis of law, and analogical extrapolation from divine law provides guidance for human law. To explicate this relationship in a way that allows engagement with secular jurisprudence remains a challenge for a Barthian approach to positive law. This engagement is desirable not as an end to itself, but in service of efforts to improve law, an aim that is consistent with Barth's endorsement of it as essential for social and political life.

III

Emil Brunner

The Orders of Creation and Law

Emil Brunner (1889–1966) was a prominent Swiss theologian whose career spanned the first half of the twentieth century. During his lifetime, he was considered, along with Barth, as one of the most influential Protestant theologians. Brunner taught most of his career in Zürich, but held visiting professorships in the United States and also spent several years toward the end of his life teaching in Japan. During the inter-war years, Brunner became known for his theological sparring with Barth regarding natural theology and the possibility of a human point of contact (*Anknüpfungpunkt*) with God. Brunner was well known in the Anglophone theological world, and he delivered the Gifford Lectures in 1947 and 1948. After his death, Brunner's reputation went into eclipse for several decades, although recently there has been renewed interest in his work.[1]

Early in his career, Brunner came into contact with the work of Christoph Blumhardt and his disciple Hermann Kutter, as well as Leonhard Ragaz, all influential figures in early-twentieth-century Protestant circles known for their strong social commitments and associations with the religious socialist movement. Other influences on Brunner's thought were Kant, from whom he derived the notion of the limits of human thought and action, Barth with his emphasis on the Word of God, and Friedrich Gogarten and his concept of the orders of creation.[2]

---

1. See, for example, McGrath, *Brunner*.

2. This is not to say that Brunner's relationship with Barth was an easy one. Jehle describes the relationship as "ambivalent" (Jehle, *Brunner*, 293). See Hart, *Theological Alliance*.

Brunner's Ethical Thought

Together with Barth, Brunner is customarily associated with neo-orthodox theology. Among the principal characteristics of this informal movement is an emphasis on the transcendence of God, the primacy of the Word of God and his gracious justification of human beings, the salvific significance of Jesus Christ, and the reality of human sinfulness. While Brunner and Barth adhered to these fundamental principles, Brunner allowed for a certain capacity of humans to comprehend and engage with divine action. He also went beyond scripture to incorporate various secular elements into his thought.[3] These moves led to conflict with Barth.

Brunner began his work on ethics in earnest in the late 1920s. At that time, he delivered a series of lectures in Germany and Holland that became the basis of his first major work on ethics, *The Divine Imperative*.[4] Brunner described the book as "a systematic presentation of biblical personalism in the realm of social ethics and a comparison and contrast of the Christian and non-Christian doctrines of society."[5] It presents an ethics based on the Word of God integrated into a personalistic theology of revelation developed by Brunner and based on the work of Ferdinand Ebner and Martin Buber. Brunner defines Christian ethics as the science of human conduct determined by divine conduct.[6] The Good, understood theologically, is compliance with God's will at any particular moment.

The volume drew critical praise in Europe as well as in the United States from figures such as Reinhold Niebuhr and Paul Ramsey.[7] Brunner's biographer, Frank Jehle, sees *The Divine Imperative* as Brunner's most important book and as a milestone in the history of twentieth-century

---

3. See generally Brunner, *Man in Revolt*, 527–46.

4. This is a translation of *Das Gebot und die Ordnungen*. Although the English translation states that Brunner approved of its English title, Brunner later noted that it failed to convey the import of the German title with its reference to "command" and "orders," key concepts in the work. On the background of the composition of the book, see McGrath, *Brunner*, 78–79.

5. Brunner, "Autobiography," 10.

6. Brunner, *Divine Imperative*, 86.

7. Reinhold Niebuhr stated that "Brunner's was the first, and in my opinion still the best exposition of a social ethic from the standpoint of a Reformation theology which disavows the Biblicist tendencies of some so-called neo-orthodox to derive all moral and social standards purely from Scripture" (Niebuhr, "Orders," 265). Writing in 1962, Paul Ramsey referred to the book as a "great work" that "was timely when it appeared and remains definitive" (Ramsey, "Brunner," 250). In a recent article on Brunner, Reuter refers to the book as the "first comprehensive ethics of Reformed theology in the twentieth century" (Reuter, "Brunner," 313).

theology.[8] Upon its publication, the book was banned by the Nazi regime. After the war, it was republished and attracted wide attention. It continues to be considered a seminal work in modern Protestant ethics.

The Divine Imperative develops a fundamental motif in Brunner's ethics—the Divine Command, which for him is the source of ethical guidance and knowledge. There is no other intrinsic good. Secular notions of the Good he sees as egotistical and presumptuous. For Brunner, the Divine Command is the law of love.[9] In its light, the Good exists "simply and solely in the fact that man perceives and deliberately accepts his life is a gift from God, as a life dependent on "grace," as the state of "being justified" because it has been granted as a gift, as "justification by faith."[10] The human response to the Command is the duty to love God, and one's neighbor.[11] This duty varies in content but not in intention.[12] The Command is expressed through what Brunner terms the law and the orders of creation, but it is not equivalent to them. "It is not God's command which is to be understood as law, but . . . the law as the Divine Command."[13] The Divine Command is the Word of God that issues forth in freedom out of the divine will. It is not subject to being generalized or schematized by those who receive it.[14] It is complemented by the orders of creation, which Brunner designates as commandments. Brunner also speaks of these commandments in contrast to the Divine Command.[15] The commandments are essentially dictates of law, with law being understood here in a biblical sense as divine instruction or legislation.

Brunner's ethics is also marked by a rejection of the traditional distinction between the social and personal ethics. His personalism leads him to distinguish between the personal realm of interactions among persons, and engagements with political and social structures. Brunner differentiates between action involving persons and institutions. These represent two distinct spheres of existence, each of which prompts kinds of ethical action pertinent to that sphere. Ultimately, there is no disjuncture between being an individual and being the member of the community; both dimensions

---

8. Jehle, *Brunner*, 255.
9. Brunner, *Divine Imperative*, 133, 149.
10. Brunner, *Divine Imperative*, 116.
11. Brunner, *Divine Imperative*, 133.
12. Brunner, *Divine Imperative*, 134.
13. Brunner, *Divine Imperative*, 144–45.
14. "The Christian never has to act according to general principles, but always according to the concrete command of love" (Brunner, *Divine Imperative*, 197).
15. Brunner, *Divine Imperative*, 132.

form a unity. As Brunner declares, "The truly personal self and the community arise and cease to exist in the same act."[16]

The contextual, anti-abstract quality of Brunner's ethics parallels Barth's aversion to general ethical principles and doctrines. In contrast to Barth, Brunner's situational approach is strongly informed by personalism, which emphasizes the personal character of the encounter of humans with God and each other. Obviously, this creates a tension with law and its concern with the general and the universal. Brunner's personalism is counterbalanced by his concept of the orders of creation, which exist in the form of shared social structures reflecting divinely inspired elements of creation. The orders of creation provide some guidance for ethical action, though they are distorted by human sin and are general in nature. Personal relationships are the individual pole of ethics; the orders are the collective and social one. In this sense, the orders of creation provide a social and cultural frame for the Divine Command in its primary meaning as the law of love. They are guiding structures and provide frameworks for obedience to the Divine Command. At the same time, the orders can distort the Divine Command due to their own sinfulness. In a word, the orders of creation are ambiguous; they are both divinely sanctioned and humanly flawed.

Brunner's Ethical Writings

Emil Brunner's principal writings on ethics, particularly in relation to positive law, are contained in two books: *Das Gebot und die Ordnungen* (1932), translated as *The Divine Imperative* (1947), and *Gerechtigkeit* (1943), translated as *Justice and the Social Order* (1945). Other relevant writings appear in portions of *Christianity and Culture* (1948) and *Dogmatics III* (1960).

The Divine Imperative is divided into three parts. The first is an exposition of the insufficiency of concepts of the good in natural morality. It is an example of Brunner's eristic theology, a kind of apologetics that seeks to facilitate engagement between religious and secular perspectives.[17] The second section sets forth Brunner's version of a divine command ethic, based on the concept of the Divine Command. The requirements of the Command will vary in each situation: "The Christian is never called to act

16. Brunner, *Divine Imperative*, 288.

17. Brunner rejects traditional apologetics. The purpose of eristics, he explains, is to prove that attacks on the biblical message are "based upon errors, due to either the confusion of rationalism with reason, of positivism with science, of a critical with a skeptical attitude, or out of ignorance of the real truth which the Bible contains" (Brunner, *Christian Doctrine of God*, 98–99).

on general principles but always in accord with the concrete command of love."[18] The third section of the book presents the individual orders of creation, which include marriage, economy, family and state. These orders are established by God to provide a structure for human existence, as rooted in creation. According to John Hart, the orders of creation serve to "connect the Divine Command to the actual life of real people, provide fundamental ethical content by providing the framework for community and giving the church a common ethical base from which it can engage society and meaningful ethical discussion."[19] In this sense, the orders are both prescriptive and descriptive.

The key affirmations of *The Divine Imperative* are: (1) the source of moral guidance is the Divine Command, (2) ethical decision-making is unavoidably situational and has a social context, (3) human social practices and institutions (the orders of creation) have certain divinely established structures, (4) human social structures are corrigible and subject to divine justice and its creational orders. Brunner embraces, as Barth does, a theologically integrated vision of ethics centered on the divine reality. As Brunner states, "Every ethical consideration is connected with the whole idea of God."[20] This means for him that every human distinction must remain provisional in light of divine purpose, culminating in the eschatological community. It also means, in Paul Ramsey's interpretation, that every ethical action (and opportunity for action) should be related to divine purposes.[21] The integrative impulse in Brunner's ethics is reflected in his insistence on the coinherence of dogmatics and ethics. He refers to the interpenetration of the two disciplines, and he refuses to separate personal and social ethics.[22] Similarly, Brunner affirms that the individual and the community inseparably relate to each other. This holism pervades Brunner's ethical thought.

The onset of Nazi tyranny and the Second World War prompted an intensification and re-direction in Brunner's thinking about ethical themes.[23] *Justice and the Social Order* was written as a response to the phenomenon of totalitarianism—both fascist and communist. He sees the roots of totalitarianism in the collectivist and atheistic tendencies of some modern states, and he contends for the superiority of a biblical foundation of the state, though

18. Brunner, *Divine Imperative*, 197.
19. Hart, *Alliance*, 118.
20. Brunner, *Divine Imperative*, 85.
21. Ramsey, "Brunner," 257–58. Ramsey views Brunner's position as a response to "mistaken Christological gradualism" (Ramsey, "Brunner," 257).
22. Brunner, *Divine Imperative*, 84.
23. See generally Lovin, *Choices*, 94–95; Jehle, *Brunner*, 432–34.

one respectful of a secular era. He wishes to counteract what he perceives as a loss of ethical substance in the state. The perspective Brunner adopts in the book, as Reuter remarks, is not that of the proclaiming church, but of the "Christian statesman."[24]

Justice proposes a Christian foundation of society based on the Divine Law, which comes to the fore as the Divine Command recedes to the background. In Brunner's words, "The main thesis of the book is this alternative: either society is grounded on the Divine Law or it has to submit to the compulsion of totalitarianism, be it of the Communist or Fascist variety."[25] Significant attention in the volume is devoted to positive law and justice. Brunner believed that Nazi totalitarianism, aided by legal positivism, had undermined law and justice in Germany and was threatening to do the same elsewhere. To his mind, law and justice must be rehabilitated on the basis of absolute justice grounded in divine law.

Brunner also addresses law in his Gifford lectures, published in two volumes as *Christianity and Civilization*. There, Brunner proposes a Christian idea of culture. He surveys various cultural domains—technics, science, education, work, art, morals and law—and analyzes each of them from a theological perspective. Two chapters in the books bear directly on law and justice, and provide a concise summary of Brunner's assessment of modern positive law without, however, significantly advancing his overall analysis.

Throughout all of these writings, Brunner speaks of the orders of creation, and it requires closer scrutiny.

The Orders of Creation

Though the idea of the orders or ordinances of creation is of modern vintage, it has a lengthy provenance. Augustine spoke of a natural order intended by God; Luther conceived of three spheres of society: the spiritual, the economic and the political.[26] These spheres were divinely established, forming a framework for the social existence of the faithful. The concept of the spheres, or orders, was developed doctrinally in the nineteenth-century Luther renaissance by Adolph von Harless and in the twentieth century by Lutheran theologians such as Werner Elert and Paul Althaus.[27]

---

24. Reuter, "Brunner," 314.
25. Brunner, *Autobiography*, 14.
26. See Pannenberg, "Theology of Law," 24.
27. Pannenberg, "Theology of Law," 26. See also Rosenau, "Schöpfungsordnung," 356–58.

In the 1930s, the orders were appropriated by Elert, Althaus and others in ways that legitimized *völkisch* notions of race, culture and history. By mixing the doctrine of creation with Romantic notions of cultural identity, these interpretations of the orders of creation were put to ideological use in ways antithetical to, for example, Barth's Christocentric ethics.[28] Althaus spoke of the struggle of the rebellious, disruptive forces of modern life against divine order, and he welcomed Nazism as a remedy for social chaos.[29] As a consequence of its co-optation by the German Christians and their fellow travelers, the orders became theologically discredited. According to Martin Honecker, the orders gave way to the concept of the institution.[30] For his part, Brunner opposed any ideological perversions of the concept of the orders. But some have viewed Brunner's understanding of the orders as reflecting its own ideological distortions.[31]

Nevertheless, the orders of creation remained a significant component of Brunner's ethical vision. As the results of divine creation, the orders connect existing social structures with divine intention and purpose. "Brunner's point is that for human beings there is an inseparable link between the commandment of God and the concrete historical circumstances and natural limitations in which they are set."[32] This connection legitimizes and sanctions those circumstances while also judging them.

In *The Divine Imperative*, Brunner identifies five orders: marriage, labor, the state and law, culture, and church. Brunner defines the orders as "those existing facts of human corporate life which lie at the root of all historical life as unalterable presuppositions, which, although their historical forms may vary, are unalterable in their fundamental structure and, at the same time, relate and unite men to one another in a definite way."[33] The orders stand below, and are subject to, the Divine Command.[34]

The orders are inherently social in nature and facilitate community among individuals. For Brunner, humans are social beings, and are destined for interaction with each other. Persons are fulfilled through interpersonal complementarity, rather than through individual self-realization that ultimately, for Brunner, ends in isolation. The orders are "the means by which

---

28. Honecker, *Ethik*, 296.

29. For example, Althaus considered the introduction of the death penalty has an appropriate reaction to social disorder. See Jehle, *Brunner*, 261–62.

30. Honecker, *Ethik*, 296.

31. See Huber, *Gerechtigkeit*, 169.

32. Lovin, *Choices*, 49.

33. Brunner, *Divine Imperative*, 210.

34. Brunner, *Divine Imperative*, 67.

the divine wisdom compels men to live in community—men, that is, who through their sin have become separated from one another."[35]

The orders serve to establish and secure order. This gives them a conservative character, although Brunner also speaks of them as being revolutionary as well. They are both preservative and redemptive; preservative in that they serve to contain chaos, and redemptive in that they create the possibility of transcending justice in the direction of love. "God preserves in order to perfect."[36] Their preservative function requires that they themselves be protected, and this is the first duty of those subject to the order of state and law. At the same time, those persons also have a duty to improve the orders by making them more humane and just. This duty of amelioration is necessary because of deficiencies in the orders caused by sin. Responses to sinfulness require, in Ramsey's phrase, "inauguration of a new line of action in view of the coming kingdom of God."[37] Brunner call this duty of improvement the "second duty" respecting the orders: they are not only to be accepted but also reformed and, if necessary in extreme situations, overturned.

It is important to note that Brunner sees the orders as relative and historical. They do not exist as invariable constants of human life, but bear the weight of history and sin. One form of the distortion of the orders is their tendency to become legalized. Brunner refers to them in their legalized form as *Lex*, and as such, they resemble a kind of ideological, legalistic natural law.[38] This is often unappreciated due to Brunner's failure at times to distinguish clearly between natural law and the orders. Sometimes the two seem to be similar, while other times they contrast with each other. Certain parallels exist between the orders and natural law thought: both point to certain foundational structures of social life that shape the actions of individuals. Both stand for shared, trans-cultural structures but they are clearly not the same.

Positive law possesses the status of an order by virtue of its connection to the state and, indirectly, to divine law. These associations endow positive law with normative aspects. Though distorted by sin, it remains capable of pointing to its divine origin. In a word, as an element within an order of creation, positive law is compromised and defective yet still workable and necessary.

---

35. Brunner, *Divine Imperative*, 67.
36. Brunner, *Divine Imperative*, 214.
37. Ramsey, "Brunner," 398–99.
38. Ramsey, "Brunner," 140.

Sin affects the orders in two ways: it distorts the human ability to perceive them and conform to them; it also warps the orders themselves. At times, Brunner equates the historical variability of the orders in itself with sinfulness. "It is true that the unalterable fundamental forms of these orders are the gift of the Creator and Preserver of the world; but the forms in which they appear at any given time, which is constantly changing their historically concrete forms, is the effect of human sin, and is therefore, like all that is sinful, the object of moral conflict."[39]

Justice provides the standard for the improvement of the orders in their encounter with concrete historical circumstances.[40] The orders embody and display justice; Brunner closely relates justice and the orders.[41] This follows from his view that justice is primarily concerned with orders and institutions rather than with persons. "The idea of justice belongs, not to the sphere of personal ethics, but to the ethics of orders or institutions."[42] This reveals an affinity between the orders and classical natural law's affirmation of universal norms, something Brunner also embraces.[43]

As for the knowability of the orders, Brunner contrasts it with the knowability of justice. The content of justice can be discerned by all persons, separate and apart from knowledge of God.[44] However, innate knowledge of the orders is distorted by sin, and requires correction by the "scriptural idea of creation."[45] Yet sin diminishes the ability of humans to perceive the orders. This conflicts with Brunner's contention that the orders are knowable by all.[46] But he means that in being known, the orders are known only in part; their "significance and true nature" is discernible only within the sphere of faith. Their full theological import is available only from the standpoint of faith. This creates the central challenge, in Brunner's view, of Christian social ethics: "The most important task of the Christian ethic of society is that of throwing light upon the relation between the natural existence and understanding of the existing forms of community and the divine will, perceived by faith."[47] By this distinction, Brunner seeks a basis

---

39. Brunner, *Divine Imperative*, 337–38.
40. Brunner, *Divine Imperative*, 210.
41. "Justice is His Will as it refers to the order of His created world" (Brunner, *Civilization*, 1:116).
42. Brunner, *Justice*, 20 (translation altered).
43. Brunner, *Justice*, 104; *Divine Imperative*, 140.
44. Brunner, *Justice*, 90.
45. Brunner, *Justice*, 92.
46. Brunner, *Justice*, 335.
47. Brunner, *Justice*, 336.

for critical cooperation with the orders by believers and nonbelievers alike, each making their respective contributions.

The orders are rationally perceptible and relatively autonomous. Only a Christian perspective reveals the creative, preserving, and redemptive word of God as reflected in and through the orders.[48] Faith has a regulative function with respect to the orders, not a constituitive one.[49] Accordingly, Brunner distinguishes between the primordial, divinely ordained orders and their historically conditioned manifestations.[50] This particularly applies to law and the state.[51] The two dimensions overlap, but only incompletely. For Brunner, the Divine Command and the divine orders are in one side, and the orders of creation on the other. At the same time, "All these existing forms of community conceal within themselves Divine orders of creation."[52]

The concept of the orders of creation has long attracted criticism. They were frequently seen to represent a variant of natural law thinking, and therefore were deemed suspect from traditional Protestant perspectives.[53] For some critics the orders are inescapably ahistorical and therefore fail to do justice to the variability of social institutions and practices. Others claim that the orders are as much, if not more, the result of human action rather than divine creation. Further, the character of the orders as both divinely instituted and humanly conditioned have left some unsatisfied. As Barth complained, "What I do not understand is from what source and in what way Brunner claims to know these orders."[54]

Other criticisms address the relation of the orders to history. Pannenberg finds the orders unable to account for historical relativism, a shortcoming that he sees as leading to positivism. He urges instead a deeper understanding of the "human involvement in history."[55] This would account for the historical variability of law, which is a challenge for any theology of

---

48. Brunner, *Justice*, 200, 220, 252.

49. Brunner, *Justice*, 248, 207, 246.

50. Brunner, *Divine Imperative*, 337–38. Some commentators such as Ramsey interpret Brunner's dialectical concept of the orders in two ways: as creational and preservative. The distinction seeks to account for the character of the orders as simultaneously divinely established and historically distorted. Brunner does not use this distinction very often; Thielicke develops it in his *Theological Ethics*. See chapter 6 below.

51. Brunner, *Justice*, 84.

52. Brunner, *Divine Imperative*, 336.

53. Pannenberg distinguishes theologies of ordinances of creation from natural law in that the former does not entail a "general, abstract human nature but deals with actual forms of all specific societies." He terms the ordinances as "institutional natural law rather than a normative version" (Pannenberg, "Theology of Law," 26).

54. Barth, *CD* 3/4:20.

55. Pannenberg, "Theology of Law," 25.

law. Reinhold Niebuhr criticizes Brunner's orders for their ahistorical nature and lack of a normative dimension, without which they lose authority. "It is difficult to find this normative principle because man is a historical creature and there are no 'natural' forms in his life which have not been subjected to both the freedom and corruptions of history."[56] At least with respect to law, these criticisms are telling. Brunner does not account sufficiently for the historicity of law. Further, he does not adequately develop the significance of the character of the orders as both rationally knowable and divinely sponsored. He tends to utilize the same distinction as Barth—between partial and complete knowledge. All persons can know of the existence and contents of the order of the state and law in part, but a full understanding of their significance is only vouchsafed to the perspective of faith.

The State and Law as Orders of Creation

The character of the individual orders (marriage, economy, state, and culture) is not uniform but variable. Some are more personal, others more social; some more consistent across cultures, others more culturally relative. Even more than marriage or economy, state and law depend on historical and cultural peculiarities.

As orders, the attributes of state and law have a particular status in that they, more than the other orders, are clearly related to human sinfulness. Somewhat inconsistently, Brunner from time to time declares that this deprives the state and law of their status as an order of creation: "There are also orders which, although they belong to the presuppositions of the present life . . . still cannot be described as belonging to the created or natural order, because they only have any meaning owing to the fact of sin. The most important of these orders is that of the State and the Law."[57] In a footnote to this sentence, Brunner qualifies this somewhat by stating that he is referring to their present form, with their dependence on coercion. Nevertheless, Brunner sees the state as the most ethically attenuated order of creation. Its role is to create space for the other orders of creation.[58]

The state's relation to sin is evident in its dependence on force. Its principal responsibility is to maintain order, and its main instrument for doing so is coercive law. But it does so at a price, for it diminishes the state's status

---

56. Niebuhr, "Orders," 266. Niebuhr also criticizes the orders for their minimalism.

57. Brunner, *Divine Imperative*, 212.

58. "All the state ought to do is to make a place for the autonomous life of these institutions: economy, marriage and scientific work" (Brunner, *Divine Imperative*, 458).

as an order of creation. "In so far as the state is . . . a mode of force, it cannot be understood from the standpoint of creation."[59] For Brunner, the state is based on power, not on justice.[60] Even a tyrannical state is still a state. At the same time, the state is the most comprehensive organization, meaning that it encompasses more dimensions of social life than other institutions.[61] Its purpose is the formation of community, and in so far as it carries out this purpose it remains an order of creation. Consequently, Brunner views the state ambivalently. It tends to be self-aggrandizing and to usurp prerogatives of the individual. Further, it derives its capacity for justice from positive law, which also stands at a distance from justice. "No state has ever sprung forth from the principles of justice."[62]

For Brunner, law is formally an order of creation and materially a product of specific political and cultural circumstances. It has an identifiable origin and foundation; it also possesses relative autonomy. Law's grounding in primordial order gives it a metaphysical anchoring, and endows it with certain religious awe expressed in an intuitive sense of justice that precedes positive law. "The God-given meaning of the state" is law.[63] In *Justice*, Brunner equates this primordial structure and meaning with a sense of ordered proportionality.

While their status as a created order grounds the state and law theologically, their mundane manifestations render them in need of continual improvement. Both state and law exist in a tension between origin and reality. They neither are fully consecrated by their origin, nor nullified by their structural sinfulness. Hence: "There is no Christian or non-Christian form of the state."[64] This follows from Brunner's conviction that faith plays a regulative and not constitutive role in public affairs, meaning that it does not prescribe the structure of the state or the content of the law so much as polices them for distortions and encourages their improvement. This allows Brunner to say that law, though grounded in divine law and justice, is binding on all, Christian and non-Christian alike, given its function of maintaining order.

59. Brunner, *Justice*, 72.
60. Brunner, *Divine Imperative*, 446.
61. "The state is the widest, most embracing circle of organization" (Brunner, *Justice*, 138).
62. Brunner, *Divine Imperative*, 463.
63. Brunner, *Divine Imperative*, 449. In the original text, the word used is "*Recht*"; the English translation renders it here as "justice" even though the word "*Gerechtigkeit*" (justice) appears elsewhere on the same page. Further, the translation renders "*Recht*" as "law" in another sentence in the same paragraph.
64. Brunner, *Divine Imperative*, 445.

Law, for Brunner, is a creation of the state. As such, it is subordinate to, and maintained and enforced by it. Law shares in the ethical ambiguity of the state itself by being contingent in form and content, coercive in enforcement, and ethical in its expression of cultural values and dispensing of justice.[65] States inevitably utilize coercion as a matter of necessity, but such coercion is a result of sin and is not divinely willed. This gives the state a sense of tragic necessity: "The state is the product of collective sin."[66] Coercion is intrinsic to a state's legal system.[67] "The fundamental characteristic of the state is not right but might."[68] Power is divinely sanctioned and is therefore instrumentally good while susceptible to egotistical misuse.

Brunner's conception of law's relation to the state contrasts with that of several of the writers considered here. Barth sees the two as largely independent of each other. Pannenberg also considers law as preceding the state, while Thielicke does not. As we have seen, Brunner is somewhat inconsistent on this point. While he says that law gives rise to the state, he also declares that "Law itself is, in principle, independent of the state."[69] A close relation of law and state tends to stress the political character of law, while a looser one tends to emphasize law's sociological and anthropological character. In the case of a close state-law relation, law is politically contextualized and shaped by constitutional norms that are ultimately political. In the obverse case, more weight is given to law's social form and function. It then provides a broader basis for the development of human rights than that of a specific legal order.

Law

Eleven years separate Brunner's two books that most deeply deal with law—*The Divine Imperative* and *Justice and the Social Order*. During that interval, Brunner witnessed the Nazi seizure of power and the outbreak of the Second World War and its catastrophic consequences. It is not surprising that Brunner's thinking on law evolved significantly in light of these events. In the earlier volume, positive law is approached more formally, with less attention devoted to its material content and more to its relation to the state and power. In the later book, Brunner concentrates more on the relationship

---

65. Brunner, *Divine Imperative*, 443.
66. Brunner, *Divine Imperative*, 445.
67. Brunner, *Divine Imperative*, 446.
68. Brunner, *Justice*, 196; *Divine Imperative*, 446.
69. Brunner, *Civilization*, 1:106.

between law and justice. The books must be considered together for a full picture of Brunner's understanding of positive law.

In *The Divine Imperative*, law is a creation of the state.[70] "As soon as a State exists—in some way or another—law exists."[71] The state establishes law in order to promote and preserve human community. Here, Brunner defines law as "the actual, effective, comparatively permanent, and to some extent familiar, order of the conditions which constitute human community, as it springs from the State."[72]

As its product, law supports the state and shares its dependence on power and coercion. But in its role of promoting community, law must be concerned with justice. Given this dual vocation, law is not reducible to a function of either power or justice. The dependence of law on power raises the question of the role of justice; its aspiration toward justice raises the question of the role of coercion.

In *Justice*, Brunner revises concept of law in a way that concentrates on its relation to justice. The focus now is on the nature of justice and its relation to the orders of creation. The personalism of *The Divine Imperative* is replaced by a concentration on the nature of law itself. In that earlier book, Brunner proclaimed that law is not primarily concerned with justice; in fact, it has "practically nothing" to do with justice.[73] That earlier view is replaced with a theory of the substantial relation between the two.

Brunner develops this through close attention to classical notions of justice. Law must create and maintain order, but it must also continue to address ancient questions of distribution and remediation. It must regulate and adjudicate the claims of persons, and this requires determination of whether, and if so what, is owed by one to another. One commentator (Reuter) contends that Brunner conceives of the doctrine of justice exclusively as the doctrine of the appropriate distribution of *suum cuique* in terms of what is due (*das Gehörige*).[74] Although other aspects are also considered (such as divine justice), Brunner devotes primary attention to justice's distributive function.

Later, Brunner expanded on these views in *Christianity and Civilization* (1948) (delivered as the Gifford lectures in St. Andrews, Scotland). There, he presents a historical-evolutionary conception of law, emphasizing a primordial relation between law and social custom (*Sitte*) that predates the

---

70. Brunner, *Divine Imperative*, 445.
71. Brunner, *Divine Imperative*, 448.
72. Brunner, *Divine Imperative*, 448.
73. Brunner, *Divine Imperative*, 208.
74. Reuter, *Rechtsbegriffe*, 99. Huber shares this view. See Huber, *Gerechtigkeit*, 202.

state and positive law. Originally, law and custom were scarcely distinguishable. They interpenetrated each other; Brunner cites English common law as an example of this interaction.[75] Law became distinct and autonomous as custom declined: "Where social custom is strong, only a minimum of legal prescription is necessary."[76] The demise of custom was prompted by the rise of individualism and decreasing social cohesion. The evolution from law's dependence on custom to a close reliance on the state was facilitated by the legal codifications of the eighteenth and nineteenth centuries reflecting the Enlightenment's rationalist views of law. The principal result of the decline of custom and the rise of state authority was a diminished connection between law and morality.[77] The state came to dominate law: "The state is no longer under the law but above it."[78] This dominance, he believes, became evident in the growing formalism of law. Brunner means by this that law came to be identified by its source rather than its content, corresponding to a basic precept of positivism. Increasingly, law expanded to include various administrative activities of the state, matters that have little to do with traditional notions of law. The rise of the totalitarian state was abetted by the instrumentalization and demoralization of law.

Although this theory of the genesis of law differs from the more state-centric idea of law in Brunner's earlier books, they are not inconsistent. The state is built on the foundation of pre-existing communities, and political institutions arose and replaced these less formal, customary social arrangements. As state and law have become more formalized in increasingly complex societies, they are more procedurally complex and morally agnostic. In the case of law, this facilitates a positivistic outlook. Positivism furthers the moral degeneration of law by undermining the relation between law and morality. By underwriting the expansion of state authority, law contributes to its own subversion and creates an opening for totalitarianism.

As noted, Brunner's thinking about law evolved between *The Divine Imperative* and *Justice*. The dependence of law on the state is much less emphasized in *Justice*, a development understandable in light of the Nazi experience. In the later book, law comes to derive its normative weight more from justice than from the orders. Justice lacks the status of an order of creation, for it is both absolute and relative, static and dynamic. But it nevertheless inheres in the orders. Brunner retains the notion of the orders in

---

75. Brunner, *Civilization*, 2:101.
76. Brunner, *Civilization*, 2:101.
77. Brunner, *Civilization*, 2:106.
78. Brunner, *Civilization*, 2:107.

all of his writings on law but progressively de-emphasizes their relevance to it. Justice becomes the primary foundation of law.

Law and Power

Given the relation between the state and law, Brunner discerns a close association between law and power. Individuals and groups are constantly engaged in the struggle for power, which Brunner defines as "the use of physical means to compel another person to do what we wish."[79] Law is both an expression of power and a means of controlling it. "The most important means to order power is law, which in itself is nothing but "ordered power" or "order of power."[80] Power, states Brunner, "is the irrational element in the life of the state; law is its rational factor."[81] Law depends upon both reason and justice. Its proper functioning relies on stability, predictability, generality, and universality—all rational criteria. A just law, for Brunner, is a law that "allows the rights of man and the claims of the community established by creation to assert themselves."[82]

While law is an instrument in the struggle among social groups, it is also concerned with the question of what is due to the members of those groups in their mutual relations.[83] Law mediates between power and justice by seeking a balance of interests.[84] Given this role, there is a moment of truth in both positivist (law as social/political fact) and idealist (law as rightness) notions of law. Viewed theologically, law exists at the intersection of creation and sin; it evidences creation and its ordering capacity. It also bears the consequences of the distorting effects of sin. As such, it is a hybrid institution and set of practices based less on compromise than on a kind of *coincidentia oppositorum*. Barth's emphasis on reconciliation is largely absent here; Brunner simultaneously affirms the coercive function of law as well as its ethical potential. As is evident in *The Divine Imperative*, law is an element of an interim social ethic that rejects positivism and idealism as comprehensive accounts in favor of realism leavened by justice.

While law is subject to the harsh realities of the power relations that exist within a state, it is not reducible to them. Justice continues to inhere

---

79. Brunner, *Divine Imperative*, 452. The original text uses the word *Macht*, which is rendered in the English translation as "force."

80. Brunner, *Civilization*, 2:116.

81. Brunner, *Divine Imperative*, 449.

82. Brunner, *Justice*, 210.

83. Brunner, *Justice*, 29.

84. Brunner, *Divine Imperative*, 449.

in law's substance and administration.[85] Law is rescued from amorality by justice. And law helps elevate the state to the threshold of morality. "Force is based on power; through law the coercive power of the state becomes a moral entity."[86]

Law and Legitimacy

Power is not the only means law has to secure compliance; it also relies on legitimacy. Brunner sees legitimacy as based on shared intuitions about law and justice. His position resembles that of the German jurist and philosopher Gustav Radbruch in his postwar writings. Radbruch posited a feeling for law (*Rechtsgefühl*) as the basis for his idea of right law (*richtiges Recht*). Radbruch's legal feeling does not identify, however, which norms should apply to positive law. Similarly, Brunner speaks of an intuitive sense of rightness in law that is the basis of respect for law and the true source of legal authority.[87] Instead of feeling-based legitimacy, Brunner ties legitimacy to rights. Just law, as noted, "allows the rights of man in the claims of the community established by creation to assert themselves."[88] The authority of law ultimately rests on the respect of those subject to it.[89] Legitimacy is not only a matter of moral authority but also of the power and usefulness of law. This is a pragmatic description of legality. The power of law is ultimately based on recognition rather than coercion.[90]

The critical variable in law is human variance from the orders of creation: "The greater the actual deviation of the human situation from God's order . . . the more widely must a system of positive law deviate from the creative ordinance of God."[91] Human deficiency requires the adaptation of law. Yet other factors may require the evolution of law as well. Technological change, demographic developments, evolving anthropological and political understandings all contribute to dynamism in law. While plausible as far as it goes, Brunner's account of the static and dynamic dimensions of law understates the complexity of law's development. The internal logic and rationality of law also contributes to its development.

---

85. Brunner, *Divine Imperative*, 449.
86. Brunner, *Divine Imperative*, 452–53.
87. See Pöhl, *Problem*, 177.
88. Brunner, *Justice*, 210.
89. Brunner, *Divine Imperative*, 451.
90. Brunner, *Divine Imperative*, 451.
91. Brunner, *Justice*, 102.

One of the manifestations of just law is that it preserves order and prevents anarchy. In particular, Brunner stresses the importance of the stability of law: "The law [depends] upon its reliable rigidity, upon the fact that laws cannot be deflected in any direction."[92] Law's rigidity is alleviated by the elasticity of equity, which heeds individual circumstances and the needs of the common good.[93]

In conceptualizing law's relation to justice in this manner, Brunner seeks to strike a balance between realism and idealism. The realistic element is expressed in his emphasis on law's mutability and dependence on power; its idealism lies in its orientation to divine order and internal justice. Ultimately, the legitimacy of law stands or falls on its capacity for justice.

Justice

Though law is subject to endless distortions and perversions, justice is its lodestar. Brunner's most extensive treatment of justice appears in *Justice*. There, he selectively appropriates elements of classical notions of justice and aligns them with his conceptions of the orders of creation and divine justice. He proceeds from Aristotle's notion of justice as concerned with the appropriate distribution of social benefits and detriments. This is an essential component of a just social order for Brunner.[94] But equality is not only a matter of equivalence because persons with different capabilities inhabit dissimilar situations. Simple equality is an abstraction; Brunner labels it a "mere fiction of justice."[95] Standing by itself, it is abstract and remote from mundane reality. "The idea of equality can never be more than a regulatory principle; it can never be a constitutive principle of the actual formation of law."[96]

In essence, Brunner fuses Aristotle's notion of equality as *suum cuique* with the idea of a transcendent metaphysical order. For him, justice is basically but not exclusively egalitarian.[97] In fact, it essentially seems to be both egalitarian and non-egalitarian. For Brunner, there is no such thing as simple equality in the sense of each receiving an equal share. Instead, there is complex equality, or equality in the context of individual differences.

---

92. Brunner, *Justice*, 451.

93. Brunner, *Justice*, 451.

94. The proposition that "justice consists in rendering to each person his due is the fundamental principle of all natural law" (Brunner, *Justice*, 86).

95. Brunner, *Justice*, 27.

96. Brunner, *Divine Imperative*, 450.

97. "Justice is equality" (Brunner, *Divine Imperative*, 26).

Equality and inequality relate to different aspects of persons; equality to the ontological and inequality to the ontic. The personal element is concerned with unlikeness: "The more justice is concerned with the relations between persons, the less the differences between the persons can be disregarded."[98]

Justice's concern for individual differences is expressed in equity, which tempers law's rigidity and limitations. Brunner views equity affirmatively.[99] But his concept of it is more ambitious than traditional understandings in that it is concerned not only with the relations between persons, but also with the well-being of community. As for Aquinas, law for Brunner is directed to the common good.

The tension between equality and inequality (or "unlikeness," which Brunner prefers) elevates the issue of justice to a metaphysical level. In Brunner's view, justice is anchored in and inspired by divine justice, according to which each person is divinely created as equal and endowed with equal rights. The divine law of justice also provides for a "primal allocation" of the basic life requirements of each person. Yet specific needs, individual to specific persons, also exist and must be respected. Brunner further contends that inequality makes persons dependent on each other, leading them to community. The diversity of needs and abilities constitutes the basis of community.

This primal order is metaphysical and reflected in the orders of creation.[100] Law is concerned with rights and claims; justice is the "precept of the orders of creation accommodated to concrete historical circumstance."[101] Justice and law primarily relate to orders in all their fallenness; love precedes and exceeds justice since it is the divine essence. Since the orders reflect divine will, justice does as well, though indirectly. "We cannot be just, our laws cannot create an order of justice if these natural facts are not acknowledged and respected as lying in the will of God."[102]

Because it encompasses both equality and inequality, justice can only be adequately comprehended theologically. It must mediate between those poles: "The real problem of justice . . . is always whether it is the equality

---

98. Brunner, *Divine Imperative*, 29.

99. "Equity makes it plain that justice cannot be conceived in legal terms" (Brunner, *Divine Imperative*, 182).

100. "Justice is something holy; it is backed by divine order, divine necessity" (Brunner, *Civilization*, 1:107). Once justice is detached from its religious basis, it becomes a "conventional fiction" (Brunner, *Justice*, 110).

101. Brunner, *Justice*, 210.

102. Brunner, *Justice*, 210.

or inequality which matters, or whether, in spite of their actual inequality, people must be treated equally or unequally."[103]

The doctrinal basis of equality is the divine image. "The doctrine of *imago Dei* is the fundamental principle of the Protestant doctrine of justice."[104] It establishes a common human dignity among persons. Equality, Brunner cautions, should be conceived not only in terms of justice but also as the "unconditional imperative of love."[105] This means that equality has a transcendent dimension that surpasses the criteria of justice since it is rooted in the divine-human relationship.

Ultimately, equality prevails over inequality. Equality is an eschatological affirmation, resulting from Christ's universal embrace of all humanity. In the interim, the requirements of justice apply. Inequality entails interdependence and cooperation among persons, yet this takes the shape of social hierarchies, dominance, and subservience. They are provisional and not final.

Brunner also introduces a distinction within justice itself by differentiating between absolute and relative justice. Absolute justice relates to the order of creation; relative justice to the mundane order.[106] Brunner warns against confusing the two of them, for that can result in abstract fanaticism instead of justice.[107] Relative justice relates to the coercive law of the state, mitigating it and making it "serviceable." But it cannot transform its intrinsic nature. "Every positive system of justice is a compromise between the truly just and what is possible."[108] Similar to the duties applicable to the orders of creation—maintenance and improvement—Brunner holds that justice requires a duty to preserve and better it. While, by and large, historical Christianity has often had a conservative understanding of social justice, its understanding of absolute justice requires the improvement of positive law and relative justice. This is the essential element in Brunner's idea of critical cooperation with the orders. A further distinction Brunner makes is between permanent and variable elements of justice—its static and dynamic aspects. Brunner deals with this question in *Justice*, and he frames it in terms of the distinction between absolute and relative justice. Static justice is absolute, divine justice; dynamic justice is justice subject to changing historical circumstances.[109]

---

103. Brunner, *Justice*, 30 (translation altered).
104. Brunner, *Justice*, 36.
105. Brunner, *Civilization*, 1:118.
106. Brunner, *Justice*, 98.
107. Brunner, *Justice*, 99.
108. Brunner, *Justice*, 101.
109. Brunner, *Justice*, 96.

Is there a specifically Christian form of justice? Brunner believes there is. It combines equality and inequality and is anchored in the divine will as "determined by the conception of God's order of creation."[110] He contends that the Christian idea of justice is more complete and adequate than other understandings. It affirms both the equality and inequality of persons, and is more realistic for doing so. Brunner sees the combination of the equality and inequality as complementary yet always subject to conflict. This tension is rooted in Brunner's effort to avoid the extremes of collectivism and individualism while preserving the elements of truth in each of them.[111]

How are justice and law connected? Brunner sees a connection on two levels. First, they are both grounded in divine law. Second, they are linked through the concept of "just law." A just law combines realism and principle. The justness of law is not simply a matter of defining and adjudicating the rights of persons and the claims of the community, for that leaves open the nature of those rights and claims. A just law must also be equitable.

Justice stands over positive law: "Justice is the ultimate standard, transcending all man-made law."[112] It gives law its ethical weight, it connects law with the orders of creation, and is the basis for a repudiation of positivism. And law is essential for justice, for it determines whether an entitlement to equality exists. Yet their relation is not without tension. Justice is congruent with law in the order of creation, but conflicts with it in the realm of positive law.[113] Law is too human and too compromised by human defect to be adequate to the demands of justice. For its part, justice requires something more to complete it—love.

Justice and Love

For Brunner, a central task of a theory of justice is to define the relation of justice and love.[114] This is not a simple undertaking in view of the complexity of the concepts of law, justice, and love that Brunner develops. As he conceives it, justice has various facets that stand in interrelated tension. At times, justice is identified with law, and at other times it is contrasted with it.[115] Justice also has various forms: "true justice," "divine justice," and "rela-

---

110. Brunner, *Justice*, 89.
111. See Reuter, "Brunner," 314–15.
112. Ibid., 23–24.
113. Ibid., 23.
114. Brunner, "Niebuhr," 30.
115. Compare, Brunner, *Justice*, 21 (justice inseparable from law), 182 (true justice not conceivable legally), 125 (justice radically different from law).

tive justice." Further, justice for Brunner has a dualistic relation to love. It is primarily concerned with both equality and inequality in the context of institutions and systems. In contrast, love belongs to the personal, relational realm of justice-transcending agape.

While sometimes Brunner describes justice and love as supporting each other, one remembers more vividly his distinguishing between them. "Justice belongs to the world of systems, not to the world of persons."[116] "Love is always related to persons, never to things."[117] There is an echo here of Luther's two kingdoms, one also discernible in Brunner's differentiation between divine and mundane justice, and between the Divine Command and the orders of creation. Justice is impersonal and objective, abstract and rational; love is concrete and personal, non-deliberate and non-general.[118] Love encompasses justice, but never does less than what justice requires. Law may express and serve the interests of love (indirectly) and justice (directly). But it does so only incompletely, and in the case of love, surreptitiously.

Paul Ramsey has noted an evolution in Brunner's thinking between *The Divine Imperative* and *Justice* leading to a more conservative and even authoritarian outlook and a more dualistic notion of the relation of law, justice, and love. In the earlier book, the relation between love and justice forms a bridge for transformation of justice by love in the direction of more humaneness and completeness. They remain distinct, reflecting Brunner's idea that justice and love are at home in different realms. Justice takes precedence over love in the social realm, though love may express itself in the "interstitial spaces" of that realm.[119] Love, in turn, informs justice by "keeping justice just."[120] In this sense, justice and love are interdependent and interactive—together they cooperate in enabling community fulfilled in love.

The relation is different in *Justice*. In it, Ramsey finds that Brunner moves in the direction of a more dualistic concept of justice and love. Brunner distinguishes more sharply between justice and love in the context of a more conservative social vision.[121] Their relation is more of contrast than cooperation. While the transformational element of *The Divine Imperative* does not completely disappear from Brunner's ethics, it is now more subdued. Love becomes more focused on the realm of the individual and

116. Brunner, *Justice*, 128.
117. Brunner, *Justice*, 16.
118. Brunner, *Justice*, 450.
119. Ramsey, "Brunner," 245.
120. Ramsey, "Brunner," 245.

121. Jehle remarks that in *The Divine Imperative* Brunner "was more open and less authoritarian" (Jehle, *Brunner*, 442). He finds that Brunner had become more pessimistic by the time of the writing of *Justice*.

personal, limiting its relevance for institutionally oriented justice. In their separation, each becomes more partial in nature, more distanced from "the whole idea of God." This development also alters the Christian duty to make the social order more just and more humane by segmenting the motives for action into separate realms. The answer to this dualism, Ramsey contends, "is again to connect *every* ethical consideration with the *whole* idea of God, this time with man's second duty of searching for ways to make secular order is not only more just but more humane and more full of the spirit of love without unfitting them for the purpose for which they exist as orders."[122]

The Attack on Positivism

The interaction that Brunner envisions between justice and law is further illustrated by his critiques of positivism and natural law. Despite his acceptance of some of its elements, in both *The Divine Imperative* and *Justice* Brunner seeks to discredit positivist conceptions of law. In essence, positivism lacks a sense of justice and sees law as "nothing but an expression of the actual conditions of power."[123] It is an outgrowth of a positivist understanding of history that culminates in relativism.[124] In *Justice*, Brunner argues that positivism was a contributing cause of the rise of the totalitarian state.[125] Like others who reflected on that catastrophe, Brunner blamed positivism for neutralizing law as a moral force, rendering it an instrument of totalitarian oppression. This thesis is now historically contested.[126] It also goes against the implicit positivism of some established Protestant attitudes toward positive law.[127]

The chief failing of positivism in Brunner's eyes is that it leads to moral relativism and the abandonment of any critical criterion for the critique of positive law. As he writes in *Justice*, "Either there is a sacred law . . . or that sacred law is a mere dream and law is nothing but another name for the chance products of the actual elements of power in a political field of force."[128] Since Brunner sees the state and law as an order of creation, he rejects understandings of the relation between the state and law as only based on power. The positivist premise, Brunner believes, is also contradicted by

122. Ramsey, "Brunner," 258.
123. Ramsey, "Brunner," 448.
124. Ramsey, "Brunner," 686.
125. Brunner, *Justice*, 6.
126. See, for example, Lippman, "Law in the Third Reich," 429.
127. Wolf, "Recht," 1960.
128. Brunner, *Justice*, 8.

an intuitive sense of justice possessed by the common person. This sense rests on a prior intuition of the intrinsic demands of justice. He writes, "No doubt there is a sense or feeling of justice in every human being."[129]

In an essay entitled "What Is Justice?," Hans Kelsen challenges Brunner's dismissal of positivism. For Kelsen, Brunner's notion of relative justice cannot avoid relativism and leaves him no alternative to positivism. This is because, Kelsen argues, "There can no more be a relative alongside an absolute justice, than there can be an absolute alongside a relative."[130] Since Brunner admits the existence of relative justice, no criterion of absolute justice is available for a critique of positive law. Brunner must therefore accept some version of positivism. Kelsen's position depends on the assumption that absolute and relative justice are incommensurate, but his real problem is with the concept of absolute justice. For Brunner, absolute justice stands at the heart of his theology of law. Without it, one is left with an ungrounded, shadow of law, fully vulnerable to political abuse and moral perversion.

Natural Law

Unlike most of his Protestant contemporaries, Brunner is associated with an affirmative embrace of natural law.[131] Indeed, natural law has significant influence on his conception of justice. At the same time, Brunner often distances himself from natural law. For example, he rejects the role of conscience in traditional theories of natural law.[132] The priority of divine action and will, the impact of sin, so prominent in his anthropology, and the role of the state all counteract natural law tendencies in Brunner's thought.

In *The Divine Imperative*, Brunner displays a degree of reticence towards natural law because of semantic confusion about its meaning. This is qualified somewhat in *Justice*, where he affirms the necessity of natural law, though not in that name.[133] The question of just distribution at the heart of natural law is also a question pertinent to the orders of creation of family, economy, culture, state, and law. In a sense, the orders of creation provide the same moral pressure as natural law for establishing justice and directing that each person be given his or her due. Justice secures a

129. Brunner, *Civilization*, 1:106.

130. Kelsen, "Justice," 26.

131. See generally Herr, *Naturrecht*, who contends that Brunner is "the only Protestant theologian who attempted to develop a doctrine of natural law on the basis of biblical revelation" (Herr, *Naturrecht*, 166).

132. McGrath, *Brunner*, 189.

133. Some commentators speculated this change is due to the dire circumstances of totalitarianism. See Herr, *Naturrecht*, 167–68, 171.

"primal allocation."[134] Christian tradition, Brunner contends, equated the two: "The law of nature for Christianity meant simply and solely the order of creation."[135] This also applies to natural justice, which is also supported by a divine order. "Underlying the *suum cuique* there is the order of creation, the will of the Creator which determines what is each man's due."[136] This order is presupposed by justice but transcended and fulfilled by love.[137] Although he warns that the concept of natural law under that name as "hopelessly confused and misunderstood,"[138] he advocates a "Christian version" of natural law that reflects the divine orders of creation.[139] This affirms the basic principle of rendering to each person her due. This is based in the created order but is elaborated biblically and theologically through the created order and in Jesus's teaching.

Brunner criticizes rationalized versions of natural law for prioritizing the independence of each individual at the expense of the community.[140] Associations of individuals, rather than community, are the basis for contemporary collective identity. Inorganic groupings have replaced communal structures. For example, rationalistic distortions of natural law led to individualistic forms of liberalism that lack a notion of a social body. The remedy for this distortion is not a separate source of knowledge in competition with natural law, but development of a critical criterion applicable to positive law. Natural law can and must criticize positive law without undermining it, except in the case of resistance to an unjust law.

Brunner sees his conception of natural law as congruent with positive law in that it determines what is fixed and fitting. "It lies in the nature of law to fix, to settle."[141] This fixing exists prior to positive law. It is an essential prolegomenon to positive law, but in no way can substitute for it.

---

134. Herr, *Naturrecht*, 49.

135. Brunner, *Justice*, 90.

136. Brunner, *Justice*, 48.

137. Brunner, *Justice*, 50.

138. Brunner, *Justice*, 87.

139. Brunner, *Justice*, 89.

140. Brunner discusses natural law in *Christianity and Civilization*. There, he traces a rationalist form of it to Grotius. It is marked by a detachment of justice from its metaphysical/religious bases, and by a "one-sided" identification of justice and equality. See Brunner, *Civilization*, 1:110.

141. Brunner, *Civilization*, 1:21.

Concluding Observations

Brunner presents a predominantly affirmative concept of positive law. He acknowledges the relative autonomy of law, its secularity, and its rationality without considering any of its characteristics as definitive. In vigorously affirming the connection between law and justice, he rejects conceptions of law merely as a state-centered, administrative apparatus for dispute resolution and the maintenance of order. And while Brunner properly observes that there is much in law that is irrelevant to justice, that is not the case for all law. Criminal law and much of civil and commercial law is concerned with providing for fairness and equitable conduct; constitutional law secures basic rights in relation to political ideals. Brunner affirms the importance of critical cooperation with law in order to work for its improvement. One misses an equally vigorous affirmation in Barth, Thielicke, and Wolf.

At the same time, Brunner's theology and ethics of law suffers from limitations in his concept of justice. As Wolfgang Huber remarks, not only does Brunner "exclusively relate his concept of justice to the Aristotelian tradition, but he also selects one element of that tradition, namely the equivalence of justice with *suum cuique*."[142] This leads him to concentrate on the relation of equality and inequality. The principle of *suum cuique* does not, in and of itself, reflect adequately the agapaic dimension of Christian ethics. To be fair, Brunner warns that justice does not exist in any perfect form, and must be transcended by divine sovereignty and love.[143] Nevertheless while admitting justice's abstract character, he goes on to claim that the best approximation of its definition is the principle of *suum cuique* as expressed in the rational-egalitarian law of nature as informed by Stoicism and a Christian notion of creation.[144]

Creation establishes differences among persons, resulting in unlikeness and inequality. These inequalities must be addressed where possible, but other values are also important. As noted, Brunner admits that equality "can never be more than a regulative principle; it can never be a constitutive principle of the actual formation of law."[145] Presumably, this would have led him to develop a more expansive idea of justice that includes procedural and substantive fairness, along with legal stability and predictability. It would help to overcome the dualism Brunner implies between justice and love.

---

142. Huber, *Gerechtigkeit*, 202.
143. Brunner, *Divine Imperative*, 450.
144. Brunner, *Divine Imperative*, 450.
145. Brunner, *Divine Imperative*, 450.

Brunner anchors justice in a metaphysical/religious, specifically Christian, foundation. Does he provide sufficient warrant for this contention? How does this align with the pluralistic premise? While Christianity affirms the essential equality of persons, it is not alone in doing so. Democracy is also premised on equality. Obviously, the existence of secular grounds for equality does not disqualify metaphysical/religious ones. But the converse is also true. To attempt to answer these questions would lead too far afield. But a related question should be addressed: whether metaphysical/religious commitments can cooperatively interact with, and complement, other worldviews. Brunner believes those metaphysical commitments are essential, but he envisions that Christians and others can coalesce around the concept of justice. He states: "Justice is a topic where Christian and non-Christian thinking meet, where they have common ground without being identical."[146] This may be a pragmatic move, but it can have beneficial results.

Brunner is aware that modern western societies are not theocratic, and their legal systems are relatively autonomous. Obviously, Christian perspectives are not privileged over secular ones. To Brunner's credit, he appreciates the difficulties and dangers of mixing the ultimate with the penultimate. He rejects a Christological grounding of positive law for this reason, asking, "What . . . does it mean for a lawyer, who is working on a new penal code, to acknowledge the Kingship of Christ?"[147] To his mind, this shows that "this whole Christological ethic is pure fantasy; at its best it would have no result; at its worst it would lead to that ancient utopian mixture of spiritual and secular elements, of the Kingdom of Christ and the State, or to the no less unpleasant confusion between Church and State which occurs in some of the efforts which a been made to unite theocracy with "ecclesiocracy."[148]

Given the dynamism of societies, positive law must continually evolve. Justice has a role to play in this process. Relative justice is of primary relevance for positive law in its incrementally corrective capacity, yet absolute justice is also aspirationally important. Brunner's idea of justice supports both activities, but it is limited by its focus on equality and inequality at the expense of values such as integrity, fairness, and the development of human capabilities.

146. Brunner, *Civilization*, 1:108.

147. Brunner, *Christian Doctrine of Creation*, 320.

148. Brunner, *Christian Doctrine of Creation*, 320. See also where Brunner criticizes the effort to "deduce the order of law and the state from the historical event of Christ, the cross of Christ. How fantastic this deduction is must be plain to any unprejudiced mind. Even jurists consciously standing on the ground of Christian faith reject it" (Brunner, *Justice*, 272).

Finally, the anthropological elements in Brunner's theology of positive law are constructively provocative. His notion of complementarity with its idea that humans are dependent on each other for wholeness stands as an antithesis to conceptions of legal community based on atomistic individualism. This enriches ethical reflection on law by avoiding one-sided emphases on either the individual or the communal. This is not to say that the tension between them is eliminated, rather it both endures and is transcended. Brunner writes, "The real individual and the real community are not related to each other by tension, but by a relation of identity; the truly personal and the truly communal is one and the same thing—it is love."[149]

---

149. Brunner, *Divine Imperative*, 638.

IV

Jacques Ellul

The Foundation of Law

Jacques Ellul (1913–94) stands in contrast to most of the other figures treated in this book. Not formally trained as a theologian, Ellul was a law professor his entire career, although many of his numerous publications (approximately 50 books and over 600 articles) deal with theological, ethical, and biblical topics. A French Protestant, he was influenced by the Reformed tradition as mediated by Karl Barth; Kierkegaard was a strong influence on him as well. Born in Bordeaux into a religiously indifferent household, Ellul developed an early interest in Marx. He retained an interest in Marxian social analysis throughout his career, declaring it to be the most powerful and insightful approach to social analysis available.[1] Although Ellul identified himself as a Christian, he felt that Christianity on its own lacked the ability to fathom and address social problems adequately. This led him to combine elements of Christianity and Marxism in his social and cultural writings.

During his intellectually formative years, Ellul traveled in diverse circles, spending time with some Catholic personalists (the *Esprit* movement), anarchists, and socialists (the *Ordre Nouveau*). He ended up studying law and was named professor of law in Strasburg in 1938. He was dismissed from his teaching position in 1940 by the Vichy regime and spent the war years farming and participating in the resistance movement, as well as helping Jews to escape the Nazis and their French collaborators.[2] In 1944, Ellul regained his professorship at the University of Bordeaux in legal studies, and in addition lectured and wrote extensively on sociology.

1. Sturm, "Ellul," 562.

2. Ellul's formative years and wartime experiences are detailed in Lovekin, *Technique*, 129–36.

After the war, Ellul became a deputy mayor of Bordeaux, an experience that exposed him to the challenges of political administration. He also became involved in ecclesiastical activities, both by forming Protestant associations and by serving as a member of the national council of the Reformed Church in France. Later, Ellul also became active in the World Council of Churches. His experiences with these organizations yielded certain frustrations for him. In the case of the World Council of Churches, it culminated in an open break in 1966 as a result of what Ellul termed its "theological superficiality and social *naïveté*" in its endorsement of certain Third World liberation theologies.[3] Ellul published widely until his death in 1994 on a variety of subjects: ethics, theology, sociology, cultural criticism, biblical exegesis, social history, and law. Many of his works have been translated into English.

Ellul is often described as a lay theologian, which is accurate but potentially misleading. He was well acquainted with continental theology, and displayed a deft sophistication in his handling of theological concepts and texts. Further, he maintained personal contact with some of the prominent theological figures of the day, above all, Barth. At the same time, Ellul saw himself as a lay person whose primary professional field was the law.

Ellul's major work on law, *The Theological Foundation of Law*, appeared in a German translation in 1946 shortly after its publication in France, and rapidly became influential in post-war discussions among German Protestant theologians and jurists about the theological foundations of law, natural law, and the relation of law, theology and religion.[4] He was seen as closely allied theologically with Karl Barth. Barth himself referred to Ellul's work in his own writings, and studied Ellul's *Theological Foundation of Law* in a seminar with theology students.[5] Currently, Ellul's influence in the theology and ethics of law is limited, although from time to time studies appear contending that this neglect is undeserved and that Ellul deserves greater attention.[6] Several societies currently exist that are dedicated to preserving his legacy and promoting interest in his writings.[7]

---

3. Sturm, "Ellul," 563.

4. See Herr, *Naturrecht*, 77, who refers to Ellul's theology of law as "pointing the way" in postwar Protestant discussions of law in Germany.

5. Busch, *Barth*, 388.

6. For example, see Lohmann, "Recht bei Ellul"; Goddard, *Living the Word*.

7. For example, the International Ellul Society maintains an active publishing program related to his work.

Ellul's Theological/Ethical Vision

Provocatively, Ellul professes a disinterest in theology. He states that, as an abstract activity, theology "bores me immeasurably.... What is important to me is that which belongs to the ethical domain and the existential domain, in other words, what is close to life, to reality."[8] Ellul did not produce any systematic or doctrinal works of theology; rather his concern was "to provide Christians with the means of thinking *for themselves* the meaning of their involvement in the modern world."[9] Yet theological themes suffused his writings, such as *The Ethics of Freedom*.

Ellul's theological vision draws on themes of estrangement and reconciliation. Between these two poles is the theater of divine action, antecedent to and sovereign over any human action. According to one commentator, for Ellul "the central theme of Christian theology is God's incessant contention with the world."[10] While Ellul works out the implications of these motifs primarily in ethical rather than theological or doctrinal terms, his concept of ethics is broad and includes theological dimensions.[11]

Ellul describes his methodology as based on dialectic, grounded in his discovery "that in the world we live in there are no means of thinking and acquiring knowledge that are not of the dialectical nature."[12] He understands dialectic in terms of counterpoint, confrontation and contradiction rather than a kind of culminating synthesis or amalgamation. In one of his later books, Ellul speaks of the dialectic between two elements as involving both alienation and connection.[13] His interest in dialectic is attributable, at least partly, to Barth who emphasizes divine freedom and action in interaction with human existence. Ellul also shares with Barth an emphasis on biblical texts as the medium of revelation. His reading of these texts is holistic in the sense of basing interpretation on the totality of Scripture and not on individual passages.[14] In Ellul's reading of them, the biblical texts are unified by a conviction of the central significance of Jesus Christ.

---

8. Ellul, *In Season*, 220.
9. Ellul, *In Season*, 6.
10. Sturm, "Ellul," 561
11. Greenman, *Understanding Jacques Ellul*, 121.
12. Ellul, *In Season*, 201.

13. "Thus the relation between two factors can only be a dialectical and critical one. Noetically, we can only affirm two contradictions, pressing contradiction to the limit. Actively, we can only introduce the element of mutual criticism" (Ellul, *What I Believe*, 44).

14. On Barth's influence on Ellul's interpretation of biblical texts, see Bromiley, "Barth's Influence on Jacques Ellul," 36–39.

Ellul draws sharp distinctions between Christian morality and natural morality. The former is focused on God's will; the latter to its own idea of the good. They are not the same: "The good morality is acquainted with is not the same thing as God's will."[15] The primary source of moral guidance is divine will. It exists in a tension with the existing order, with its reliance on technique. There is a double movement at work in Christian ethics: one movement of distancing and liberation from the institutional structures of the social and political world, and the second involving the emergence of the love of God and neighbor as paramount concerns. Like Barth and Brunner, the good for Ellul is associated solely with the divine will, which is discernible in situations, not in structures. Social and political arrangements are necessary for ordered life, but they are incapable of embodying the good. Ellul terms these systemic arrangements "moralities." They resemble Brunner's or Thielicke's orders of preservation, but lack creational status and are ultimately insufficient to realize fully the possibilities of Christian existence.

Like Barth and Brunner, Ellul rejects any notion of Christian ethics as consisting of rules, principles or slogans.[16] As Gene Outka observes, Ellul refuses to decode Christian conceptions.[17] Such decoding invites substitution of human conceptualizations for divine guidance and authority. Ellul writes: "It is the will of God which determines what is good, and there is no good which exists outside of that decision."[18] This will is discernible only in specific circumstances and this is particularly the case with law. "Human law does not proceed by deriving principles but by discerning concrete situations, by judging historical facts, more or less justly in the light of the righteousness of God."[19]

Ellul contends that every society requires some form of morality, which he terms "natural morality." While natural morality is "useless" for Christians, it is necessary for social life. But he cautions against any attempt to extend the believer's understanding of the good to non-believers. "One of the essential rules of the Christian life is never to ask a non-Christian to conduct himself like a Christian."[20] Ellul shows sensitivity here to the circumstances of pluralism. His theological contextualization of positive law tends, however, to downplay this sensitivity.

---

15. Ellul, *To Will & To Do*, 73.
16. Ellul, *Presence*, 12.
17. Outka, "Ellul," 178.
18. Ellul, *To Will & To Do*, 6.
19. Ellul, *Theological Foundation of Law*, 93.
20. Ellul, *To Will & To Do*, 104.

Indeed, Ellul's ethical vision is pervaded with the tension between the actual circumstances of life and the revealed truth of divine purpose. Ellul describes this tension as "agonistic" in the sense of adversarial struggle between divine goodness and sinful humanity. He stresses the importance of being "present to the modern world" while not being ensnared by it with its tainted, confining reality. Entrenchment in a closed subgroup is, in his view, an unsatisfactory alternative. The ethical task, for Ellul, is one of faithful presence, not of seeking to resolve the tension inherent in the existence of the believer in the contemporary world preoccupied with technique and propaganda. He is insistent on the necessity of engaging actual circumstances without capitulating to them. As Ellul writes in a volume entitled *What I Believe*: "I have found it impossible to join Christianity and the world into a single whole. . . . From another angle, it seems no less certain to me that we cannot think in a Christian way in isolation from the concrete reality of society."[21]

Ellul's Writings on Law

Ellul's writings on law are an underappreciated and neglected part of his corpus. This is ironical in light of the fact that Ellul spent his career as a professor of law. Much more attention has been devoted to his sociological writings and particularly to his writings on technology, such as *The Technological Society* and *The Technological Bluff*. Nowadays Ellul is perhaps best known as a critic of technology, politics (in books such as *The Politics of God and the Politics of Man*), and religion and ethics (in *The Ethics of Freedom*). The lack of engagement with his writings on law in Anglophone circles is partly due to the fact that his major work on law (*The Theological Foundation of Law*) was not translated into English until almost a decade and a half after its translation into German. Upon its appearance in English, it seemed to belong to a different historical era, and it did. The book attracted more attention in Germany, appearing at a time of renewed interest in natural law, which Ellul discusses at fair length in the volume. Also, the Nuremberg war crimes trials were underway at the time, and this heightened public interest in questions about the basis of law. Ellul's reception in Germany was aided by his theological relationship with Barth, although it is sometimes thought to be more substantial than it in fact was.[22] The theological affinity between

---

21. Ellul, *What I Believe*, 43.

22. See Bromiley, "Barth's Influence on Jacques Ellul," 33: "Ellul is no unqualified Barthian."

Ellul and Barth is particularly evident in their Christocentrism, as well as in their views of revelation and scripture.

The Theological Foundation of Law was cited frequently in postwar era discussions about law among theologians and jurists such as Barth, Thielicke, Ernst Wolf, and Erik Wolf. Ellul also figured in discussions by the newly reconstituted Protestant church in Germany about the nature of law and its theological foundation in the conferences that took place in the late 1940s and 1950s in Gottingen, Treysa, and Hemer, Germany. Ellul's volume on law drew particular attention in the May 1949 meeting of German jurists and theologians in Göttingen convened by the Council of the Evangelical Church in Germany. It was discussed in some depth in the two primary papers delivered at the conference by Ernst Wolf and Ulrich Scheuner.[23] At the time, Ellul was viewed as offering a middle way between the established camps of Barthian Christocentrism and the natural law-related thought of Brunner and others. His approach represented a rejection of scholastic and philosophical versions of natural law, while affirming the relevance of theological perspectives for positive law. According to Lena Foljanty, Ellul took seriously both Protestant skepticism about natural law as well as the need for a Protestant version of natural law.[24] As described in the preceding chapter on Brunner, the suitability of natural law as an influence for positive law was a much-discussed question in the period of postwar reconstruction. It was in many ways an obvious response to the totalitarian experience, and represented an established tradition, antithetical to any racial or national tribalism. Brunner and Ellul assessed the prospects for a revival of natural law. They came to opposing conclusions: Brunner was generally optimistic, while Ellul's skepticism outweighed his sense that the times demanded a revival of natural law.

Throughout his career, Ellul returned from time to time to questions of law, religion, and ethics. Regrettably, many of these later publications have not been collected or translated. His thinking on law continued to evolve throughout his career; Ellul himself speaks of having developed four different understandings of law in his writings.[25] As noted, most of the secondary literature on Ellul fails to deal with his legal thought in any detail. When it is treated, it occurs in isolation from his other writings, especially his sociological and cultural analyses.[26]

---

23. They appear, along with a report on the conference, in Dombois, *Kirche und Recht*.

24. Foljanty, *Rechtstheologie*, 157.

25. Goddard, *Living the Word*, 207.

26. An exception is Andrew Goddard's book on Ellul that appeared in 2001.

In one of the best studies available on Ellul, Andrew Goddard notes the evolution of Ellul's thinking on law over several decades, including several revisions and reversals. This makes it problematical to speak of Ellul's understanding of law as if it were consistent and cohesive. But most of the legal claims that preoccupied him are contained in *The Theological Foundation of Law*. The focus here is on that book as Ellul's most extensive and developed statement on human law, with some reference to his later writings.

As with the other thinkers treated in this book, Ellul is dissatisfied with the prevailing jurisprudential alternatives of the day: positivism and idealism, including varieties of natural law. He believes that these alternatives fail to attend to social realities: idealist theories are abstract and remote, positivist ones reduce law to enactments of law detached from normative considerations. It is hard to overemphasize Ellul's concern with the actual realities of law. "The lived relationship between people and the law" is the center of Ellul's focus.[27] His notion of law encompasses not only its established legal institutions, but all forms of social ordering directed toward the creation and maintenance of order out of disorder. The perennial urge to structure the unruly realms of time, space and relationships creates a human inclination to law. "At the heart of the creator of law lies in the attempt by humans to establish an order in the world and thus to escape the alienation experienced in their natural and social milieu."[28]

The theme of the book is "not to determine what law with a Christian content is; rather, it is to find out what the Lordship of Jesus Christ means for law (law as it exists), and what function God has assigned to law."[29] Outside of a Christological orientation, there can be no true understanding of justice, which is solely to be found in the divine will and judgment. Ellul holds fast to a notion of law as a secular phenomenon. The question then is one of applying Christocentric sovereignty to a human institution: "Law is secular and is part of a secular world. But this is a world where Jesus Christ is King."[30] To frame the question in this way emphasizes both (1) the non-theocratic, mundane nature of law, and (2) the place of law's claimed autonomy in a divine economy of reconciliation.

---

27. Goddard, *Living the Word*, 209.
28. Goddard, *Living the Word*, 211.
29. Goddard, *Living the Word*, 211.
30. Goddard, *Living the Word*, 211.

Natural Law

The opening chapter of *The Theological Foundation of Law* deals with natural law, which Ellul observes is "now reappearing, after about a century and a half of partial eclipse."[31] In general, he is anything but optimistic about its viability. For him, natural law is static, implicitly deistic, anti-eschatological, unscriptural, lacking in a valid basis for justice, and ultimately non-Christian.[32] It is not grounded in divine justice, disregards human sinfulness, and reflects human presumptuousness, disqualifying it as a source of, or resource for, positive law.

Ellul analyzes natural law both conceptually and historically, focusing on its Western manifestations.[33] He devotes considerable effort to identifying natural law and to describing the deficiencies in its customary understanding. In the first place, natural law is not an idea but a phenomenon and a "concrete event in history."[34] Ellul views traditional notions of natural law as anthropocentrically oriented and opposed to law that is theocentric and theologically grounded. The problems he identifies in natural law lie at a deep level; they involve the philosophical assumptions underlying particular conceptions of natural law. One of the book's principal arguments is that law's grounding is not self-contained and autonomous, but rather is dependent on a deeper foundation—in his case, a theological one.

From a historical perspective, Ellul posits a threefold evolution of natural law from its religious origins in priestly sanctions, to a legalized phase, in which religious and magical elements are purged and natural law becomes infused with the mores and practices of the state. In the third stage, natural law comes under the control of, and becomes wholly a creation of, the state. It becomes increasingly rationalized and technical, which robs it of its spontaneity and concern with justice, leaving it a "consecrated abstraction."[35] Ellul sees this as an irreversible process: there is no possibility to recover previous forms of natural law once they have been displaced by successive ones.

---

31. Ellul, *Theological Foundation of Law*, 8.

32. Ellul states, "The doctrine of natural law as a Christian doctrine is . . . ruled out at every point" (Ellul, *Theological Foundation of Law*, 68). Ellul proceeds to state twelve deficiencies of natural law from the perspective of divine law, including that divine law is created by God, is Christocentric, and is neither based on human nature nor subject to discernment by natural knowledge.

33. Ellul, *Theological Foundation of Law*, 17. He disclaims any intention of being comprehensive in his treatment of natural law.

34. Ellul, *Theological Foundation of Law*, 14.

35. Ellul, *Theological Foundation of Law*, 3.

Ellul believes that, under contemporary circumstances, natural law is outdated. From its origins until the eighteenth century, it was principally concerned with private law and individuals. Subsequently, it became focused on public law and the social and institutional aspects of law; it has also entered into different domains of law.[36] Natural law has become more varied and variable as social and cultural circumstances have evolved. At the same time, it has become rationalized through attempts to develop a universalized concept of human nature and to define goodness independently of divine revelation. This attempted universalization, Ellul believes, is a presumptuous effort to abstract law from time, while in fact it deprives it of dynamism and hope.

Conceptually, Ellul differentiates among philosophical, juridical, and phenomenological theories of natural law. Philosophical theories are grounded in reason, and are remote from juridical experience and social institutions. Its hallmarks are rationalization and theorization; both phenomena are characteristic of the impending decay of legal traditions. Philosophical theories of natural law fail to consider the institutions and practices of actual societies and, as a result, they have little or nothing to do with law itself. This is an important consideration for Ellul. In his eyes, remoteness from legal reality disqualifies both philosophical and theological theories of natural law. "We can admit a theory of law only if it relates to actual legal practices."[37] Ellul specifically references Roman law and French Enlightenment-era theories in this connection. In contrast, a "juridical" concept of natural law treats it not as a moral ideal but as a juridical fact. Nor is it a criterion of justice, "but an *aggregation of institutions and rules* which can be named, described and circumscribed."[38]

But Ellul's sharpest critique of natural law is based on theological grounds. For him, it is Christ, not nature, that is the basis of human law. The divine-human covenant constitutes humans as legally competent, and Christ is the goal and fulfillment of the covenant.[39] Further, he sees natural law as an attempt to derive a creation-based notion of humanity that unites Christians and non-Christians and, as such, it is an "effort at reconciliation beyond grace." To his mind, this is "absolutely inadmissible."[40] Creation is a dynamic process, tending to an eschatological conclusion; natural law tends to stasis. More fundamentally, the meaning of human institutions such

---

36. Ellul, *Theological Foundation of Law*, 9.
37. Ellul, *Theological Foundation of Law*, 21.
38. Ellul, *Theological Foundation of Law*, 26.
39. See Herr, *Naturrecht*, 75.
40. Ellul, *Theological Foundation of Law*, 11.

as law and justice can only become apparent in reference to God. In this context, Ellul sharply distinguishes between the divine and human realms, consigning law to the latter. As a human institution, natural law remains inescapably human. "Natural law is nothing but absolutized terrestrial law."[41]

Without reservation, Ellul advocates a theocentric idea of law, one dependent on a divine foundation. Natural law, to the extent that it can even be said legitimately to exist, should be concerned with institutions, rules, and social reality, not with rationalization and abstract norms. He sees similarities between earlier epochs and his contemporary situation. Law has now entered a technical phase and natural law is no longer tenable, its sense of justice replaced by sanctions and technique. Ellul contends, "It seems wholly illusory either to work for the construction of a new natural law which fails to satisfy both the common thinking of contemporary man and the modern concept of law, or to debate the necessity or the existence of natural law as a theory."[42] With this judgment, Ellul writes off the postwar revival of natural law, finding it an untenable basis for legal reconstruction amid the ruin of law under totalitarianism.

Despite his rejection of most natural law theories, Ellul concedes that a pragmatic version of natural law exists that contains elements useful for positive law. This pragmatic version has certain characteristics that occur across different cultural and political contexts. They are (1) the existence of law; (2) a fundamental similarity in substantive content in fields as criminal law, marriage, property and contract and (3) a common intuition that law "is constituted neither as an arbitrary creation on the part of the state nor as an automatic result of social and economic conditions."[43] The third characteristic means for Ellul that while political and social conditions may influence the nature of law, the ultimate, "refining factor" in the creation of law is the human being herself. Taken together, these commonalities point to a certain kind of natural law dimension to all human law, constituting elements of a common legal foundation that are "cornerstones of any theory of law."[44]

But Ellul does not see these common features as amounting to anything like natural law. The evolutionary social and cultural forces he discerns in contemporary society oppose the revival of natural law. Indeed, all law is imperiled by trends in modern societies. Law is becoming progressively more technical, and its preoccupation with technique marginalizes

---

41. Ellul, *Theological Foundation of Law*, 64.
42. Ellul, *Theological Foundation of Law*, 35.
43. Ellul, *Theological Foundation of Law*, 29.
44. Ellul, *Theological Foundation of Law*, 30.

and eventually suppresses justice. The result is technical law, generated by the application of technique to law. Technique, with its procedural preoccupations and emphasis on social expedience, overwhelms the primordial element of justice.[45] Without a regulating element, juridical technique, like all technique, generates a self-absorbed dynamism and becomes blind to other considerations.[46] Law becomes preoccupied with instrumentalized means serving material interests and becomes deaf to the demands of justice. The situation arises in which, according to one commentator, "A teleology of order has substituted itself for a teleology of justice."[47]

Consequently, for Ellul, natural law belongs to the past rather than to the present or future. It has certain affirmative characteristics: it attests to the inevitability of law as a vital feature of social life and expresses a substantive concern with justice, reflecting political and economic circumstances without being reducible to them. These constitute the legacy of natural law, and are present even in secularized, technical law. But that legacy is endangered by the technical mindset. Law is threatened with the loss of its character as law, and with a descent into the status of an administrative apparatus that blindly facilitates a cacophony of unexamined ends.

It should come as no surprise that Ellul's depiction of natural law has proven controversial. As an interdisciplinary construct, it combines history, theology, philosophy, jurisprudence, and cultural criticism in a distinctive way. While his notion of the various historical stages of natural law is illuminating, his analysis is colored, strongly if not excessively, by his theological presuppositions about the infirmities of human law. These presuppositions lead Ellul to a straightened view of the capability of humans to create valid law. Timothy Fort has criticized Ellul's negative view of the human capacity for developing law and justice, contending that in such an extreme form it diminishes human responsibility and invites decadence.[48] Another critic has contended that Ellul's minimalist assessment of human capabilities amounts to a denial that women and men have been made in the divine image.[49] It is certainly the case that Ellul has a jaundiced view of natural law and presents it in unappealing terms. His emphasis on deficiencies serves to prepare an affirmative case for a theological grounding of law, which is developed in Ellul's treatment of divine law.

45. Ellul defines technique as "the totality of methods rationally arrived at and having absolute efficiency (for a given stage of development) in every field of human activity" (Ellul, *Technological Society*, xxv).

46. Ellul, *Theological Foundation of Law*, 32.

47. Dujancourt, "Law," 10.

48. Fort, *Law and Religion*, 23.

49. Charles, *Natural Law*, 135–36.

Law and Divine Law

Against the backdrop of his sober assessment of natural law, Ellul proposes an alternate vision of human law—one rooted in divine law.[50] This involves recognition that contemporary notions of law are deficient in their concern for justice and righteousness—two key elements for Ellul's scriptural understanding of law. He identifies two manifestations of righteousness in the Hebrew Bible: judging (*shpht*) and righteousness (*sdq*). Though different, they relate to each other, with the result that justice provides guidance and culminates in mercy. Divine righteousness is linked inextricably with human justice: the two cannot be separated, but serve to illuminate each other. "To the extent that human justice is patterned after divine righteousness, the one cannot be apprehended without the other."[51] Ellul sets out three expressions of divine righteousness in relation to human justice: (1) transcendence (which connotes comprehensiveness and ultimacy), (2) judgment of the insufficiencies of human justice, and (3) an eschatological orientation, according to which the world, including law, will be judged.

Divine righteousness is embodied in Jesus Christ. Ellul's Christocentrism comes to the fore at this point. "Law," he declares, "is entirely Christocentric."[52] It is the ground and basis of divine justice, an important notion for Ellul. Divine justice is a mode of divine action and serves as the basis and criterion for human law. It is dynamic and personal, not eternal and objective. Yet it is not the source of human law. Although Ellul contends in an early essay that the Old Testament concept of law constitutes a template for human law,[53] he subsequently rejects that position in *The Theological Foundation of Law*. Divine justice is transcendent. It is "supremely expressed" in mercy, articulated concretely in specific historical contexts, with its ultimate and culminating expression in Jesus Christ: "All the characteristics of God's righteousness are united and embodied in the life, the death, and the resurrection of Jesus Christ."[54] This means that law is oriented to the person—both divine and human. Ellul declares that "What is important in the discussion of the problem of justice, including legal justice, is

---

50. Goddard points out that there are linguistic difficulties in rendering Ellul's terminology in English. Ellul speaks of *droit divin*, which Goddard suggests should be translated as "divine right." But this obscures the term's parallelism with *droit humain*. *Droit*, like *Recht*, connotes both law and right, for which there is no single Anglophone cognate. See Cassin, *Dictionary of Untranslatables*, s.v. "Droit."

51. Ellul, *Theological Foundation of Law*, 39.

52. Ellul, *Theological Foundation of Law*, 69.

53. Ellul quoted in Goddard, *Living the Word*, 299.

54. Ellul, *Theological Foundation of Law*, 42.

the absolute centrality of the person of Jesus Christ."[55] The relation between divine and human justice is mutually interactive, or dialectical (in Ellul's understanding). It involves both affirmation and condemnation, judgment and acceptance. On the one hand, all human justice is unjust; on the other hand, to reject human justice is unjust and therefore opposed to God's will.[56] The authority for this interpretation of divine justice is, again, scripture.

Theologically, Ellul is dismissive of human law. As already noted, he combines this theological rejection with provisional, pragmatic acceptance, or at least tolerance, of natural law as a variety of human law. As human law, natural law is inferior to divine law. Although it has contact with divine law, this contact does not rescue it from the deficiencies of its human authors. It is not religious but human and is consequently constrained: "Law in our understanding cannot have a Christian content."[57]

Ellul further contends that to the extent law is considered autonomous, it is incompatible with scripture. "Whether it be a legal principle or a system, whether rational or mystical, law by itself, as an autonomous entity, does not exist in the Bible."[58] This statement conveys a defining characteristic of Ellul's ethical thought: its biblical character. He openly declares that the criterion of his thought is Biblical revelation.[59] In part, Ellul appropriated this stance from Barth. Bromiley points out that Ellul's view of scripture resembles Barth's in the central position it has in his thought.[60]

Ellul's insistence on the absolute priority of divine law over human law has led one critic to accuse him of advocating "theocratic monism."[61] That criticism has a certain plausibility, at least as far as the normative authority of law is concerned. Ellul grants human law no dignity of its own, it depends for its legitimacy solely and derivatively on divine law. Throughout *The Theological Foundation of Law*, Ellul tends to diminish the status of human law as an amalgam of more or less unsuccessful attempts to create viable justice on its own, apart from divine guidance. At the same time, he concedes a certain social and political validity to positive law. That is to say that Ellul sees human law dialectically—in terms of a dialectic between religious affirmation and social reality.

---

55. Ellul, *Theological Foundation of Law*, 44.
56. Ellul, *Theological Foundation of Law*, 39–44.
57. Ellul, *Theological Foundation of Law*, 13.
58. Ellul, *Theological Foundation of Law*, 45.
59. Ellul, *To Will & To Do*, 1.
60. Bromiley, "Barth's Influence on Jacques Ellul," 47.
61. Lohmann, "Recht bei Ellul," 128.

Law as a Dialectical Social Reality

The dialectical character of law reflects its location in a force field of contrasting and often opposing tensions—between divine and human, means and ends, procedure and substance, past and future, and justice and expediency. Divine law is an expression of divine justice and serves as the ground of human law. In and of itself, human law is hopelessly deficient and incapable of realizing its own potential. It is rehabilitated by divine law. Law is fundamentally concerned with justice, and this means that human justice is ordered in accordance with divine justice.

Ellul approaches human law from various contrasting perspectives. Sociologically, he sees the scope of law as defined by denomination (in the sense of naming) and function.[62] Whatever is denoted as 'juridical' qualifies as some kind of law; whatever functions as an institution and procedure for maintaining a normative social order also is seen as law. Viewed anthropologically, law is a universal human phenomenon; it is an attempt to develop structures for structuring time, space and human relationships with the aim of maintaining order.[63] Theologically, law is a divine-human phenomenon in which the source of law (divine justice) judges the validity of its human counterpart (human law), and concludes that it is altogether lacking.

In Ellul's understanding, behind its profusion of cultural forms law is a human creation, a universal human phenomenon, one that is inescapably normative. In seeking to create uniform, stable standards of applicability throughout a political community, law represents an attempt to impose structure on time, space and human interactions. This structuring activity reflects values of the society, including, but not limited to, justice. Values, for Ellul, are human creations that express "the imperative in relation to which [a person] judges himself."[64] Law's normativity is a consequence of its value orientation. The values reflected in law are typically conflicting and corrigible and this forces law to be dynamic and evolutionary. This does not undermine such values, rather it underscores the linkage between them and their social context. Indeed, the embeddedness of value is important in Ellul's eyes. Values are validated by their appearance in law.[65] By this,

---

62. See footnotes 133–36 below and accompanying text regarding Ellul's sociological critique of law.

63. Ellul writes in a 1965 essay, "It seems to me that in reality law is made in order to establish a *livable* situation in the midst of conflict and disorder" (Ellul quoted in Goddard, *Living the Word*, 211).

64. Ellul quoted in Goddard, *Living the Word*, 212.

65. "Law is effectively what establishes a simultaneous relationship between people's values and their conduct and creates the milieu in which these values can be realized" (Ellul quoted in Goddard, *Living the Word*, 218).

Ellul emphasizes the actual and concrete reality of law as experienced by those subject to it, and not only by its technicians and administrators. Law embodies and applies these informing values in and through its procedural and substantive dimensions.

Ellul reinforces this pragmatic, approximate idea of law by identifying the content of law in terms of order and judgment. By order, he means the preservative arrangements within a society that allow it to be organized and avoid chaos. Judgment is eschatological; it involves the use of force and also requires a constant exercise of discretion. Judgment is a recurrent theme in Ellul's writing. In the context of human law, it is essentially an ethical, rather than juridical action. It is the exercise of pragmatic justice. It is a proximate and provisional activity, a human act of "laying down a law and re-establishing or establishing order."[66] Judgment is divinely imposed but humanly executed. It is a relational-participatory act, neither abstract nor purely theoretical. It takes place in the juridical realm, but also elsewhere, exercised by juridical actors but also by laypersons. Judgment "is at the center of human law."[67] As for the material criteria of judgment, they are not directly concerned with divine order and the furtherance of law. The tools of judgment are a juridical vocabulary, categories and principles. Their articulation and development is a pragmatic, realistic activity, illuminating the eschatological tension in the act of judgment. As an activity, it is poised between the preservation of creation and its future transformation. Any detachment of judgment from this context causes it to degenerate into the arbitrary manipulation of power.

Ellul's notion of judgment involves participation by all citizens in the realm of law while entrusting particular legal activities to juridical actors. At its heart, this is a personalized view of how law is administered and developed. It appropriately points out the necessity of law for the protection of human rights and the maintenance of human institutions. At the same time, this is vague and leaves unanswered how individual acts of judgment coalesce into collective legal activity. Ellul's situational voluntarism seems to undercut the social nature of law. Even if law is seen as an interactional, communicative institution, it is not easy to see how discrete acts of individual judgment coalesce into coherent legal activity. If judgment is a function of pragmatic justice in the defense of human rights, then Ellul's emphasis on judgment is more plausible, but still fails to address adequately how it is integrated with the judgments of others.

---

66. Ellul, *Theological Foundation of Law*, 109.
67. Ellul, *Theological Foundation of Law*, 111.

Ellul also emphasizes the role of judgment within juridical procedure. Judgment is a meaning-creating practice within law. Somewhat cryptically, he declares that law's meaning is expressed when judgment is prophetic and compassionate. The act of human judgment is imitative of divine judgment; it depends upon God's power and is responsible to it. This thesis is somewhat obscure since Ellul does not explain the basis for this relation between divine and human judgment. Is it founded on analogy, emulation, or something else?

Perhaps Ellul has in mind something like the following. The act of judging is possibly a kind of mimesis of divine judging in that it defines justice within a specific situation, and does so compassionately, in the Ellulian sense of being directed to actual situations.[68] Divine judging and justice manifested in Jesus Christ is pragmatic justice. Human law falls far short of realizing divine justice, but it can do so incrementally, resembling it in its approximation of justness.

Ellul's attention to the meaning and purpose of law contrasts with most schools of contemporary jurisprudential theory. His understanding is distinctive for its emphasis on the central significance of institutions and rights and human law and the soberly pragmatic and non-normative character of that law. Here again, Ellul argues for a vigorously theological context for law, while at the same time arguing for law's secularity. How do these two notions align? The theological context of law is essential for Ellul, and apart from it, law is reduced to an ensemble of legal technique and administrative regulation, morally adrift and subject to fluctuating, expedient dispositions. But Ellul says too little about how justice affects the quotidian functioning of law, and this gives his exposition a somewhat abstract and distanced character. As for law's secularity, it appears that Ellul sees it partly as the consequence of human alienation from God, and partly a reflection of necessary human involvement in maintaining an ordered creation. In any event, human law is, Ellul contends, a dialectical reality.

Covenant and Eschatology: Theological Elements of Law

A concept that figures prominently in Ellul's approach to law is covenant.[69] Along with creation and eschatology, it is one of the theological bases of his analysis of law. He describes it as an "act of God's choosing, or electing, a

---

68. Ellul, *Theological Foundation of Law*, 119.
69. Ellul, *Theological Foundation of Law*, 75.

partner"; it is "an act of mercy."[70] Its "truly striking element" is judgment.[71] In the act of judgment, God demonstrates his justice, pardons and extends his covenant. As such, covenant is significant because it connects divine and human law and serves both as a source and element of human law. Ellul refers to human law as an "intermediary entity, existing between covenant and the last judgment."[72] Covenant exists alongside the other constituent elements of law: institutions and human rights.

Ellul notes that covenant is a form of contract of adhesion, being a contract imposed by one party with superior bargaining position on another party.[73] This is a rather curious reference because adhesion contracts are disfavored in law; perhaps Ellul alludes to it to show an affirmative relation between divine and human law.[74] It may also stem from Ellul's conviction that divine justice is preeminently expressed in acts of judgment arising out of violations of the covenant between God and humanity. Ellul prefers this covenantal form of divine justice over ideas of it as objective or eternal. In other words, divine law is a kind of divinely established covenantal condition that "establishes a law, his law over against man."[75] Covenantal justice is always accompanied by mercy, embodied above all in Jesus Christ. It connects divine justice and human law.

The priority of divine justice leads Ellul to a Barthian denunciation of human law: "Anything man builds up under the name of law, is precisely non-law."[76] As with Barth, however, this condemnation is not absolute, for that would amount to opposition to God's will. Reconciliation of these contrasting stances is achieved through the incarnate person of Christ, the personified intersection of the divine and the human. A wholesale and absolute rejection of human law is therefore impossible. There is no way, for Ellul, around the figure of Christ: "What is important in the discussion of the problem of justice, including legal justice, is the absolute centrality of

---

70. Ellul, *Theological Foundation of Law*, 50.

71. Ellul, *Theological Foundation of Law*, 50.

72. Ellul, *Theological Foundation of Law*, 94.

73. Both Barth and Wolf approvingly refer to Ellul's characterization.

74. In Goddard's interpretation, Ellul is arguing that "the very fact that God's covenant is in the form of human legal conventions demonstrates that he appropriates human law to make his will known to us and this has important implications for all human law" (Goddard, *Living the Word*, 235). This seems an accurate interpretation of Ellul's intention, but it suggests a certain anthropomorphism and somewhat problematic notion of divine action, in which a human prototype generates a divine appropriation of it.

75. Ellul, *Theological Foundation of Law*, 55.

76. Ellul, *Theological Foundation of Law*, 49.

the person of Jesus Christ."⁷⁷ The covenantal dimension of law is only one of several dimensions. It is insufficient on its own to justify law. "Law is not valid on account of its origin in, or relationship to, the covenant."⁷⁸

There is also an eschatological aspect of law that must be seen in light of the *parousia*. Law is appropriated and transformed by God into an instrument of condemnation of human sin and injustice, preserving the human community until its future consummation.⁷⁹ This is the eschatological dimension of law, one that condemns as well as preserves. It condemns not to damn, but to prepare for forgiveness and acceptance. Condemnation is an act of transformative reversal. "At the end of its history, God will authenticate this law and in some way incorporate it into the reign of his righteousness."⁸⁰ The antithesis of *sedeqah* and *mishpat* will be overcome, and justice will be finally whole and complete, law will be purified through the purging of its unjust elements.

The completion of law is dependent on its eschatological fulfillment, which is anticipated in its covenantal origin.⁸¹ The eschatological dimension of law frees it from any tendency toward idealism, something Ellul constantly rejects. Eschatology forces law to be concerned with its end, not with some abstract order of value. It also discourages law from aspiring to ultimate ends. "We must immediately warn against the idea that law could be a means to bring about the kingdom of God."⁸² Law's purpose is more provisional: it is to preserve the world through protection of human rights and the maintenance of order for its eschatological reckoning. This purposive, facilitative character of law elevates it over social or economic contingencies. Ellul refers to the "partially independent character of law."⁸³ By this he means that while law reflects the social and economic circumstances in which it is embedded, it is not reducible to them. It achieves this relative independence through its connection with preservation and judgment. These connections allow it to transcend mere autonomy. If law becomes an end unto itself, it loses its ability to promote corrective justice. It becomes instrumental and decadent, and forfeits its critical perspectives on social

---

77. Ellul, *Theological Foundation of Law*, 44.
78. Ellul, *Theological Foundation of Law*, 97.
79. Ellul, *Theological Foundation of Law*, 91.
80. Ellul, *Theological Foundation of Law*, 98.
81. Ellul writes, "Whatever the origin of law, it has its validity only in this fulfillment, and law itself is necessarily linked to this fulfillment because its origin is linked to the covenant" (Ellul, *Theological Foundation of Law*, 99).
82. Ellul, *Theological Foundation of Law*, 101.
83. Ellul, *Theological Foundation of Law*, 103.

and economic arrangements and abandons its "preserving mission."[84] Yet law must not be religiously presumptuous. Despite its theological vocation, law remains secular and lacks any explicit moral or religious content.

Law as covenant reflects its vocation in the context of the economy of salvation. Yet it is unclear how this role is made manifest if it leaves no traces on the substance of law. Is it simply a consequence of Ellul's theological framing of law? Perhaps, but it also seems to involve something intrinsic to law: its relation to the preservation and maintenance of creation, though this would be at odds with law's secularity. Perhaps it is a reflection of the relation of law to justice, rooted in a vision of society consisting of individuals whose rights may not be sacrificed for social expediency.

Ellul has been credited with emphasizing the idea of covenant within law. This fits with Ellul's predilection for concepts that are at home in both theological and legal contexts, and that resonate in each domain. His usage of covenant demonstrates a kind of analogical or prototypical relation of theological and legal concepts. Covenant is particularly suited for this usage, given its extensive provenance in scripture, theology and law. Conceptually, it is both theological and legal in origin and connotation, combining promise, commitment, obligation, reliance, trust and enforceability.[85]

Both Barth and Erik Wolf endorse Ellul's use of covenant to express an affirmative connection between divine and human law.[86] Pannenberg on the other hand raises several reservations. He considers Ellul's use of covenant to be an advance beyond Barth's Christocentrism but faults his failure to relate it to the other two elements of human law—rights and institutions. Further, he finds Ellul's use of covenant to be "eclectic" in its combination of elements of the theology of ordinances (institution) and natural law (human rights).[87] "It would have been better," Pannenberg contends, "to demonstrate the validity of the theology of ordinances and natural law within the structure of the covenant itself."[88] Covenant assumes some operative capacity of humans as covenantal parties, but the rights incident to that status remain undefined. Finally, Ellul's handling of the concept of covenant, in Pannenberg's view, fails to take into account the full riches of the history of

---

84. Ellul, *Theological Foundation of Law*, 105.

85. Ellul speaks of covenant as a "successively renewed unilateral contract" whose "meaning is far from being limited to one historical situation" (Ellul, *Theological Foundation of Law*, 102).

86. See Barth, *CD* 4/1:25; Wolf *Recht des Nächstens*, 51.

87. Pannenberg, "Theology of Law," 36.

88. Pannenberg, "Theology of Law," 37.

God's activity summed up in an especially pregnant manner in the concept of covenant."[89]

The Sources/Components of Human Law

In addition to covenant, Ellul identifies three components of human law: institutions, rights, and justice as foundations of human law. Like covenant, they are grounded both in divine law and human law, and are entrusted to humans for their development and maintenance. Ellul speaks of them both as elements and sources of human law. This is suggestive but imprecise. It is unclear how institutions are a source of law, other than in a general sense as a means through which law is developed and administered. How are human rights derived, and how are they grounded? It is not clear. Nor is it obvious how justice, Christocentrically conceived, generates secular law. Perhaps Ellul means that justice acts on law through equity, rendering it more humane. Let us consider these in turn.

Institutions

The first source/element of law is institution, which Ellul defines as a "body of juridical rules oriented towards a common goal, constituting an enduring entity which is independent of man's will in imposing itself on man in certain circumstances." It is a body "with organic and objective existence."[90] As examples, he cites marriage and property. While their historical origins are uncertain, Ellul holds that they are divinely created, "organically linked to Christ," and humanly influenced.

Law interacts with institutions by giving them form and shape that vary among cultures and times. In being divinely established, institutions resemble orders of creation and preservation, though Ellul avoids that terminology. Instead, he emphasizes the malleability and variability of institutions. Ellul admits that institutions share the same susceptibility to ideological distortion and therefore are ambiguous. Further, institutions have a certain autonomous status and dignity, and are neither exclusively human creations nor intended merely for human convenience or pleasure.[91]

---

89. Pannenberg, "Theology of Law," 37.
90. Ellul, *Theological Foundation of Law*, 76.
91. Ellul, *Theological Foundation of Law*, 78.

They are a "fundamental part of creation," divinely fashioned "as are trees or the light or the angels."[92]

Marriage, the state, commerce, and property are all examples of institutions, and they are universal and inherently obscure in origin. Ellul links them to creation, referring to them as "organisms" willed by God. How do institutions compare with Brunner's orders of creation? They share the characteristic of a divine, creational origin; they are not human creations.[93] Further, they serve the purpose of fulfilling the work of salvation. Ellul emphasizes that institutions exist on their own, independent of human beings, who are tasked with living by them and adjusting them to present circumstances. "They are an element of law, but basically they are a creation of God."[94] In emphasizing the role of the institution in law, Ellul aligns himself with other thinkers in proposing it as an alternative to the idea of orders of creation untainted by historical associations of *völkisch* theology.

How do institutions relate to law? A relation is secured through the concept of order. A primordial order exists that is structured by law or, as Ellul phrases it, is formulated by law.[95] This order is divinely created and takes the form of institutions. While not all institutions are juridical in nature, several are, including marriage, property and exchange. In short, Ellul conceives of institutions as a kind of social-ethical infrastructure that orders human existence and provides scaffolding for legal norms and procedures that occupy the interstices between primordial institutions. Ellul states: "it will be the task of human law to give actual form to God-given institutions and to fill the gaps between them."[96] Institutions are constantly evolving for their social context is in flux. "Law must constantly evolve in order to remain responsive to the needs of God's creatures."[97]

An epistemological question exists concerning the theological meaning of Ellul's institutions. To say that they are scripturally derived and Christocentric in nature rests on certain presumptions that are not universally understood or accepted. The scriptural warrants to which Ellul appeals are ambiguous. A more promising approach might be to see institutions as anthropological-social constructs. But Ellul wants to connect institutions to creation, and that requires a more developed and nuanced idea of creation than Ellul offers. Furthermore, grounding institutions in creation courts the

---

92. Ellul, *Theological Foundation of Law*, 78.
93. Ellul, *Theological Foundation of Law*, 78.
94. Ellul, *Theological Foundation of Law*, 79.
95. Ellul, *Theological Foundation of Law*, 79.
96. Ellul, *Theological Foundation of Law*, 79.
97. Ellul, *Theological Foundation of Law*, 108.

danger of theologized or sacralized law. Ellul opposes this, but his theory appears vulnerable on this point. He perhaps believes the character and function of institutions can also be explained anthropologically. Pannenberg, for example, believes that proto-legal practices in societies and early developmental stages can be interpreted as expressive of basic human proclivities. Their religious character may be posited anthropologically rather than doctrinally.[98] The same challenges to the orders of creation apply to institutions as well: how do we know of their divine origin?

Ellul's notion of institution has some affinities with natural law, particularly in its universal and ubiquitous character and independence from cultural context. But institutions require human articulation and development. "Man determines the actual form of the institution."[99] And juridical institutions have "a wide margin of invention and application in man's juridical enterprise."[100] Human elaboration of institutions are not based on justice but on the preservation of order consonant with certain human rights. This is pragmatic justice, not pure justice.

Rights

Rights are granted to humans in the divine-human covenant; preeminently in the new covenant of Jesus Christ. As such, they are divinely bestowed rather than natural. They relate to humans as communal beings rather than as atomistic individuals, the latter being a modern phenomenon. "Man cannot have any rights except as part of society, and society is stable only when man enjoys his rights."[101] He refuses to ascribe any specific content to such rights, considering it to be "essentially contingent and variable" and dependent on social exigency and historical circumstance.[102]

Ellul identifies two general characteristics of rights. First, they "exist in order that man may accomplish something" and, second, they are acknowledged by man himself.[103] He believes that, despite their variability in content, rights include a concern for self-preservation, suggesting a kind of foundational, biological-ethical claim to life. This, along with rights derivative of it, can only be established through an act of self-assertion in pursuit of the necessities of existence. Rights impose a duty of recognition of the

98. See Pannenberg, "Theology of Law," 38–45.
99. Ellul, *Theological Foundation of Law*, 109.
100. Ellul, *Theological Foundation of Law*, 107.
101. Ellul, *Theological Foundation of Law*, 80.
102. Ellul, *Theological Foundation of Law*, 89.
103. Ellul, *Theological Foundation of Law*, 89.

rights of others, establishing reciprocity as a fundamental social and legal practice. Ellul appeals to the biblical Parable of the Wicked Judge (Luke 18:1–8) in support of this notion, contending that the judgment in favor of the widow was prompted by the earnestness of her appeals, not by any action or virtue of the unjust judge.

But how do rights relate to covenant? Ellul seeks to integrate them into the covenant by contending that they are necessary to qualify humans as covenant partners. They enable human persons to hear and respond to the divine pronouncement of covenant. Concerned with the creation and preservation of the world, rights are the enabling conditions of human participation in covenanting.

The content of the rights is regrettably vague. Self-preservation, for example, is a morally ambivalent notion. It may be exaggerated; it may be mixed with self-concern, ego, and self-aggrandizement. To contend that rights are content-variable is to leave many questions unresolved. Ellul seems to be drawing on some basic claim to existence. But this not worked out satisfactorily, and its limits are not drawn. Further, he does not spell out the purpose of rights beyond creating the capacity to be covenantal partners. If rights have a divine origin and are conditional on their proper orientation to their source, then law must accede to them, rather than seeing them as created by law. One is reminded of the role of rights in Barth's early ethics. There, rights constituted the primary data of law, though they were more possessory and individualized in nature than with Ellul. They inevitably conflict and clash, so the management of the collision of rights is a primary task of law for Barth. In Ellul's case, it is less clear how these primordial rights relate to legal rights. Nor does he articulate law's role in managing the conflict of rights. Neither writer correlates rights to obligations, though Barth sees the experience of right-collisions as ethically significant, and Ellul states that reciprocity is essential in the exercise of rights.

Institutions and rights serve as mediating concepts between the theological frame and the secular content of law. Schüller criticizes Ellul for failing to explain how these human rights are known. For this and other reasons, he finds Ellul's theory about rights to be "hardly convincing."[104] If human rights serve to secure the necessary conditions for life, then they are obvious and uncontestable. If they mean something more, they remain underdeveloped.

---

104. Schüller, *Herrschaft Christi*, 193.

Justice

Of the *trias* of institutions, rights and justice, justice is the least developed by Ellul.[105] He does not attempt to present an elaborated concept, reasoning that such an effort would be fruitless. For him, justice is a practice of pragmatic adjustment rather than a substantive concept. It consists of prudential potentiality rather than ethical virtue. "Justice is no more than a certain adjustment to convenient and pragmatic criteria, chosen by man for organizing the environment in which he lives. For this reason, it is impossible to ascribe a content to human justice."[106] The character of human justice is a result of its nature as pragmatic justice that is essentially potential in character. This position is curious, given its importance for human law and for the other two constitutive elements of law: institutions and rights.

Ellul's definitions of "law" and "justice" anticipate these views. As noted, he typically speaks of law as a juridical institution, a description that emphasizes its mundane nature and its procedural character. In contrast, justice is concerned with judgment and mercy. It transcends the juridical plane while at the same time legitimizing law. Law is "nothing other than an expression of justice."[107] Law is law by virtue of justice.

It is clear from these statements that Ellul sees human justice as discontinuous with divine justice.[108] Yet, as Schüller points out, both realms share the word "justice." He interprets Ellul as proposing an analogy between human justice with its concern for the preservation of human societies and the divine desire for the preservation of all creation. Both ultimately promote the divine will—human justice indirectly and unknowingly, and divine justice openly and directly.[109] Schüller's interpretation has a certain plausibility, but it overlooks the rift that Ellul posits between the divine and the human. Only divine initiative can connect them. Humans are only capable of approximations of justice, and can only receptively emulate them.

Scripture affirms, Ellul asserts, that humanity cannot know what justice is based on its own faculties and resources. Justice can only be grounded in divine righteousness, not on law. Righteousness and justice are inextricably linked, but righteousness is most fully present in acts of divine judgment

---

105. In an analysis of Ellul's major work on ethics, *The Ethics of Freedom*, Outka observes that "there is little room for justice in Ellul's ethics" (Outka, "Ellul," 200).

106. Ellul, *Theological Foundation of Law*, 93.

107. Ellul, *Theological Foundation of Law*, 37.

108. Ellul approvingly quotes Max Huber: "Justice cannot be defined" (Ellul, *Theological Foundation of Law*, 86).

109. Schüller, *Herrschaft Christi*, 195.

in response to transgression and disobedience.[110] Righteousness is bound to judgment through grace, yet their relation is only known through wisdom. While Ellul posits a relation of antithesis and similarity between divine and human justice, he also submits that, in the eschatological future, the differences will be overcome in a divine act of culmination. God will ultimately authenticate human law and overcome the distinction between *tsdq* and *shpht*.[111]

One might describe human justice as "adjectival" or nominalist justice, in that it is only manifested indirectly through various media such as institutions and human rights. It is not available in an unmediated way. Perhaps this is why Ellul claims that human justice has no content.[112] As pragmatic justice, it performs an ordering, shaping activity, and in giving form to institutions and rights. The limited capabilities of human justice distinguish it from divine righteousness: "This kind of justice provides no link between man's justice in God's righteousness."[113]

Ellul dismisses conventional Aristotelian kinds of justice (distributive and retributive) and is disinterested in other substantive notions of justice. As he sees it, justice serves a regulatory function, policing and supporting the other load-bearing pillars of the legal order—institutions and rights. Human justice supports the immanent purpose of human law and therefore bears a mundane orientation. In contrast, divine justice and righteousness have a transcendent focus, and are principally concerned with justification and salvation, not social concerns.

Obviously, this does not mean that justice is unimportant for Ellul. Justice is essential for law, preventing its decline into mere technique. He asserts that law essentially expresses and corresponds to justice. Further, human justice is dependent upon divine justice, which is rooted in divine wisdom. The relation between the two is one of similarity and incommensurability. While human justice is corrigible, functional, and immanent, divine justice ultimate, corrective, and transcendent. While human justice is at least partly rational, divine justice partakes of divine inscrutability.

Ellul posits two sources of divine justice: divine judgment and wisdom.[114] Divine judgments are "pronounced according to the rights of man" and thus contributes to human law through those rights.[115] Judgment is

---

110. Ellul, *Theological Foundation of Law*, 87.
111. Ellul, *Theological Foundation of Law*, 94–99.
112. Ellul, *Theological Foundation of Law*, 93.
113. Ellul, *Theological Foundation of Law*, 93.
114. Ellul, *Theological Foundation of Law*, 88.
115. Ellul, *Theological Foundation of Law*, 49.

manifested through historical acts; for example, covenants are acts of divine judgment. Wisdom is a quality of judgment. Ellul's position on these matters depends on scriptural and theological premises that are not fully explicated. His rejection of natural law minimizes any natural source of insight. Schüller argues that Ellul, at least implicitly, nevertheless draws on natural law elements. While Ellul states that reason provides some basis for a criterion to evaluate justice, he does little to establish a connection between reason and divine justice. Ultimately, it is indiscernible except through revelation.

In Ellul's reading of the Biblical texts, justice is most fundamentally a divine attribute that stands in judgmental opposition to naturalistic notions of justice. "Strictly speaking, everything that natural man does is unjust."[116] Righteousness and human justice are not opposed concepts, but form a unified continuum. Note here that Ellul speaks of divine righteousness as the source of divine justice. This suggests that Ellul sees *sedaqah* as the more substantial component of divine justice instead of *shpht*, which represents a more anthropomorphic idea of justice in its "human, external and social aspect."[117] Righteousness suggests transcendence in the sense of a complete reckoning with human misdeeds as well as in the merciful forgiveness of them.

"Both the knowing and doing of justice proceed from this wisdom: you will understand and you will walk."[118] This is a performative idea of justice, pragmatic in character, concerned with the fulfillment of justice, and anti-theoretical in import. On the one hand, Ellul contends that there is no way to link divine and human justice substantively. On the other hand, they are connected through the ongoing action of God in judgment, forgiveness and preservation. Justice is also embodied in the person of Jesus Christ. He stands for the restorative forgiveness of sins, showing that justice is always linked to grace and forgiveness.[119] Ellul even states that, to a degree, justice is grace in itself.[120]

The inherent tension between *shpht* and *sedaqah*, between righteousness and justice, judgment and mercy remains unresolved in Ellul's thinking. Neither dialectic nor formal synthesis is capable of reconciling them. This can only be done Christologically: "God himself has given us his synthesis in Jesus Christ."[121] This synthesis holds that the life of the "person

---

116. Ellul, *Theological Foundation of Law*, 40.
117. Ellul, *Theological Foundation of Law*, 38.
118. Ellul, *Theological Foundation of Law*, 88.
119. Ellul, *Theological Foundation of Law*, 29.
120. Ellul, *Theological Foundation of Law*, 98.
121. Ellul, *Theological Foundation of Law*, 41.

of Jesus Christ is righteousness."[122] Jesus' trial before Pilate shows both the injustice and the validity of human law—injustice through the judgment of human justice and validity through Jesus' submission to it. As both judge and reconciler, Jesus Christ enacts human justice and divine righteousness. This is the point of contact between the two.[123] Ellul criticizes Brunner for severing divine righteousness from human justice, leading to a hierarchy of different justices. Instead, Ellul speaks of an incarnational transformation of human justice. Justice is unitary. "Either all justice is founded, realized and qualified by the Son of God, or there is nothing."[124]

Law informed by justice is the opposite of any positivist notion of law that, formalistically, is defined solely by its manner of enactment by a political community. Hart's rule of recognition is not a principle of justice. Ellul also speaks of secular law as a fiction, or as precariously situated on the brink of meaninglessness, preserved only by divine tolerance. This is the situation in which technical law finds itself, in which it "ceases to be measured against a certain sentiment or idea of justice and becomes purely a combination of technical rules."[125] It is vulnerable to co-optation for expedient ends, and remains dependent on the threat of sanction to secure compliance.

Without a connection to justice, law tends toward irrelevance and insignificance. The twilight of law, for Ellul, is its descent into technical law. Technical law is law that has forfeited any reference to value, and is instead concerned with organization and regulation. In a word, it is law that is no longer law but regulation.[126] He finds Christian tradition to be pessimistic about law when it is not tied to justice.[127] Institutions and human rights embody justice, and all three are indispensable for maintaining human law.

Law, State, and Society

Only toward the end of *The Theological Foundation of Law* does Ellul takes up the question of the relation of law and the state. He finds it to be a perennial question in theology, legal philosophy and ethics. The later Barth and Brunner represent what seems to be the majority view in modern Protestant theology in seeing law as a creation of the state, largely subordinating law

122. Ellul, *Theological Foundation of Law*, 41.
123. Ellul, *Theological Foundation of Law*, 43.
124. Ellul, *Theological Foundation of Law*, 45.
125. Ellul, *Theological Foundation of Law*, 31.
126. Goddard, *Living the Word*, 24.
127. Ellul, *Theological Foundation of Law*, 85.

to the state.[128] In contrast, Ellul asserts the independence of law from the state. "Law does not receive anything from the state."[129] In fact, the state is dependent on law. "The state only exists . . . because law exists."[130]

What, then, is the role of the state in the law? It essentially involves the enforcement and what Ellul calls the "guardianship" of law. The state enforces law, and the need for enforcement distinguishes law from morality. Law depends on enforcement, morality does not. Ellul suggests that without enforcement law has not yet become "genuine law."[131] This creates a relation of mutual dependence between the state and law. Enforcement alone does not establish the authority of law—that is alone a consequence of human law's dependence on divine law. Unfortunately, as is frequently the case, Ellul does not expand on this point. This involves the concept of legitimacy, but Ellul does not devote much attention to it.

Though Ellul does not say so, he is making the often asserted point that law depends on moral suasion as well as coercive sanction. This is different from his idea of human dependence on divine law. That dependence rests on a biblically informed idea of legal authority, according to which God is the divine source and authority for law. Obviously, this is not universally accepted, and it also conflicts with Ellul's insistence that the state should be secular. Responsibility for declaring and defending the dependence of human law would seem to appropriately rest with the church and other communities of faith. As Ellul says, the church's role "is essentially to make evident the existence of a justice other than juridical justice."[132] Ellul's reference to non-juridical justice hints that the dependence of human law on divine law is a kind of ulterior normative dependence. This would be in line with other statements he makes that Christianity should not prescribe the substantive content of positive law.[133] Ellul advocates here a kind of prophetic witness, consisting of proclamation and manifestation. The church proclaims divine righteousness in acts of merciful judgment, and manifests its adherence to this divine justice, rather than to the flawed and provisional justice of human society. Put otherwise, it addresses the Word to human law. This requires of the church have the protections of all legal bodies, with the "fundamental freedom to proclaim the word of God."[134]

128. As noted above, Brunner is not consistent on this point.
129. Ibid., 123.
130. Ibid.
131. Ibid., 125.
132. Ibid., 133.
133. Goddard, *Living the Word*, 62.
134. Goddard, *Living the Word*, 132.

This echoes Barth's understanding of the role of the church in the "Christian Community", but without Barth's more nuanced notion of how the two realms relate to each other. But while Ellul lacks Barth's acute insights here, he does offer more specific ideas of how the church interacts with law through its proclamations. For example, it does so through advocacy of human rights. (Ellul accuses the church of being silent for three centuries regarding these rights.) This requires critical monitoring of law, maintaining the limits of law, judging the legal system, and "rectifying" the law.[135] These are responsibilities, Ellul stresses, of the whole church community, not only of formal ecclesiastical bodies. These obligations in turn require the church to instruct its members about law, its foundations and purposes. Such tasks prescribe an important, affirmative role for faith communities in connection with positive law.

This is consonant with the pluralistic premise defended in these pages. Obviously, questions remain regarding the content of institutions and rights, and about the relation of divine and human justice, something of central importance for Ellul.

The Sociological Critique of Law

Many, if not most, expositions of Ellul treat his sociological and theological writings separately, if not in isolation. In the public perception of Ellul, his sociological analyses attract primary attention, with books such as *The Technological Society* most widely noted among his publications. Ellul's work on sociological topics, such as technique, technology and propaganda, attracted mainstream attention during his career. The lasting influence of these works has been questioned.[136] Yet his analyses are incisive and open up uncommon perspectives on contemporary law.

According to Goddard, Ellul's sociological project can be viewed as a quest to understand law's specific characteristics and function in society.[137] Ellul's interpretation of contemporary law relies extensively on the concept of technique. For him, this is a predominant characteristic of contemporary cultures. It is one of the three characteristics that mark modern law; they are technicalization, specialization, and amoralization. Law is technical in that law has become preoccupied with means instead of ends, and refuses the idea that law should have goals. It has become subverted by a fatuous concern with fact and expediency at the expense of normativity. Law has

---

135. Goddard, *Living the Word*, 136.
136. Borgmann, *Technology*, 9–10.
137. Goddard, *Living the Word*, 209.

become institutionalized and is increasingly concerned with particular interests to the detriment of common goods. It has become specialized in its ongoing co-optation by the state through its administrative and bureaucratic capacities, enlisted in the pursuit of political power. Law has become a surrogate for social morality, and has become an arena for the adjudication of political and cultural disputes.[138]

The danger of the influence of technique on law is that it replaces justice and human preservation as the goals of law with lesser ends—order and efficiency. Ellul sees this as a lesson of history. According to Mark Aultman, Ellul's interpretation of the past led him to conclude that societies of a certain degree of legal evolution have ended by substituting security and order for justice as the ideal end of law.[139] In the course of these historical processes, the state tends to annex law to itself by transmuting values of justice and morality into state-defined goods. This undermines law, for "the state is created *for the benefit of law.*"[140] As a consequence of its subversion by the state, law is ineffective in contemporary society. This means that law has lost its original relation to divine law and become something other than itself.[141]

Ellul's sociological insights correlate with his critique of human law in *The Theological Foundation of Law*. Law has become unmoored, deprived of its moral foundations, and has fallen under the sway of the dictates of technique. The erosion of commonly held values and principles expressed in law is a crucial factor of its current crisis. Even though Ellul denies that justice is directly embodied in law, contemporary confusions over values have undermined the relation between justice and law, resulting in a hollowing out and marginalization of law.

Ellul seeks to keep his sociological and theological reflections apart, viewing them as independent endeavors, distinct in method and content. As he declared shortly before his death in 1994, "I have always tried to prevent my theology from influencing my sociological research and my comprehension of the world from distorting my reading of the Bible. These are two domains, to methods, two distinct interests. Only after the separation, one begins to perceive relationships."[142]

But this is questionable. One can respect the differences between the two fields without keeping them apart. Ellul's sociological and theological

---

138. Hunter, "Law, Religion," 1079.

139. Aultman, "Technology," 55.

140. Ellul, *Theological Foundation of Law*, 123.

141. See Goddard, "Law, Rights," 5, stating that because of technique, Ellul sees that law has undergone such a total transformation that it is no longer truly law.

142. Goddard, *Living the Word*, 155.

analyses complement each other. Goddard suggests that a dialectical relationship exists between Ellul's sociological and theological analyses. His social analyses discern a fundamental rupture between the divine and human world; his theological vision describes the possibility of a restored communion between the divine and human. Ellul's emphasis on the social dimension of law is a valuable contribution of his reflections on law, and stands in contrast to the more socially distanced perspectives of many theologians.

Concluding Observations

When the English translation of *The Theological Foundation of Law* appeared in the United States, it received a mostly critical reception. One reviewer recommended that Ellul read Reinhold Niebuhr.[143] Many of the critical comments were specifically directed to Ellul's stringent separation of divine law and human law, and his failure to describe satisfactorily how the former could influence the latter. Ellul argues, concluded one reviewer, "against any orderly manner of appropriating divine law . . . in juristic experience."[144] In fairness, it bears noting that Ellul revised his views after *The Theological Foundation of Law*. In later writings, he restated the Christocentric character of his notion of law, but limited its relevance to believers.[145] But, tellingly, he never renounced the book itself.

Now, seven decades after its publication, does *The Theological Foundation of Law* have any contemporary relevance, or is it essentially a relic of post-war Barthian Christocentrism? With its robust affirmation of the priority of divine law, it seems somewhat dated, reflecting the urgency of immediate postwar era and the concern of many theologians to establish Christ as the criterion of human society, including law. Despite Ellul's affirmations of law's secularity of law, he firmly insists on the definitive significance of Jesus Christ for human law.

Ellul clearly believes that theology has a role to play in reminding law of its vocation and possibilities. Much of the current condition of law is the result of the relentless incursion of technique into the legal realm. Ellul sees this as a broad cultural phenomenon that cannot be reversed, only incrementally remediated. Law would seem to be a significant instrument for opposing technique, but it has fallen under the thrall of the political power of the state. This seems to leave only the way of prophetic resistance. Curiously, Ellul balances prophetic denunciations of contemporary law

---

143. Cobb, "Review," 286.
144. Carney, "Review," 44.
145. Lohmann, "Recht bei Ellul," 130.

with declarations of the necessity of pluralism and of law's secularity. To the extent these developments result from causes Ellul condemns (such as denial of law's roots in divine law and justice) one would expect him to reject secularity and pluralism. He does not do this because of his realism and attention to social circumstances. He speaks of the necessity of Christianity giving a jurist "complete clarity concerning the world."[146] Ultimately, Ellul's vision of law leads to an ethics of law for the faithful. A more robust, affirmative notion of justice would open up other options for critique and engagement with law, but Ellul's Christocentrism, and its indictment of human justice limits this option for secular sensibilities. Ellul has made a genuine contribution to a theologically informed vision of law, but one that is constrained by contemporary pluralism.

A wholesale dismissal of Ellul's work is unwarranted. It continues to be valuable, not so much as a comprehensive theory of law, but for the incisiveness of many of its elements. Friedrich Lohmann, while acknowledging the contemporary lack of interest in Ellul's writings on law, contends that they remain instructive for the following reasons: (1) they demonstrate the viability of theological engagement with law as a significant segment of social reality; (2) they show that law offers a realm of actual social interaction with which theology can engage and avoid abstraction and remoteness; and (3) they emphasize the necessity of connecting law with ethics and eschatology.[147] On their own, these reasons validate dialogue between law and theology and ethics. At the same time, they limit the appeal of Ellul's theology of law in that it flows mostly from theology to law.

Indeed, Ellul's negative notion of human law is a stumbling block for theological—jurisprudential dialogue. He rightfully points out the deficient justice of human law, but he depreciates human law and justice on the basis of the unapproachable transcendence of divine justice and law. He does this on theological grounds, among them his anthropology and view of human society. No author considered in this book is as unremitting in seeing the relation of the divine and human law as disjunctively as Ellul. Ultimately, he sees human law as he does because of the way he sees the human. But in order to participate in public debates about law, other vocabularies and modes of expression are necessary.

A possible point of contact of his assessment of law and secular jurisprudence is Ellul's sociological critique of law and the impact of technology and technique on it.[148] That critique raises the question of justice in law

---

146. Quoted in Goddard, *Living the Word*, 51–52.

147. Lohmann, "Recht bei Ellul," 129–32.

148. An instructive example of this possible approach can be found in Aultman,

from a social perspective rather than a theological one, while leaving room for theological/ethical insights.

While discussions of justice's relation to law may seem to endanger law's autonomy, this need not be the case if placed in the context of Ellul's critique of contemporary law. This is not to suppress theological insights, but to put them in a context of interdisciplinary discussion. Such discussion need not and should not take place only in theological terms if theology is comprehensive in scope and seeks "complete clarity."

"Technology and the End of Law," which contains a close analysis of Ellul's thinking on these topics.

V

Erik Wolf

The Law of the Neighbor

Outside of Germanophone Europe, Erik Wolf is the least well-known of the authors treated in this book. This is not surprising given that virtually none of his writings have been translated into English.[1] Wolf (1902–77) was a German jurist and law professor who wrote extensively on law, jurisprudence, theology, philosophy, and history of law as well as church law. His work was influential in theological and legal circles in postwar Germany. Along with Hans Dombois and Johannes Heckel, Wolf is associated with the turn towards the theology of law as a response to the experience of National Socialism. Wolf's work attracts little critical attention nowadays, but his writings on the theology of law remain provocative for their novel conceptualizations and theoretical verve.

Wolf spent his entire career teaching at various German universities, for the most part in Freiburg. He is linked with two very different figures: Martin Heidegger, who also taught in Freiburg, and Karl Barth. Wolf developed significant personal relationships with each of them, and his writings bears noticeable traces of their influence on him. Wolf was also in frequent contact with Brunner and Ellul. His works were cited favorably by Barth and were discussed by Pannenberg, Thielicke, and others. He was involved in the postwar discussions in Germany about Christianity on the basis of positive law, such as those that took place in the church-sponsored conferences held in Göttingen and Treysa in 1949 and 1950. His role in these discussions, as well as his publications, would seem to justify some consideration of his work.

1. I have located only a brief encyclopedia entry in English by him about J. Althusius. See Wolf, "Althusius."

But Wolf is a thinker with a complicated history. In the 1930s, Wolf was first a sympathizer and later a member of the Nazi party. Towards the end of that decade, he became involved with the Confessing Church, and participated to some extent in resistance activities in Freiburg. After the war and after undergoing the denazification process conducted by French occupation authorities, he resumed his academic career as a professor of law until his retirement in the 1970s. Increasingly, he devoted his energies to church law and the theology of law. Wolf's career, then, is one of a Nazi supporter, a resistance figure, and a jurist with strong theological interests.

Wolf's association with the Nazi party came early in his career, while he was still in his twenties. Such involvement was not unusual for an academic jurist in Germany at the time; more than a few legal academics followed the same path as Wolf did.[2] Given this personal history, it might seem repugnant to credit his work with any attention here. At the same time, as in the case of Heidegger, author and work can arguably be separated, at least to some extent. Further, there is debate about the depth and extent of Wolf's involvement with Nazism. Some scholars argue that Wolf's involvement with Nazism was limited in time and scope, and resulted from his youth and suggestibility. Wolf's later involvement in resistance and church activities (which continued for several decades) indicate that he turned away from fascist politics. Others dispute whether this, in fact, was the case.

Some attention to his past, particularly his involvement with Nazism, is helpful for understanding his theology of law and his historical context. Lena Foljanty, a German legal historian, has recently argued that the postwar interest in Germany in the theology of law and natural law must be seen as an attempt by some to expiate the shame and guilt of those associated with the Nazi movement. One of those figures was Erik Wolf.

A Tangled Legacy

The 1930s were the critical decade for Wolf's involvement with Nazism. Some basic facts are uncontested: Wolf joined the League of National Socialist Lawyers in the summer of 1933, and he became a member of the Nazi party in May 1937. In October 1933 he was appointed dean of the law school in Freiburg by Heidegger, then the rector of the university. Wolf's

---

2. For example, Johannes Heckel, professor of law in Munich and author of *Lex Charitatus*, was an advisor to the leader of the Nazi-inspired German Christian movement, *Reichsbischof* Ludwig Müller, and Walter Schönfeld, a prominent law professor in Tübingen, was also a member of the Nazi party. See Foljanty, "Rechtstheologie," 221n29. Also see generally Müller, *Hitler's Justice*, for a somewhat polemical account of the involvement of the legal professoriat in Germany with the Nazi movement.

activities at the time demonstrated some ardor for Nazi ideology, though he later contended he was largely nonpolitical and his involvement was prompted by professional reasons. In December 1933, Wolf delivered a lecture in Freiburg entitled "The Ideal of Law in the National Socialist State" in which he argued in favor of *Volkstum* (national character) and *Führertum* (leadership) as sources of law.[3] In the summer semester of 1934, Wolf taught courses on law and National Socialism and on criminal law in the National Socialist state. He produced other publications on the role of law in the Nazi state, endorsing ideas such as the significance of race in defining national identity, and emphasizing the priority of the national community over the individual.[4] According to the racial criteria Wolf endorsed, those who were not members of the national race were only entitled to lesser rights.

Wolf's tenure as dean of the law faculty in Freiburg was short-lived. Actions he took to change and rejuvenate the law faculty along Nazi-inspired lines promoted by Heidegger included paramilitary exercises and labor service.[5] In the face of faculty resistance to these measures, Wolf resigned the deanship in March 1934, having served only around six months.

Toward the end of the 1930s, Wolf became involved to some extent with resistance activities in Freiburg. He cooperated with the local resistance group centered around Gerhard Ritter, a prominent historian. He had some limited contact with the resistance circle headed by Admiral Canarius in Berlin, of which Dietrich Bonhoeffer was a member. Wolf, along with others, met with Bonhoeffer in Freiburg in October 1942. In 1942, the Freiburg resistance group produced a memorandum addressing the future orientation of postwar Germany. Wolf coauthored a section of the memorandum addressing the future legal order of Germany that affirmed a connection between religion and law. The relation would not be based on natural law but rather on biblical guidelines derived from scripture and the Decalogue. In autumn 1944, several members of the Freiburg circle were arrested, and Wolf was interrogated by the Gestapo about his activities, but somehow avoided arrest. In addition to these resistance activities, Wolf was also active to some extent in the Confessing Church during the war years. He assisted in the legal defense of Martin Niemöller, the Berlin pastor incarcerated for his public resistance to the Hitler regime.

Wolf's evolution from NSDAP member to Confessing Church supporter and regime opponent is evaluated in conflicting ways by different

---

3. Several excerpts of the lecture appear in Staff, *Justiz*, 149, 156, 158.

4. Wolf's article is described and analyzed in Hatzel, "Nationalsozialistisches Rechtsdenken," 530.

5. Safranski, *Heidegger*, 270. Also see Faye, *Heidegger*, 174–77.

scholars. Some describe Wolf's involvement with National Socialism basically as a brief episode of youthful enthusiasm that quickly passed and was replaced by his resistance activities. Alexander Hollerbach, a law professor and one of Wolf's former students, admits that in the early 1930s Wolf "became entangled in the political turbulence surrounding the universities" but argues that "he quickly disengaged himself from the influence of National Socialist ideology."[6] Wolf's writings about law and Nazism were, Hollerbach contends, "borne by an optimistic expectation that a renovation in legal thought and practice in the service of the people was underway, in which social pacification was a presupposition for the overcoming of the crisis in bourgeois society."[7] In Hollerbach's view, while these writings contained "shocking misinterpretations and mistakes," they represented a discrete and limited episode.[8] Wolf's subsequent involvement in the Confessing Church and his postwar ecclesiastical activities indicate, according to Hollerbach, that his interest in Nazi ideology was short-lived.

Hollerbach's interpretation is supported by others. In an important study of the Protestant theology of law that appeared in 1968, Wilhelm Steinmüller writes of Wolf, "Only for a short time was he overwhelmed by National Socialism. . . . But very soon he saw through the illusion."[9] He goes on to claim that Wolf had reoriented his efforts toward the Confessing Church by the end of 1933, which does not explain why Wolf joined the Nazi party in 1937.

Others interpret Wolf's history differently. A French philosopher, Emmanuel Faye, contends in a book published in 2009 entitled *Heidegger: The Introduction of Nazism into Philosophy in Light of the Unpublished Seminars of 1933–1935* that Wolf, in fact, remained an ardent Nazi fellow-traveler who was enthralled by Heidegger and became "the closest of Heidegger's close friends."[10] He argues that Wolf was also impressed by the writings of Alfred Rosenberg, the Nazi propagandist, and Carl Schmitt, the Nazi legal philosopher. Further, Faye claims that Wolf "carefully concealed the radical nature of his Nazi involvement" in the postwar years, and did not, even then, disown his writings of the 1930s supportive of Nazi ideology.[11] In response,

---

6. Hollerbach, "Wolf," 523. Hollerbach elsewhere attributes Wolf's involvement to his "youthful suggestibility." Hollerbach, "Wirken," 52n23 and accompanying text.

7. Hollerbach, "Wolf," 337. Hollerbach goes on to state that in none of his writings about Nazism did Wolf express total affirmation of it.

8. Hollerbach, "Wirken," 53n26 and accompanying text.

9. Steinmüller, *Rechtstheologie*, 269.

10. Faye, *Heidegger*, 173.

11. Faye, *Heidegger*, 188.

Hollerbach has criticized Faye's portrayal of Wolf as based on a prejudiced interpretation of the relevant sources.[12]

Lena Foljanty takes an intermediate position between Faye and Hollerbach. She believes that Wolf's movement away from National Socialism is evident in writings that appeared in 1936 and that he effectively made a break from it in 1937.[13] However, she sees Wolf's activities in the Confessing Church as motivated more by an interest in ecclesiastical reform than by opposition to the regime. His aim was to prepare the way for the emergence of a re-established, unified Protestant church in Germany after the war.[14] Foljanty further contends that Wolf's activities during and after the war were driven by repentance for his Nazi activities. She cites a lengthy letter drafted by Wolf to Karl Barth that was never sent in which Wolf describes at length the intellectual environment of the early years of his career as well as his own personal development. In it, he wistfully refers to the mistakes he made connected with his involvement with the Nazi movement, and at the same time expresses resentment about what he considered to be revisionist accusations against him.

Foljanty sees Wolf's postwar activity as part of a broader wave of interest among some German jurists in the relation of law and religion, and especially in theological interpretations of law (*Rechtstheologie*). For some, this led to natural law; others inclined to more overtly theological positions, such as Barth's Christocentrism. The latter group included Wolf and Dombois, both of whom turned to theological interpretations of law and produced numerous books and essays on the relation of law to scripture and various theological loci such as grace, love, and justice. These publications were informed by the belief that law is dependent upon faith. In 1946, Wolf wrote that "Christian existence is the best presupposition for a just establishment of law."[15] Many jurists had become skeptical of the ethical potential of law as a result of the Nazi experience and looked to theology as a means to regain it. According to Foljanty, these theological-legal writings were motivated by a desire to rehabilitate their authors' ambiguous wartime reputations, articulate a basis for future opposition to illegal state action, and reaffirm the presence of an ethical dimension in law.

As it stands, the historical record of Wolf's involvement with National Socialism is ambiguous. That he joined the Nazi party and publicly supported its policies, at least for some time, is clear, as was his later work with

---

12. Hollerbach, "Brief," 347.
13. Foljanty, *Recht*, 140.
14. Foljanty, *Recht*, 142.
15. Wolf, "Biblische Weisung," 33.

the Confessing Church and participation in resistance activities. Opportunism played a role in the postwar rejection of Nazism by members of Wolf's generation. The circumstances surrounding Wolf's involvement with the Nazi movement will likely, as in Heidegger's case, remain clouded. As the facts now stand, Wolf's reputation is clouded, to say the least.

The Way to *Rechtstheologie*

Wolf's long career led him through various fields of law. He published prolifically, producing articles on criminal law to widely read standard works on German legal history, a volume on law in classical German poetry, a six-volume work on law in Greek antiquity, numerous essays on the theology of law, and a massive volume on ecclesiastical law. Many of his theological and philosophical writings were collected in three posthumously published volumes. Rather than attempt a survey of this large corpus of work, the primary focus here will be on a single work published in 1958 under the title *Recht des Nächsten* (*Law of the Neighbor*).[16] It is the most prominent of Wolf's writings on the theology of law, one that Hollerbach considers a key work in Wolf's *oeuvre*.[17] In aid of its interpretation, two later essays by Wolf interpreting *Recht des Nächsten* are also referenced.

In *Recht des Nächsten*, Wolf proposes a distinctive understanding of the relation of philosophy, theology, and law. His views appear, upon first encounter, idiosyncratic. Comprehension of them is not helped by the oracular style of the essay, reminiscent of Heidegger. Fortunately, an essay published by Wolf on the philosophy of law shortly before *Recht des Nächsten* provides helpful terminological clarification.[18] In that essay, Wolf distinguishes sharply between theology and philosophy. On the one hand, theology thematizes the relation of being to God. On the other hand, "Philosophy inquires about Being, the philosophy of law about Being in Law."[19] Philosophy poses questions about ontology (the giveness of being-there (*Dasein*)), ethics (the obligatoriness of being-there), logic (the presentness (*Vorgegebenheit*) of being-there), and metaphysics (the surrender (*Hingegebenheit*)) of being-there.

These areas of philosophical inquiry are replicated in the philosophy of law with its subdivisions of the ontology of law, the ethics of law, legal

---

16. Subsequent references to the book will be capitalized; references to the concept of the law of the neighbor will not.
17. Hollerbach, "Wirken," 48n3 and accompanying text.
18. Wolf, "Rechtsphilosophie," 69–82.
19. Wolf, "Rechtsphilosophie," 69.

logic and the metaphysics of law. Of particular significance for Wolf are the ontology and ethics of law. The first "interrogates law about its reality in institutions and norms" in order to determine whether what is designated as law truly is law.[20] It is concerned with identifying what law is, with determining what makes law. The ethics of law asks about the obligatory authority of law, as expressed in principles and postulates, in order to determine if law is as it should be.

The major conceptions of law are positivism, in which law is a given object; rationalism, in which law is found in the subject as a function of understanding; voluntarism, in which law is a given purpose, and phenomenology, in which law is a given activity. Wolf suggests that law is not a system or complex of possessory rights and obligations so much as a particular state of being and way of acting consistent with the demands of justice. Law is most truly present when one exists, so to speak, in accord with the law, in the sense of being just and acting justly. It is less a matter of complying with rules. This ontological-existential notion of law provides a basis for Wolf to speak of both personal and social dimensions of law. Human rights and obligations relate to the human person in her singularity, while interactions and transactions with fellow persons demonstrate the social dimension of law.

An ethics of law is concerned with the question of law's purpose: what should law be? This is the question of justice. "The justice of law is the theme of the ethics of law, just as the authenticity of law is the theme of legal ontology."[21]

Legal philosophy cannot provide stable and enduring answers to its own questions; it leads to the theology of law. It is concerned with the basis of law in divine interaction with human beings. This is only possible when law, as a form of personal existence, is enabled by the divine action of endowing human beings with the capacities of hearing, speaking and responding. Only when law is related to an understanding of persons as divinely imaged beings do the fundamental phenomena of being in law come into view—personality and solidarity.[22] These are communicated in and through biblical directives ("*biblische Weisungen*"). Wolf develops these basic *existentials* more fully in *Recht des Nächsten*.[23]

20. Wolf, "Rechtsphilosophie," 70.

21. Wolf, "Rechtsphilosophie," 76.

22. Wolf describes personality and solidarity alternately as phenomena and rights. As he describes them, they resemble Heidegger's existentials.

23. "Used as a noun, the term 'existential' *(Existenzial)* denotes one of the broad fundamental possibilities of *Dasein's* being, in analogy to the term category which denotes one of the basic formal characters of an object" (Macquarrie, *Existentialist Theology*, 34).

Law of the Neighbor

Recht des Nächsten was originally delivered in 1957 as a lecture on the occasion of the five hundredth anniversary of the founding of the university in Freiburg. Wolf subsequently published it in 1958 with extensive footnotes and references that ran longer than the text of the lecture itself. The published version was dedicated to Karl Barth.

The essay evidences the significant influence of both Heidegger and Barth on Wolf. In addition to their cooperation as university administrators in 1933–34, Heidegger and Wolf jointly taught seminars. Wolf adopted Heidegger's phenomenological-existential approach as a method of describing the role of law in human existence, drawing upon Heidegger's method of close semantic analysis of classical texts, a technique Wolf also used in his volumes on ancient Greek notions of law. In *Recht des Nächsten*, he also employs unique and somewhat idiosyncratic terminology, and in some cases borrowed and adapted neologisms from Heidegger's writings. At the same time, Wolf moves beyond Heidegger's anthropocentric hermeneutic in pursuit of theological concerns; it is safe to say that *Recht des Nächsten* would never have come from Heidegger's pen.

When Wolf and Barth first came into contact in June 1945, they were already acquainted with each other's writings. Their relationship evolved into a friendship, marked by a degree of personal warmth.[24] The two men visited each other from time to time and corresponded. They valued each other's work; Barth favorably refers to Wolf regarding the nature of community in the section of the *Church Dogmatics* on the order of the community.[25] Wolf cites Barth over fifty times in *Recht des Nächsten*, more than any other author. In a letter he wrote to Barth in 1956 while composing the essay, Wolf emphasizes how much he learned from Barth's *Dogmatics*.[26] Wolf's references to Barth in the essay show that he especially drew on Barth's notion of human personhood as a basis for his concept of the neighbor. Their theological outlooks shared similarities but also displayed differences. Both had sensibilities informed by the Reformed tradition, each extensively interpreted Biblical texts, and both adhered to a strong Christocentric focus, although their understandings of its implications differed. Particularly in his earlier work, Barth emphasized the sovereignty of God while Wolf attached more significance to creation and its orders. These differences in theological accent resonated in their respective theologies of law. Given the contrasts between them, one commentator (Steinmüller) concludes that

---

24. Hollerbach, "Wirken," 58n57 and accompanying text.
25. Barth, *CD* 4/1:25.
26. Bauer-Tornack, *Wolf*, 344.

Wolf's theology of law cannot be described as Barthian. Instead, he finds it to be *sui generis*, and more open for Lutheran perspectives than Barth's.[27] Indeed, Wolf has been interpreted as staking out (along with Jacques Ellul), a middle ground between Barth and Brunner.[28]

Recht des Nächsten employs a phenomenological and existential approach to what Wolf considers the fundamental phenomena of human selfhood and sociality. In essence, the neighbor relation is the center of human law, even of positivist versions of it. To establish this position, he poses several fundamental questions, including: What is law? How is it rooted in human-selfhood and society? What is its relation to love? In order to answer them, Wolf looks to what he terms the transcendent basis of law revealed in the fundamental human phenomena of rights of personality and solidarity. They stand in a dialectical relationship to each other, and together constitute the authentic possibilities of the personal and the social dimensions of existence.

In its published form, *Recht des Nächsten* is a dense, compact work. It summarizes the basic elements of Wolf's theology of law in distinctive concepts such being-in-law, and is replete with insights that can be simultaneously incisive and cryptic. For its brevity, the essay is ambitious; it ranges across expanses of philosophical and theological terrain. Wolf self-consciously treads the boundary between philosophy and theology, and between human and divine law, aspiring to speak to both jurists and theologians through an existentialist philosophical theology of law.

Personhood and Law

By the time of *Recht des Nächsten*, Wolf had come to believe that philosophy cannot satisfactorily resolve questions of personhood or justice. In his view, the multiplicity of theories about their nature reflects an insurmountable confusion of approaches and theories. So as a first step in the essay, Wolf seeks to clear away misapprehensions about law, personhood, and the relation of selves to God and to each other.

Ontology poses questions about the nature of being in its giveness according to the various dimensions of intellect, will, and thought. Similarly, legal ontology, which Wolf describes as a regional ontology, interrogates law about its reality as expressed in institutions and norms, and does so under the perspectives of positivism, rationalism, voluntarism and phenomenology. Each of these approaches illuminates an aspect of existent being without

---

27. Steinmüller, *Rechtstheologie*, 1:444.
28. Foljanty, *Recht*, 156–59.

reaching the fundamental questions of origin and destiny contained in "being in law." Legal philosophy is not able to overcome the ontological opposition between being in law and "being obligated in law." This terminology posits a difference between being subject to law and living up to the law, between an attitude of mere legal compliance and more robust commitment to law and its possibilities for human interaction. "Legal philosophy is grounded in and flows into the theology of law . . . because neither legal ontology nor legal ethics can ask or answer the question of the whence and whither of "being in law" and "being as one should be in law."[29] This is the tension between is and ought in one's relation to law. It points to the ultimate, divine source of obligation: "Being in law is opened up through the exhortation of God."[30]

This leads to a deeper level of reflection. Divine law, expressed in and through neighbor-law, reconciles the tension between is and ought: "The insight into what law is (by itself and before God) liberates one from the saving alternative between legal reality and legal value; it rejects the position that the ontology of law excludes an ethic of law."[31] On the level of human existence, the tension between "is" and "ought" remains. Law incorporates the tension between is and ought. As Steinmüller puts it, "The dialectic of *Sein* and *Sollen* is now relocated into the interior of existential law."[32] It creates and maintains order, but also strives for justice, the element of ought within law. Personhood arises out of the responsive answer of a human being to the call of God (mediated through Christ as the brother of all persons). Wolf calls this the primordial right of personality. It initiates the self into a covenantal relationship with God, giving her a divine likeness that underlies all other human rights. The vertical relation between self and God is intersected by the horizontal relation among self and other selves that are also in vertical relation to God. The intersecting horizontal relationships of selves forms the right of solidarity. These vertical and horizontal relations share a common origin and essence—community with God.[33] Neither individuality nor sociality alone has the final word, for they belong together. These intersecting axes symbolize the law of the neighbor.[34] It precedes any

---

29. This distinction echoes Kant's (and others') contrast of is (*sein*) and ought (*sollen*).

30. Wolf, "Rechtsphilosophie," 80.

31. Wolf, "Rechtsphilosophie," 19.

32. Steinmüller, *Rechtstheologie*, 1:271.

33. Wolf's conception here is reminiscent of H. R. Niebuhr's view of the social nature of selves: "To be a self in the presence of other selves is not a derivative experience but is primordial" (Niebuhr, *Responsible Self*, 71).

34. The figure of intersecting lines echoes Barth, who speaks of the horizontal encounter of fellow human beings and the vertical encounter with God. See Barth, *CD* 4/2:442.

human conception of law, whether it is seen as inherent in nature, reason or history, as a notion of natural rights based on individuality or sociology, or as a utilitarian or egalitarian distributive scheme.

In this manner, Wolf locates law within the structure of human existence. That structure should not be conceived abstractly, for it belongs in the concrete context of social existence. How are these structures to be understood non-abstractly? Wolf proposes a theological-personalistic perspective. Persons are called into being by God, summoned to transcendence and conditioned by responsibility.[35] This vocation constitutes the basic right of personality. It must be respected by all political and social powers.

The law of the neighbor overcomes the apparent antinomy between law as concerned with the individual (as the subject and bearer of legal rights) and as concerned with the community (as the source of law). It does not do so by the arbitrated resolution of conflicts but through uncovering the dimension of unity in difference. "Neighbor" implies both self and other, as well as a relationship between them. The basic axioms of personality and solidarity are the "foundational ground and guidelines" for these differing, yet complementary, ways of being: as an individual and as a member of society.[36] Personality is rooted in covenant-grounded responsibility before God, solidarity secures fraternal/sororal relations with others. Neither the person, understood as an "individual," nor a group of persons understood as a collective, is the source of law. Rather, relation is primary, and out of relation law arises. In this regard, Wolf proposes a kind of personal relationalism similar to Brunner's, and applies it to law.

Law and Love

The essence of the relationships implied in personality (divine-human) and solidarity (human-human) is love.[37] This prompts the question of the relation between law and love. He asks: "Is [the] divisive isolation of law and love perhaps responsible for the fact that the task of all law—in the given circumstances of natural and social inequality to grant and secure to each his due—remains unsolved?"[38]

---

35. Wolf, *Recht des Nächsten*, 16. Wolf cites Romano Guardini in support: "The human being is constituted to hear in that place. He is supposed to be the answering being" (Guardini, *Welt und Person*, 165).

36. Wolf, *Recht des Nächsten*, 20.

37. Wolf, "Dialektik," 116. This essay, published in 1961, is described by Wolf as an expanded paraphrase of the first page of *Recht des Nächsten*. See Wolf, "Dialektik," 115.

38. Wolf, *Recht des Nächsten*, 11–12.

Law and love are often viewed as excluding each other, a position Wolf attributes to Rudolph Sohm and Emil Brunner. Law is responsible for order; it embodies regularity and generality though its substantive content may vary. Law is vulnerable to distortion and political misuse caused by human sinfulness. In contrast, love is personal and specific, and is expressed in caritative acts. These differences notwithstanding, Wolf draws love and law into close relation, contesting Sohm's and Brunner's assumptions that they are incompatible because love weakens law's normative authority, undermines its universality, and relativizes its demands. These assumptions reflect a positivist idea of law as directives enacted according to prescribed procedures. Wolf rejects them as based on an abstract, generalized idea of legality. The divine-human relation and the neighbor relation are not opposed to law. Law does not begin where love ends, nor does law consist merely of positivist regulations.

Instead, Wolf contends that love neither limits, supplements, nor contradicts law; it relates to it dialectically. He claims that there cannot be any human relation without an element of love. Love participates in the neighbor relation by virtue of the divine-human covenant, outside of which persons do not authentically exist.[39] It is grounded in the neighbor relation and law indirectly expresses it. In fact, he asserts that law is only discernible in the context of the neighbor-relation.[40] Obviously, social order requires law, but love needs law as well to avoid becoming individualistic and sentimental. Law requires love if it is not to decline into loveless order without equity, clemency, burden-sharing, or respect for individual relationships.[41] Love and law must be seen, he believes, as inseparable.

Rather than viewing love in shallow, secularized terms, Wolf envisions it as a capacity that enables humans to respond to divine love by loving both God and neighbor. Love relates to law because law seeks justice and cannot adequately envision it on its own. Justice needs love to avoid descent into cold indifference. In this sense, Wolf contends that the relation between law and love is dialectical.[42] Neither displaces, overwhelms or minimizes the other. Law cannot alone inspire the moral necessity for social order. It can identify the neighbor, guide treatment of her, and prescribe how it may be practically approached.[43]

39. Wolf, "Dialektik," 120.

40. "Law can at all only really be encountered, only found in, the neighbor-relation" (Wolf, "Dialektik," 116).

41. Wolf, "Dialektik," 137.

42. Steinmüller contends, "Law and love are ... dialectically one. Love without law is unordered love, law without love is unloving, unjust law" (Steinmüller, *Rechtstheologie*, 1:409).

43. Wolf, "Dialektik," 136.

This connection between love and law has implications for the theology of law. For Wolf, a refusal to see the neighbor-relation as a legal relation is to return to outmoded patterns of theological and legal thinking, and to deny the divine-human relationship that underlies law.[44] Love is not a marginal supplement to law. It is part of its essence: "The neighbor relation is that of love."[45]

Justice and Law

Curiously, Wolf has relatively little to say about justice in *Recht des Nächsten*. This is because justice is the essence of an ethics of law and, together with the ontology of law, it is subsumed in the theology of law to which Wolf devotes his primary attention. Law and justice stand in the same relation to each other as "is" does to "ought." They remain separate and distinct, of equal dignity, yet related. The essence of justice, Wolf declares, is relation and function.[46] Relation is concerned with proportion and equality; function with appropriateness and correctness. These elements are expressed in three forms: as orderliness, usefulness and value. This *trias* secures the preservation of order, protection of interest, and promotion of an ethos of law. Without these manifestations, law would become unjust order, a perverse inversion of its vocation.

According to Wolf, there are multiple models of justice, each underwritten by a different philosophical perspective. A formal notion of justice deals with the just distribution of goods and services. A material model of justice examines the nature of equality and inequality, and a relativist notion of justice deals with cultural values and goods rather than questions of distribution or inequality. He considers the classical definition of justice—giving each her due—to be excessively formal. In contrast, natural law provides a material definition of justice. For him, this means that justice is not a unitary concept, but relates differently to the realms of things, persons and society. In the specific context of law, justice is a matter of value, function, and order; collectively these values serve to secure legality, promote legal security, order, usefulness, and legitimacy. They exist in a "trialectic" relation to each other, together forming the determinative criterion of law.[47]

Without justice, law deteriorates into a perverse order in which personhood is undermined and recognition of others' rights is replaced by

---

44. Wolf, "Dialektik," 135.
45. Wolf, "Dialektik," 116.
46. Wolf, "Rechtsphilosophie," 79.
47. Wolf, "Rechtsphilosophie," 79.

self-seeking. While justice is essential for preserving law as law, it is not self-supporting. Instead, Wolf suggests somewhat obliquely, justice is too riven and indistinct to stand on its own, and is threatened with relativism unless grounded. A theological foundation of justice is indispensable. "Justice is the directing Word of God: the 'biblical directive.'"[48]

Ultimately, then, law and justice are guided by divine authority. Human law bears a likeness to divine law in its concern with justice; its difference lies in a tendency to neglect the neighbor in favor of self-regard or ideological distortion. Wolf sees human law and justice as aspiring toward a social order defined by law and devoted to the needs of the weak.[49] But even a just legal order must satisfy the requirements of law: legal stability and appropriateness.

The Neighbor

Who is a neighbor for Wolf? When a person acknowledges another's personality, that person becomes a neighbor. This occurs in the act of encounter: "The status of neighbor, ontologically understood, is concrete encounter."[50] This involves nearness and directedness in time and space to fellow humans, in body and spirit. Christ is the paradigmatic brother and neighbor, standing at the intersection of the vertical axis of the divine call and the horizontal axis of interpersonal relations. Neighbor-status is a counterpart to personality, and solidarity brings neighbors into relation. When the two rights of personality and solidarity are understood in Christian terms, solidarity can be expressed as Christocratic brotherhood in which Christ is affirmed as its center.

The law of the neighbor is fulfilled in the orders of Christocracy and brotherhood. They form the substance of law.[51] Christocracy is grounded in the divine covenant, and it reflects God's commitment to humanity. Brotherhood is based on divine law, and is mediated through biblical directives. These two concepts relate to each other dialectically, not in a relation of cancellation (*Aufhebung*) but in mutual coinherence.[52] Accordingly, the elements of the dialectic are not Christocracy and brotherhood, but brotherly

---

48. Wolf, "Rechtsphilosophie," 80.
49. Wolf, "Biblische Weisung," 194.
50. Wolf, "Biblische Weisung," 28.
51. Bauer-Tornack, *Wolf*, 347.
52. Steinmüller suggests that Wolf replaces his previous notion of dialectic as the diastasis of antithesis with a dialectic of coinherence and correspondence. See Steinmüller, *Rechtstheologie*, 1:406.

Christocracy and Christocratic brotherhood. Through this structure, dialectic gives rise to analogy: neighborly law becomes an analogue to divine law.

Neighbors are not only Christians but also non-Christians. Wolf appeals to Barth on this point, who contends that the divinity of God is expressed in an encompassing love for all persons, and the humanity of God refuses the exclusion of any person.[53] While the full theological significance of this love is uniquely appreciable by Christians, all persons are capable of recognizing neighbors. Two consequences follow. First, the law of the neighbor is more of a prolegomenon to law than a source or basis of law. Wolf distinguishes it from law that creates individual rights. "Because the law of the neighbor does not accrue to a person, no subjective rights follow from it." Further, being a neighbor is "a reciprocal, objective relationship, not unilateral-subjective behavior or only a disposition."[54] Society arises out of personal relations. Existentially, we do not encounter society, only persons. And law is most fulfilled when we encounter others not only as persons but also as neighbors. What is Wolf trying to achieve with the distinction between neighbor law and positive law? In part, it seems that he wants to emphasize the inadequacy of positive law to do justice to persons because it is incapable of seeing them in relation to their ultimate value and meaning.

Positive Law, Natural Law and Biblical Directives

What, then, does the law of the neighbor mean for positive law? Fundamentally, it excludes natural law as a basis for positive law. Wolf finds natural law inadequate to express the relational qualities of personality and solidarity. He wrote extensively on natural law, including a volume treating it that appeared in 1955 entitled *Das Problem des Naturrechts* (The Problem of Natural Law). In it, Wolf concludes that natural law, like other theories of law, is conceptually plural rather than homogenous. It encompasses a multiplicity of conceptions of law and justice. Natural law is inherently ambiguous because of the historical contingency of human understanding and as a result of the openness of the eschatological future. "What law truly is will be first revealed in the final judgment, when God gives each person her essential due."[55]

Second, neighbor law undergirds positive law. Wolf writes: "In so far as one respects the law of the neighbor and acts on his neighborly duties, he

53. Wolf, *Recht des Nächsten*, 33.
54. Wolf, *Recht des Nächsten*, 68.
55. Wolf, "Gerechtigkeit," 28.

also lays the theological foundation for a common 'positive' legal order between Christians and non-Christians."[56] This suggests a positive legal order is dependent on neighbor law. The language here is that of the grounding of law, with its problematical suggestion of the dependence of positive law on a suprapositive basis for its legitimacy.

To an extent, natural law fulfils this grounding role for positive law. It affirms the duty of all to embrace law in its affirmative, humanizing capacity. Natural law also serves as a guideline for positive law in seeking to establish a criterion of justice. But Wolf sees the ability of humans to discern both absolute and natural justice as constrained by the limitations of reason and human sinfulness that efface the divine image in humans. Natural law is therefore of positive, though limited, value.

Instead of natural law, Wolf proposes biblical directives. Derived from scripture, they consist of principles that guide the conduct of individuals and institutions in accord with true law. He rejects unreflective biblicism. Further, he contends that the biblical directives cannot be posited in general terms, but can only be perceived situationally in the context of interaction with neighbors.[57] In this sense, the neighbor relation, in enabling the discernment of the biblical directives, is the ground and center of law.[58]

Wolf's notion of the biblical directives is indebted to Barth and Kierkegaard. He draws upon Barth's idea of analogy, yet moves beyond it to fashion the directives as a bridge from divine law to human law. From Kierkegaard, Wolf derives a dialectic that affirms difference and rejects identity, thereby acknowledging the infinite distance between divine and human law. Steinmüller describes this concept of dialectic as an "apophatic" dialectic of overlapping relations, and declares dialectic to be Wolf's basic thought-figure (*Denkform*).[59] The apophatic quality results from a preference for negation over affirmation in describing the dialectical relation. This would explain Wolf's reluctance to elaborate on dialectical assertions about the relation of divine and human law.

The directives relate dialectically to human law, sharing both commonalities and differences. Wolf does not describe them in detail; one can imagine they include justice and equity. Yet the directives and the divine law behind them, have priority over human law. They serve to maintain the relation of divine and human law, especially with regard to justice. Kerstin

---

56. Wolf, "Gerechtigkeit," 34.
57. Wolf, "Gerechtigkeit," 19.
58. Steinmüller, *Rechtstheologie*, 1:408.
59. Steinmüller, *Rechtstheologie*, 1:431.

Gäfgen contends that for Wolf "the biblical directives assign to human law the enduring task of realizing divine justice."[60]

Wolf proposes three principles of neighbor law derived from the biblical directives: (1) the neighbor should be allowed the benefits of law; (2) neighbors must grant each other what is owing to them under the law, rather than seeking to advance one's own rights at the expense of another; and (3) neighbors should respect the legal expectations of others rather than require their enforcement through legal means. These principles reflect a preference for a voluntary recognition of the status and claims of others that is reminiscent of the Pauline injunction of 1 Corinthians 6:1. In this sense, they transcend law without nullifying it, granting law its proper role without allowing it to define the standards for interaction with neighbors. It exalts a spirit of solidarity over emphasis on the assertion of one's own interests. In short, they prescribe an ethical attitude and behavior that is supra-legal rather than antinomian.

The church is the primary social forum for interpretation and application of the biblical directives. They cannot be directly transferred and translated into positive law. "All directives of the Bible relating to legal and social order—it must be continually repeated—are never legal provisions (*Rechtssätze*) but instead are always legal principles; never regulations, rather always directives; not norms for decision, rather norms of determination (guidelines) for the legislator, judge, administrative officials, attorney and the normal person subject to law in interaction with other members of the legal community."[61]

The directives are not to be understood simply as legal or normative demands. But if neither biblical directives, the primordial rights of personality and solidarity nor the principles of the neighbor relation are law *per se*, then what are they? They have the character of regulative guidelines. In this respect, they align with Barth's emphasis on situations over generalized rules. As Steinmüller remarks, "They [the directives] are not deductive-normative in character, rather they are legal principles and guidelines directed to the disposition and thus affect law in a regulative and directive manner."[62] The active work of the biblical directives, then, is to attest that law is ultimately grounded in divine authority, evidenced in grace and love. They alone create the possibility of human law and establish a dialectical relation between human law and divine law.

---

60. Gäfgen, *Recht*, 262.
61. Wolf, "Richtschnur," 43.
62. Steinmüller, *Rechtstheologie*, 1:411.

These biblically derived principles figure in the deliberations of conscience and also in their practical implementation. They exist at a remove from positive law and this excludes any direct effect on substantive law.[63] But Wolf is unspecific about their indirect effect on law, other than general statements about the dependence of positive human law on the neighbor relation and on the divine relation.[64] Wolf's reticence to say more suggests that the biblical directives are essentially attitudinal and motivational, and are expressed in individual actions. They lack an explicitly social dimension. If this reading of Wolf is correct, then the significance of the directives seems disproportionate to what he ascribes to it, in that he states that they legitimize mundane law and make it binding.

What is the role such directives can have in a pluralistic legal community? To American sensibilities, an appeal to the directives in support or criticism of positive law outside of a situation of civil resistance is not easy to imagine. The directives seem to be at home within a faith community. Outside of that context, they appear to bear on the willingness of individuals to treat fellow persons according to the spirit of the law as well as to its letter.

Foljanty finds that Wolf ends up, in effect, with a dual concept of law—both divine and human. Wolf attempts to avoid a dualism between them by means of a threefold affirmation of (1) the priority of divine law, (2) the deficiencies of human law, and (3) the dialectical relation between them secured through the biblical directives. But it is doubtful that he succeeds. In a sense, the biblical directives show how far Wolf distances himself from secular jurisprudence in *Recht des Nächsten* and this pushes him in the direction of dualism. In the essay, the philosophy of law merges into the theology of law. Perhaps Wolf's notion of the dialectical relation between divine and human law dissuaded him from spelling out more extensively the relation between them.

Concluding Observations—Law as All Too Human

Wolf's theology of law belongs to those attempts to interpret law as essentially Christocentric. By positing the two basic rights of personality and solidarity as the crystallizations of the biblical directives, Wolf advances beyond both Barth's Christocentrism and Brunner's orders. But his vigorous affirmation of the priority of divine law over human law, his disregard of traditional themes of jurisprudence, and his assertion of a close relation between law and love presuppose certain theological commitments.

63. Wolf, *Recht des Nächsten*, 102.
64. Wolf, "Dialektik," 115.

This has prompted critical comments about Wolf's theology of law. Huber sees it as bound to its historical context—specifically, the postwar debates in Germany about the basis of human law. For him, Wolf threatens to theologize law.[65]

Foljanty notes that, even at the time of its publication, legal theorists devoted little attention to *Recht des Nächsten*. Most of the reviews of it appeared in theological journals and several had a critical tone. In one review, Pannenberg declares that Wolf's proposals, along with other Christocentric theologies of law, reflect a certain supranatural positivism. "The relation of God in Jesus Christ is presupposed as an assertion, and conclusions are simply drawn from it for the field of law."[66] He faults Wolf for seeking regulative and structural principles for law from the revelation of Christ, such as the "very formal" basic rights of personality and solidarity. In fact, Pannenberg doubts that personality requires a Christological grounding at all since the idea of a divine-human relation is not unique to Christianity. He concludes that Wolf has conflated legal and theological elements: "Normative concepts and Christian love lie on different levels."[67]

Pannenberg's critique identifies, from a theological angle, an underlying problem in *Recht des Nächsten*. The biblical directives, the basis of the primordial rights, are problematic because Wolf does not adequately explain how they are derived nor how they actually bear on human law. They seem primarily to relate to will and disposition rather than to law's substantive content. Wolf contends that they originate in the divine covenant, as attested in scripture.[68] He contends that neighbor law is direct and binding.[69] Yet it is not clear how. In contrast, human law imposes obligations only derivatively. "All human law imposes obligations only indirectly, only in so far as it is an obligation owed to God that imposes his legal obligations on us through the neighbor-relationship."[70] But the grounding of the directives in the covenant remains largely undeveloped. The directives assist in bettering law by emphasizing the dialectic of personality and solidarity, but they do so primarily by serving as an external critique of positive law. As for many of the other writers considered here, connecting theological insights with positive law is a crucial challenge.

65. Huber, *Gerechtigkeit*, 110.
66. Pannenberg, "Wolf," 439.
67. Pannenberg, "Wolf," 440.
68. Wolf, *Recht des Nächsten*, 17.
69. "God's law (*Recht*) over human beings is absolute and unmediated" (Wolf, *Recht des Nächsten*, 18).
70. Wolf, *Recht des Nächsten*, 18.

Wolf's concentration on the biblical word as a source of directives for law—following Barth—together with his conviction that absolute justice is only available in and through God, lead him to a certain personalistic theocentrism. In *Recht des Nächsten*, justice is essentially absorbed into the primordial phenomena of personality and solidarity. It is integrated into the neighbor relation, and it finds its primary expression there. Social structures and institutions are not directly related to it, only indirectly through the expression of solidarity. Wolf interprets solidarity as concrete social love, reflecting his long-standing concern with the relation of the individual and community in law. But he sees community in personalistic-communal terms, and he does not have much to say about institutions and structures. This results from his ontological approach to law. While he provides provocative insights in interpreting law in this way, it results in a concept of law that emphasizes the individual over the social.

Further, the existential situationalism of neighbor law has little to say about how law becomes better, or what better law would look like. Not all law involves relational circumstances, or if it does, it does so tenuously. Wolf's conviction that legal philosophy must eventually lead to the theology of law threatens to instrumentalize law for theological ends.

Wolf's vision of law as divinely enjoined and ethically focused rejects positivist assumptions about law, its sources, its ethical status, and its relation to love. But its prescriptive ontology overwhelms the facticity of law. Wolf overestimates the ethical dimension of legal action, and underestimates the role of coercion in legal compliance.

How tenable is Wolf's ontological approach in a North American context? Is the law of the neighbor a plausible notion in the context of contemporary law? An anthropological ontology such as Wolf's would certainly be unusual in an Anglophone context. Such metaphysical constructs are typically viewed as being beyond the ken of jurisprudence. Wolf's ontology seeks to identify the significance law can have for social existence. This is a far remove from notions of law as based on external constraint.

In the end, we return to the person of Erik Wolf himself. Against the background of his personal history, the law of the neighbor presents an example of the ambiguity of law. This involves more than the familiar and stubborn conflict between the ideal of justice and the empirical reality of law. It is rooted in the ethically tangled quality of human conduct, and Wolf's own history attests to it.

VI

Helmut Thielicke

Law as Provisional Compromise

Helmut Thielicke (1908–86) was a prominent professor of theology and ethics in Tübingen and Hamburg during the mid-century period. A student of Paul Althaus, he was banned from teaching during the Second World War, during which he devoted himself to preaching, church work and writing. Thielicke also played a significant role in public affairs during the reconstruction of Germany, not only through academic work but also through preaching and publications. He lectured and taught in the United States on numerous occasions.[1] Many of his publications have appeared in English translation.[2]

Despite his lengthy career, numerous publications, and international reputation, Thielicke's work has been overlooked for the most part since his death. Secondary literature on him is sparse, and he is only infrequently referenced in contemporary theological writing. This perhaps reflects a degree of disapproval by the academy of his reputation as a successful preacher and public speaker, as well as his political conservatism and vigorous Lutheranism. This disregard is regrettable: one commentator, Dietz Lange, refers to Thielicke as "without a doubt one of the most interesting ethicists of his

---

1. Both Zahrnt, *Question of God*, and Bromiley, "Thielicke," provide useful summaries of Thielicke's theology and ethical thought; autobiographical details are available in Thielicke, *Notes from a Wayfarer*. A helpful discussion of the historical context of Thielicke's ethics is Lange, *Ethik in evangelischer Perspektive*, 63–75. Regarding Thielicke's public role in the postwar era of reconstruction, see Barnett, *For the Soul of the People*, 275–78.

2. In addition to parts of his work on ethics, these include translations of his systematic theology, Thielicke, *Evangelical Faith* (1974–77), as well as several monographs and volumes of essays and sermons.

time."[3] This neglect is particularly unfortunate with respect to Thielicke's reflections on law. He takes up themes in law and ethics rarely addressed by the other writers treated in this book. His insights are valuable because he addresses facets of law and the actual reality of legal problems. He has a keen sense for the distortions and misuses to which law is put. For example, Thielicke deals with the political and ideological distortions of law, the limits of law, and complex questions of guilt and punishment in criminal law.

One of his two major publications was a multivolume work on ethics (*Theologische Ethik*) he began during the Second World War and that required almost two decades to complete. The other was a three-volume systematic theology entitled *The Evangelical Faith*. Thielicke's *Theologische Ethik* is massive, comprising four large volumes and roughly three thousand pages. Thielicke himself claimed that it is probably "the most extensive work on ethics ever written."[4] Writing in 1966, Heinz Zahrnt declared it to be, after Barth's *Church Dogmatics*, the "most important work of systematic theology in the present century."[5]

Thielicke's *Ethik* is an elaborately detailed and wide-ranging work informed by a Lutheran understanding of justification by faith refracted through a critical, eschatologically oriented revision of the two kingdoms doctrine of Lutheran social ethics. Justification by faith constitutes the theological foundation of Thielicke's approach; Zahrnt suggests that Thielicke's work on ethics is essentially "an applied doctrine of justification."[6] Systematically, he applies this theological *Grundmotiv* to various spheres of personal and social life, including politics, economy, art, sexuality and law. Thielicke himself describes the task he undertook in the work to be that "of declining the doctrine of justification through all the case forms in which it appears in the grammar of our existence."[7] The *Ethik* is marked by close attention to the diverse spheres of social life, and by its rejection of casuistic approaches in favor of a comprehensive "Christian interpretation of human and historical reality"[8] in which various ethical norms persistently compete and conflict.

3. Lange, *Ethik*, 68.
4. Thielicke, *Ethik*, 3:ix.
5. Zahrnt, *Question of God*, 184.
6. Zahrnt, *Question of God*, 185.
7. Thielicke, *Ethics*, 1:xiv. There is an abridged English translation of portions of the first two volumes of the *Ethik*; it is referred to below as the *Ethics*. References are to the respective volume of the English translation if the cited material is contained in those translated volumes; otherwise the citation is to the original German edition (designated by the German title: *Ethik*), or to both German and English versions if the English translation is an abridgment of the German original.
8. Thielicke, *Ethics*, 1:xiii.

Throughout, the *Ethik* displays a markedly eschatological orientation. "Theological ethics is eschatological or it is nothing."[9] As Thielicke conceives it, human life is lived simultaneously in two aeons. One is the contemporary, historical aeon of present existence; the other is a transcendent aeon in which Christ is dominant, presiding over the entire cosmos, throughout and beyond time. This duality places the believer in a relationship of simultaneous continuity and discontinuity with the mundane spheres of existence; it is analogous to the believer's status as *simul justus et peccator*. The simultaneity of aeons creates a fundamental ambiguity in ethical existence and reflection. One participates in both aeons while belonging wholly to neither. One is in continual tension between principle and circumstance, between norm and reality. Like Kierkegaard, Thielicke is convinced that the experience of simultaneity is a fundamental characteristic of human existence. "The problem with ethics is all wrapped up in this *simul*."[10]

In contrast to many other works on ethics, Thielicke's *Ethik* treats law as an independent, substantial topic.[11] He classifies the legal sphere as the third of five zones of life (*Lebensbereiche*) dealt with in the work, preceded by politics, economics and society, and followed by sexuality and art. The main section on law appears in the third volume and amounts to more than two hundred pages.[12] Extended discussions of the relation between law and morality appear in other volumes of the work; there are separate analyses of the relationship between state and moral society,[13] on law and the concept of compromise,[14] natural law, and on the political theory of the separation of powers.[15] Although an English translation of the last volume of the *Ethik* (containing Thielicke's discussion of law) was apparently planned, it never appeared.[16] As a result, the most relevant sections of the *Ethik* for law unfortunately remain unavailable in English.

Two themes of the *Ethik* are especially relevant for Thielicke's theology of law. First, he proposes an eschatological revision of Luther's two kingdoms doctrine emphasizing the provisionality and mutability of law. This

---

9. Thielicke, *Ethics*, 1:x.

10. Thielicke, *Ethics*, 1:41.

11. All references, except as otherwise noted, are to the first German edition of the third volume (1964) and are my translations.

12. Thielicke, *Ethik*, 3:295. This third volume of the *Ethik* is actually the fourth book in the series because, as noted above, the second volume is divided into two separate books.

13. Thielicke, *Ethik*, 2/1:186-201; *Ethics*, 2:155-67.

14. Thielicke, *Ethik*, 2/2:1017-18; *Ethics*, 2:620-30.

15. Thielicke, *Ethik*, 2/2:255-87; *Ethics*, 2:482-93.

16. The section in the third volume on sexual ethics was, however, separately published in English as *The Ethics of Sex*.

relativizes law and emphasizes its role in the preservation of humanity. To be sure, grace is predominant for Thielicke, and law is a relative good but not an end unto itself.[17] Like the state, it is an interim institution.[18] This aligns with Thielicke's vision of human existence as torn but not sundered—between sin and justification, between the present and the future. Second, ethical existence is characterized by the inevitability of compromise. Law contains a co-mingling of practical as well as ethical elements, and they coexist through compromise. Both themes create a field of tension (*Spannungsfeld*) in Thielicke's theology of law in which pressure and counter-pressure contend with each other, reflecting the tension between law and ethos, and between justice and pragmatism.

Two characteristics of Thielicke's conception of law are particularly significant and merit specific mention: its provisional and its compromissory character.

Provisionality

Thielicke's ethics seek to provide an interpretation of reality as the sphere in which ethical existence is played out. By "reality," Thielicke means all that is comprehensively experienced and known—including its mundane aspects. He sees the true task of ethics as the effort to insure "that the human person and his existence is integrated into a particular structure of reality and that he has to do with this structure in his daily work."[19] His understanding of the world is that of an interim order reflecting the fundamental phenomenon of human dislocation. The world shapes human reality: "The world is not regarded as a sphere which simply stands over against humanity, it is the very form of man's being."[20] It is the "macrocosmically extended sphere of man."[21] In a sense, when a person confronts the world, she confronts herself. Consequentially, in its present character the world is thoroughly *post-lapsum*. Yet it is not wholly discontinuous with the eschatological future, and this creates a temporal tension in ethics. By this, Thielicke means that the collective circumstances of existence—namely, the world—condition human self-understanding. Further, it reflects the fact that that existence

---

17. Thielicke, *Ethik*, 3:378.

18. Thielicke writes, "When knowledge of this is kept alive, it protects against the misunderstanding that law and the legal order contains its own purpose and is therefore absolute" (Thielicke, *Ethik*, 3:379).

19. Thielicke, *Ethics*, 1:xii.

20. Thielicke, *Ethics*, 1:434.

21. Thielicke, *Ethics*, 1:434.

has a fragmented, discordant, and transient character. Ethics is concerned with "a temporary ensconcement in the world;"[22] it is a "field of tension between the old and new aeons, not only in the old one, nor in the new one."[23] Thielicke holds that ethics must engage with this tension, not attempt to escape it.

Given the pervasiveness of sinfulness in human existence in the old aeon, the world cannot be meaningfully construed in terms of established orders of creation. Instead, Thielicke speaks of "orders of divine patience" or, alternatively, of divinely instituted "emergency orders" (*Notverordnungen*).[24] The orders are broken and relative, yet they possess a degree of consistency and regularity. While they are instrumentally rather than intrinsically good, at the same time they are a "representation of the divine will."[25] To the extent the orders are necessitated and shaped by human fallibility, they do not ultimately correspond to any sort of divinely sanctioned order. Ontically, the emergency orders are ambiguous in that they represent, to a degree, institutionalizations of sin. Yet they are also preservative and constructive as well.[26] Law is such an emergency order, required by sinfulness, preservative in the structuring and regulation of human community. A legal order is also corrigible and provisional because individual and social life is historically conditioned and penultimate, not ultimate.

Compromise

The concept of compromise pervades Thielicke's *Ethik* and has particular relevance for the sphere of law. In his theological framework, ethical reflection and action must constantly balance conflicting claims and interests. Though necessary, compromise is morally ambiguous rather than intrinsically virtuous; for Thielicke, compromise is the tribute that must be paid to the fallen world.[27] Humans are themselves responsible for the inevitability of compromise because of their recalcitrance and egocentrism. To the extent these characteristics require compromise, one can say that it is an institutionalization of human rebellion.[28] As such, it requires divine forgiveness.

22. Thielicke, *Ethics*, 1:42.
23. Thielicke, *Ethics*, 1:43.
24. Thielicke, *Ethics*, 1:440.
25. Thielicke, *Ethics*, 1:440.
26. Thielicke develops the concept of the Noachite covenant as a preeminent instance of the compound of divine patience and human social necessity. See Thielicke, *Ethik*, 1:701–5; *Ethics*, 1:190–94.
27. Thielicke, *Ethics*, 1:567.
28. Thielicke, *Ethics*, 1:567.

At the same time, compromise has a positive function of preserving order, and in doing so, it emulates, however faintly, divine patience.

Compromise is sanctioned in salvation history in the Noachide covenant. In Thielicke's interpretation, that covenant represents divine accommodation of ethical imperatives to fallen, historical existence. It demonstrates God's patient preservation of a sinful world by providing for and permitting the means necessary for its preservation, including the use of force. This is the alien work of accommodation and adjustment of conflicting demands and realities.[29] Tragic consequences may result from compromise, but they are the result of human disobedience and not, as in classical thought, of indifferent, cosmic fate.

For Thielicke, compromise is an essential ethical activity. It is necessary because of a disjunction between the "abstract sphere of disposition" and the "environmental destiny of action."[30] Actions are shaped by circumstance as well as intent, and they often require steps that seem to contradict the end being pursued. He rejects, as one-sided, unconditional demands that ignore the "autonomous world of means" to which every ethical act is subject. At the same time, he opposes any watering down of ethical imperatives. There is no escape from the tension between ethical demands and resistant circumstances. Compromise is also necessary because of the provisionality of existence in the two overlapping aeons. The eschatological impetus of the future aeon presses forward while the structures of creation of the present aeon incline backwards to their origins. In essence, compromise is theologically grounded and necessitated, and is not simply a pragmatic strategy.

This reflects the human situation in its totality. The "real problem facing theological ethics" is the persistent contradiction between ends and means that intensifies as one moves from the personal into the political/social realm. Individual and social action occur in a force field between eschatological anticipation and present circumstances. In the context of this interplay, Thielicke believes that there is no single, specifically Christian position on economic, political or other social questions. Christian ethical thought offers no explicit moral imperatives; instead, the imperative is contained in the indicative. Thielicke means by this that obligation arises out of concrete circumstances and institutions; the divine "gift" of justification includes an invitation for human acceptance. Compromise is an appropriate method for balancing the imperative of action with the reality of a morally ambiguous environment. It is relevant for justice in that justice, as Thielicke conceives it, involves the accommodation of legal norms to reality. His

---

29. Zahrnt, *Question of God*, 191.
30. Thielicke, *Ethics*, 1:482.

reliance on compromise injects an element of realism into his ethics.[31] In his embrace of compromise, he rejects the primacy of Kant's good will, stressing instead the importance of the practical realization of ethical norms in the light of resistant circumstances.[32] "The only realistic ethic . . . is an ethic of compromise."[33] As Martin Honecker observes, Thielicke's interpretation of compromise is a consequence of his reformed understanding of sin and justification.[34]

Compromise always involves decision, so one could say that both compromise and decision are foundational themes in Thielicke's ethics. According to Heinz Zahrnt, compromise has almost the same significance for Thielicke that the principle of analogy has for Barth.[35]

Compromise in Law

Thielicke's emphasis on social reality, and the relative autonomy of various zones of life leads him to view law as a field of tension—between justice and pragmatism; idealism and realism; order and freedom. In light of this, compromise is an essential and pervasive practice for negotiating the tensions contained in law. Compromise rejects both irresponsible idealism and cynical reduction of law to procedures for meting out punishment and resolving conflicts. By granting compromise a place in law Thielicke demonstrates his instinctive realism. Law, as he sees it, is an ethically heterogenous enterprise in which justice is conditioned and qualified by pragmatism and practical necessity.

Compromise relates to justice and law by bringing norm and reality into ethical relation rather than allowing them to remain in opposition. Law constantly requires efforts to reach a *modus vivendi et practicandi*. This requires law to allow for, indeed to promote, compromise.[36] Law facilitates

---

31. Kreβ credits Thielicke with helping to revive the concept of compromise after Barth had dismissed it. See Kreβ, *Ethik der Rechtsordnung*, 240.

32. Honecker, *Einführung*, 236.

33. Thielicke, *Ethik*, 2/1:159. While also describing compromise as a key concept for Thielicke, Lange criticizes what he sees as Thielicke's overreliance on it. By relating compromise to themes such as the relativity of ethical realization, divine accommodation of the world through law, and the incarnation, the concept is stretched so far as to lose its contours and threatens to undermine the significance of eschatology (Lange, *Ethik*, 68). Certainly Thielicke relies heavily on compromise as a mediating concept, but he clearly locates it in the present aeon.

34. Honecker, *Einführung*, 238.

35. Zahrnt, *Question of God*, 191.

36. Thielicke, *Ethik*, 3:297-98.

compromise through its emphasis on ethical criteria in the act of decision, including proportionality, equity, predictability and justness. Without a relation to practicality, norms would be forced to yield to reality because of their remoteness from actual circumstances. Those circumstances determine, in part, how purposes are realized. Justice would be, as it often is, viewed as impractical and disregarded, or diluted and marginalized. This is the dialectic Thielicke discerns between justice and purpose. Though this is the principal element of compromise in law, it also manifests itself in other contexts, such as in the balancing of individual and collective interests, as well as in the role of the judge, which can only be a relatively, not absolutely, ethical activity.

Law's character is particularly evident in borderline and conflict situations, in which ethical considerations confront circumstances that define the outer limits of their applicability.[37] This establishes, for Thielicke, the inevitability and the necessity of compromise.

The Dialectical Nature of Law

Law, Thielicke contends, typically is seen as an ordering institution, exemplified in prescriptive regulations such as traffic laws. In this capacity, it has no particular moral content, only serving a coordinating function in matters that cannot be left up to individual discretion. It is also coercive in being enforced by sanctions. Understood in this way, law belongs to what Thielicke calls the "metaethical sphere" in that it consists of a combination of arbitrary agreements and sanctions.[38] In other sorts of activities law contains a moral dimension. They require, Thielicke believes, that law and morality be neither merged nor severed; that would be a "fateful heresy."[39] While, generally speaking, law is concerned only with outward behavior and morality with interior motive, this is not always the case. Intent and motive figure significantly in some areas of law, introducing an ethical dimension into law. Even seemingly technical provisions of law have ethical consequences—a speed limit serves to protect human life from harm caused by the careless operation of motor vehicles. In most cases, some form of human evil is sought to be prevented.

Law's dialectical character also manifests itself in the hiatus in law between its normative and pragmatic specifications, and between justice and

---

37. On the concept of borderline situation as Thielicke develops it in the *Ethics*, see Thielicke, *Ethics*, 1:578–608.

38. Thielicke, *Ethics*, 2:188.

39. Thielicke, *Ethics*, 1:158.

purpose. This introduces a dialectical tension into law. Justice is the norm that arbitrates between one's own interests and those of others. It stands above, and is superior to, the pursuit of partial interests in positive law. In this sense, justice judges positive law and reveals its contingency and partiality. Thielicke sees the deficiencies of positive law as consequences of the exaggeration of its pragmatic element. By this, he means that law generally reflects some interest or goal, and accordingly is concerned as much or more with the realization of that goal than with its justness. "Law is—as a result of the internal dialectic of an "absolute" norm of justice and relative purposefulness—seen theologically, located on the seam between norm and reality, at a place that is conceptually under pressure and can occasionally lead to border conflicts."[40]

Law is subverted when either justice or purposiveness is pursued to one extreme at the expense of countervailing considerations. The unbridled pursuit of justice through the abusive exploitation of law or extrajudicial means, such as portrayed in Kleist's novella *Michael Kohlhaas*, can undermine law by intensifying disputes and prompting retaliation. The original wrong that Michael Kohlhaas suffered was the wrongful taking of two horses; his frustrated pursuit of justice in a corrupt judicial system spurred him to a revolt against the ruling aristocracy that ended with his execution. The other extreme—the perversion of law in the pursuit of some practical objective—can be equally ruinous for law. An example of this Thielicke refers to as "ideologized law."[41] This occurs when the pragmatic element in law predominates and effectively eliminates the normative element of justice, which Thielicke calls the "controlling corrective of all pragmatisms."[42] When a pragmatic interest is absolutized and becomes the organizing center of law, then "Law becomes an instrument of the will to power and resultingly becomes a department of politics."[43] A prototypical example of ideologized law is the show trial. Thielicke refers to Communist law and show trials in the Cold War era as examples of this debasement of law.[44] In discuss-

---

40. Thielicke, *Ethik*, 3:310-11. In an earlier volume of the *Ethik*, Thielicke speaks of three basic values in law, following Gustav Radbruch: justice, purposiveness, and legal stability (Thielicke, *Ethik*, 2/2:52). He does not include the third—legal stability—in his discussion of law in the relevant section of the third volume of the *Ethik*.

41. Thielicke, *Ethik*, 2/2:52-58.

42. Thielicke, *Ethik*, 2/2:53.

43. Thielicke, *Ethik*, 2/2:53.

44. Elsewhere Thielicke contends that show trials also occur in the West, mentioning the Malmedy war crimes trials of 1946 as an example. Recent research on those trials rebuts this characterization, which Thielicke helped publicize. See Remy, *Malmedy Massacre*; Frei, *Adenauer's Germany*, 161 (on Thielicke's role).

ing these abuses, Thielicke warns against the political exploitation of law, a significant and continuing threat to its legitimacy.

Though concerned with the pursuit of purposes and objectives, law is not immune from the demands of justice. Justice and pragmatism form a polarity that cannot be dissolved through a subordination of one to the other. To prioritize pragmatism is to diminish the ethical dimension of law; to prioritize justice is to idealize law. Justice is not, Thielicke declares, an abstract, transcendent norm, but a dialectical construct that internally replicates the polarity of norm and purpose. It follows from this that justice is not simple but complex for Thielicke; it is an amalgam of countervailing concepts. Divine and human, biblical and secular, personal and material—all of these relations inhabit the concept of justice. While Thielicke addresses each of these facets separately, they share a common theme in relating to each other dialectically and pointing to the necessity of compromise.

Law, Religion and Ethics

Thielicke does not concern himself to any great extent with jurisprudential theories of law. He is more concerned with law's relation to religion and morality than with its jurisprudential nature, although he shows himself to be conversant with many of the then-current theories of law, and engages with them from time to time. Law is related to religion in two ways. First, it is historically and mythologically linked to the observance of divine commands, as pronounced and enforced by priestly judges. More significantly, there is a substantive connection between the two that is most strongly present in the question of the normativity of law. While the normative import of law is now supplied by ethics, historically religion was its source.

What, Thielicke asks, is the *norma normans* that supervenes over both ethical and legal norms? The question is complicated by the fact that positive law is characterized by internal friction rather than consistency: "The field of law is a field of tension, in which opposing and never fully reconciled forces stand in permanent conflict."[45] This tension also encompasses the relation of law and ethics. On the one hand, they stand in contrast to each other in that law governs external conduct through the threat of coercion, while ethics is concerned with personal disposition and motivation. On the other hand, law depends on ethics as a basis for its normativity.

Thielicke posits three points of contact between law and ethics. By facilitating ordered social life, law assists in creating conditions that make ethical existence possible. In this respect, law is the "ground of [morality's]

---

45. Thielicke, *Ethik*, 3:297.

possibility."⁴⁶ At the same time, moral considerations inhere in law's material content through concepts such as good faith, trust and loyalty. The relationship between the two is one of mutual coinherence rather than of unilateral dependence. Their interaction is dialectical rather than univocal. Second, law protects practices and institutions such as marriage and private property, and in doing so, it imposes moral standards, such as the duty of good faith in commercial dealings. Third, love is based on a sense of moral values that affirm ordered coexistence. Without this moral anchoring, law degenerates into a contest of power. It enables ethical conduct by creating orderly conditions for life, while ethics prevents law from lapsing into an essentially coercive institution by infusing ethical considerations (such as good faith) into legal norms.

For Thielicke, both law and ethics must both deal, each in their own way, with the consequences of a disrupted vertical relation between human beings and God. This is one of the reasons why ethical imperatives cannot be directly transposed into legal norms. That would ignore the reality of existence in the present aeon, and further would disregard the autonomy of the legal sphere. Nor can law dispense with coercion in the face of perverse assertions of human will, given its capacity for egotistical and destructive behavior. Law is rooted in divine authority and in the divine preserving will, but it also reflects the experience of human infirmity.⁴⁷

In Thielicke's view, moral autonomy in a Kantian sense is an essential element for an appreciation of the inherent limits of human society. He contends: "The primacy of individuals and their ethically related freedom must be the starting point in every doctrine of state and society."⁴⁸ While Thielicke concedes that the interior sphere of ethics may be largely legally irrelevant, it does relate to law in important ways: (1) law makes organized life and therefore morality possible; (2) law contains some basic moral assumptions, such as an obligation of loyalty in certain relationships; and (3) law is "grounded in a sense of moral value that affirms an ordering of the common life and hence also the rules for such an order."⁴⁹ Thielicke attempts to support this view by means of a negative hypothesis. If you assume law does not have an ethical dimension, then law becomes a mere political instrument for the assertion of power, dependent on coercion for compliance. It is "pragmatic pseudo-law."⁵⁰ Ultimately, law must respect the

---

46. Thielicke, *Ethik*, 2/2:192.
47. Thielicke, *Ethik*, 3:375.
48. Thielicke, *Modern Faith and Thought*, 323.
49. Thielicke, *Ethics*, 2:160.
50. Thielicke, *Ethics*, 2:160.

fundamental distinction between good and evil. "[Law] is sustained by the ethical distinction between good and evil."[51]

For Thielicke, this points to a common root of law and ethics. Both entail obedience in the context of the divine covenant as well as in social life. The difference between them is manifested in the penultimate nature of the present aeon. In this context, they are dialectically related, alternately conflicting and aligning with each other. They especially conflict in what Thielicke terms "borderline cases" or situations involving extreme circumstances that heighten the claims of each of them and raise the stakes for violation of either of them. But even in these situations, law and ethics remain in relation and do not contradict each other. This is because Thielicke believes that all law is grounded in a specific anthropology that is concerned with the ethical significance of human existence and its purpose.[52] These are, for him, ethical matters. He contends that this anthropological question forces law to "reflect on its foundations, and to ascertain whether it is in keeping with the accepted end of human beings and their existence and society, i.e., whether it is good law."[53]

Law does indeed imply a vision of the human, and makes assumptions about human needs and capabilities, about social, moral and natural environments, and about the kinds of human activities that should be promoted, discouraged or punished. But it is doubtful whether one can speak of a universal human question about purpose in these terms. It is further doubtful that such a "nonlegal—indeed an ethical—predetermination" that prompts questions about purpose necessarily leads to questions about law.

Despite its concern with pragmatism and expediency, law possesses an irreducible element of ethical sensitivity. The fundament of law is ethical in nature, Thielicke believes, and that fundament is to provide redress for injustice. Yet law must acknowledge its limitations. The problem of the unbridled pursuit of individual rights requires that law limit the unrestrained vindication of individual interest, even if that pursuit remains within the parameters of the law. The act of self-limitation, both by parties and by the legal system itself, is also an ethical aspect of law in that it contains an acknowledgment that no legal system can achieve perfect justice.

---

51. Thielicke, *Ethics*, 2:160–61.
52. Thielicke, *Ethics*, 2:163.
53. Thielicke, *Ethics*, 2:163 (translation revised).

Jurisprudence and Law

Positivism

Despite Thielicke's realism, he rejects any notion of law that slackens the tension between law's normative and pragmatic dimensions. This includes positivistic understandings of law because they do not allow for the normativity of law. Positivism, in Thielicke's view, is a philosophical position that confines itself to the content of the concrete given.[54] It lacks a sense of the wholeness of law, for that presupposes some appreciation of the tension between law's limits and the transcendent quality of justice. Positivism presumes that its constricted focus on the given constitutes the totality of positive law. It rigorously avoids questions of purpose and justice and shrinks legitimacy down to the procedural enactment without regard to norms. "To lay down laws that have no norms is lawlessness."[55] Of course, this broad indictment relates to hard, uncompromising versions of positivism, but they are by no means the only kinds of positivism.[56]

Though Thielicke rejects legal positivism as an inadequate account of law, he largely accepts a positivist notion of the creation of law. Interests are pursued by power, and power in the context of law is the essence of legal positivism.[57] This renders law and the creation of law arbitrary, not only in that power determines what is right, but because power itself lacks legitimacy. "Why [power] exists, and whether it legitimately establishes law can no longer be inquired about."[58] Like several other writers, Thielicke rejects positivism when it presumes to account for more than the genealogy of positive law. When it goes beyond that, he rejects its agnostic amorality as disruptive of the legitimacy and morality of law.

Thielicke sees this as an amoral understanding of law based on a misplaced analogy to the causal laws of nature. Its amorality results from its prioritization of power as a constituent element in the creation of law, as well as its disregard of human personhood. Thielicke pointedly rejects the assumption that law is the product of human processes analogous to natural processes; in that case, process trumps ethics. He speaks of the de-valuing of humans in legal positivism, leaving the human person to be an object of power relations rather than an agent in history.

---

54. Thielicke, *Nihilism*, 61.
55. Thielicke, *Nihilism*, 71.
56. Marmor, *Philosophy of Law*, 92–97.
57. Thielicke, *Ethik*, 3:312–13.
58. Thielicke, *Ethik*, 3:350.

Natural Law

Like several other of our writers, Thielicke views natural law with ambivalence. On the one hand, he acknowledges that its existence and importance for positive law: "ultimately all positive laws derive their legitimacy from it."[59] It is primarily known in the form of a "perceptible order of being underlying every imperative."[60] He defines the classical version of natural law as "the law which belongs to man by nature, i.e., not by virtue of his bios but by virtue of what he essentially is."[61] Its main object is human nature, and how that nature is conceived. But this gives rise to a question: how is this nature to be known? Thielicke argues that knowledge of human nature is conditioned by time and circumstance, and by the dynamics of the divine-human relationship. That relationship is based on faith, and it is anything but unchanging and universal.[62] The effect of this is to render seemingly fixed concepts inherently variable. *Suum cuique* may be constant in form, but it is not in content. That depends on the image of the human one assumes, for that defines what is due.[63] Equality is always accompanied by inequality, and what is due to each is unknowable in general terms. It is reserved to divine knowledge, to be manifested in the eschatological future.[64] In Thielicke's view, Catholic natural law theory ignores these conceptual and epistemological constraints and "ascribes a false rank to *suum cuique*, regarding it as an imperative, the expression of a given and knowable order."[65] The significance of *suum cuique* is heuristic only, by which Thielicke means that it serves to illuminate the relative justness in specific situations, not to serve as a universally discernible criterion of natural law.

While he expresses respect for the efforts expended in developing the various Catholic theories of natural law, Thielicke ultimately rejects them as untenable. The principal reason for this is the variability of the contents of natural law, and the unwarranted assumption of the existence of an intact order of being that fails to account sufficiently for sin. To his mind, secular theories of natural law represent degenerate versions of traditional theological anthropology and ethics, different in that they are based on subjective

---

59. Thielicke, *Ethics*, 1:386.
60. Thielicke, *Ethik*, 3:383.
61. Thielicke, *Ethik*, 3:392.
62. Thielicke, *Ethik*, 3:421.
63. Thielicke cites Brunner in support of this position.
64. "A truncation of eschatology seems to go hand in hand with thinking in terms of natural law" (Thielicke, *Ethics*, 1:427).
65. Thielicke, *Ethics*, 1:428.

and solipsistic premises rather than on communal and social ones. History, he declares, is the sharpest critique of natural law.

One Catholic commentator on Thielicke, Ad van Bentum, sees Thielicke's rejection of Catholic natural law as fundamentally based on a rejection of certain theological presuppositions of natural law. For example, Thielicke dismisses the idea of a creational order of being. Further, he rejects the possibility of natural knowledge of God or the *lex aeterna*, for reason cannot deduce any obligations from nature. Humans are incapable of grasping their own essence rationally—it is only possible in the context of the divine-human relation. Every other definition of human essence is developed in light of, and limited by, specific circumstances; each theory of natural law likewise assumes a notion of the human that characterizes it. The analogy of being is the source of most of these problems, as Thielicke sees it, and he opposes it. But he does allow for what he terms negative natural law, such as expressed in the negative provisions of the Decalogue, which offer limited guidance for human action. Rather than a set of deductions from nature, they express the negative consequences of certain human action, and are applicable to all: Christians and non-Christians alike. Thielicke's dismissal of reason as a source for natural law principles is derived from his understanding of the divine-human relation. Thielicke's theological anthropology limits the competence of reason, and as a consequence natural law is left without a basis sufficient for its claims.

Positive Law

Like his conception of justice, Thielicke sees positive law dialectically. It cannot be simply equated with positivism. Instead, it stands in relation to both ethos and religion, and any adequate understanding of it requires an appreciation of its relation to both of them. As is the case with Barth, a central question for Thielicke is whether a connection exists between divine law and human law. Thielicke finds divine justice to be *sui generis* and essentially discontinuous with human law.[66] The legal order serves the proximate end of facilitating the interactions of persons and containing the damage caused by human sin. Law is an order of preservation, a divinely bestowed remedy provided in response to the Fall, an emergency order.

66. Thielicke speaks interchangeably of law and justice in this context. Of course, they are not the same. While relating divine and human law, he also acknowledges their separateness. It is revealing that Thielicke frames the question of the relationship between the two kinds of law in terms of the possibility of a bridge between divine justice and distributive justice. Obviously the latter is not synonymous with either human law or with justice in its entirety, only with an aspect of it.

Thielicke states that the orders of law and state are based on distributive justice and encompass orders of distribution (civil law) and retribution (criminal law).[67] Law is primarily concerned with the appropriate honoring of the provision of goods and services and less with the needs of the individual.[68] This is because law relies upon generalized rules applicable to all citizens. Arithmetical, commutative justice is premised on human equality and does not address inequality. It is dialectically related to proportional justice because of its need for correction and adaption in order to do justice to individuals. In law, the correction is effected through the application of principles of equity.

How does divine justice relate to positive law? Despite their obvious and deep differences, they are capable of a degree of consonance. Thielicke speaks of the exemplary role divine justice can have for human law. It can and should be a reminder of the transcendence of divine justice and the limits of the human legal order. Further, it affirms the transcendent status of persons participating in that order and for whose sake it exists. The divine covenant conditions the penultimate and provisional order of positive law, endowing it with dignity and contextualizing it as a transition point between creation and the eschatological future of the kingdom. In possessing an interim status, human law shuns presumptuousness. In being aware of the pattern of divine justice, it avoids pretentiousness and admonishes against inordinate preoccupation with immanent ends. Obviously, these attributes are only discernible from the perspective of divine law. Like Brunner and Ellul, Thielicke here proposes a hierarchical relationship between the two kinds of law that rests on certain theological presuppositions about the nature of divine law.

Thielicke does not flesh out thoroughly the relation between divine and human law beyond these rather general statements. The theological interactions he describes may be cogent and persuasive from a perspective of belief, but he says little or nothing to explain how these theological interactions are to be understood in light of the pluralistic premise. For an ethic that emphasizes its relation to reality, this is surprising and unfortunate. Thielicke's concept of divine law complicates engagement with secular law. This is a problem, for if law is to play the role that Thielicke envisions for it, secular legal theorists must have some understanding of it.

---

67. Thielicke, *Ethics*, 1:342, 377.
68. Thielicke, *Ethics*, 1:339.

Criminal Law

A significant portion of the section on law in the *Ethik* is devoted to criminal law, and this demonstrates the importance of Thielicke attaches to this field of law. There are theological reasons for this concentration. As Huber points out, Lutheran tradition has viewed criminal law as paradigmatic for law in its entirety.[69] Given Thielicke's Lutheran orientation, it is not surprising that he views of criminal law as "that most appropriate exemplary case for the theological treatment of law."[70] Criminal law must deal with the interplay of subjective and moral considerations internal to the criminal, as well as with objective acts and omissions that are externally observable. Conflicts can exist between the redemptive heart of divine justice and the punitive rigor of human law.

Many of the writers studied in this book devote some attention to criminal law, particularly the death penalty, but few examine the nature of criminal liability and punishment to the extent that Thielicke does. He treats topics of guilt, punishment, responsibility and deterrence in some detail, extensively discussing relevant legal theories. In his view, criminal law is distinctive for its concern with anthropology.[71] This reflects the importance of the concept of personhood in determining guilt and punishment. While a crime is defined in terms of objective elements of an offense, the intentions and mental state of the accused are also relevant for the determination of guilt. But the treatment of them in criminal law reveals the limitations of legal anthropology in its failure to see the criminal in relative rather than absolute terms. A relative perspective of an accused means seeing her in her social context. "Within law, a human being is not simply an absolute ethical person, whose being stands in relation to a practical logos, but is instead a relative person whose being is substantially defined in terms of a relationship to the legal community."[72] Both the criminal and the legal community stand in relation to each other. Solidarity binds them, and each owes duties to the other. A crime is prosecuted on behalf of the legal community as an offense against it. The community owes the criminal recognition of her

---

69. Huber, *Gerechtigkeit*, 342. Reuter contends that Thielicke's theological construction of law leads to the view that punishment is the main problem to be considered, and therefore he understands law from the perspective of punishment rather than punishment from that of law. See Reuter, *Rechtsethik*, 173. While this statement goes a bit too far in speaking of law generally (concepts such as compromise and emergency orders of preservation form the theological frame for law), it points out an assumption operative in Thielicke's understanding of criminal law.

70. Thielicke, *Ethik*, 3:373.

71. Thielicke, *Ethik*, 3:405.

72. Thielicke, *Ethik*, 3:408.

moral personhood; she is a partner in relationship. Thielicke believes that guilt is only meaningful in the context of personhood. He sees punishment in terms of atonement (or expiation) (*Sühne*). "Atonement is the assumption of punishment through acceptance of it. It, rather than deterrence, is the purpose of punishment."[73] At the time Thielicke was writing, this was an established view in Lutheran social ethics. At the same time it also had its opponents, such as Barth, who rejected it on Christocentric grounds. Barth argued in favor of a pedagogical view of punishment in which punishment is intended to assist in rehabilitation of the prisoner.[74] The legal community is authorized to mete out punishment, but it must also recognize its share of responsibility for the criminal act. This leads Thielicke to speak of the legal community as being causally implicated in crimes committed against it.[75]

Although Thielicke's views of criminal law generally align with the mainstream of traditional Lutheran thinking, they represent an effort to think through certain theoretical and practical aspects of criminal law by means of theological engagement with jurisprudential theory. He recognizes that the secular state does not share this perspective, and in cases of conflict between the state and the church, the church must acknowledge the priority of the state. What is ethically important for Thielicke in criminal law is the possibility of personal rehabilitation. But his understanding of punishment and rehabilitation is overlaid with an emphasis on atonement to an extent that it creates the possibility of a confusion of divine judgment with human punishment.[76] Nevertheless, Thielicke's attention to criminal law acknowledges its importance for theological and ethical reflection on law. For many, criminal law is emblematic of law as a whole. Engagement with it, as Thielicke shows, is a necessary part of a theology of law.

Law and Justice

Underlying all of Thielicke's reflections on law is the concept of justice. For him, justice is a complex concept that incorporates ethical and pragmatic elements. He analyzes justice phenomenologically, historically, and theologically. The result is a multi-faceted, internally differentiated concept

73. Thielicke, *Ethik*, 3:410.

74. Honecker, *Grundriß*, 597.

75. This is reminiscent of Reinhold Niebuhr's statement: "The society which punishes criminals is never so conscious as it might be of the degree to which it is tainted with, and responsible for, the very sins which it abhors and punishes" (Niebuhr, *Interpretation*, 47).

76. On this point, see Huber, *Gerechtigkeit*, 342.

of justice, replete with internal polarities and tensions. As he often does, Thielicke examines justice in terms of practical contexts and under the pressure of concrete situations. Unlike Brunner, Thielicke finds justice irreducible to a single, basic principle. Instead, it is defined in terms of encounters with practical reality. Thielicke's notion of justice is not so much a guiding principle as an interpretative frame in which justification contends with sinfulness, and ideals with reality.

Viewed phenomenologically, justice contains a tension between partial and complete justice. This is the tension inherent in compromise. In practice, justice is always perspectival—it depends on the individual who assesses the justness of an action from her own point of view. Every value order is perspectival according to the valuing agent; consequently, society is characterized by a plurality of value orders. Every concrete representation of justice is inescapably partial. Justice does not exclude partiality, inescapably it reflects it. "The just person is always an advocate of partial order *vis a vis* other partial orders."[77]

The "Magna Charta" of justice is the *suum cuique* principle, but Thielicke believes it, by itself, to be incapable of supplying a satisfactory definition of justice. This is because of the irreducible fact of differences among persons, such that it is impossible to determine the entitlement as well as the preferences of each person. Human difference manifests itself in all human activity, especially in matters of moral and cultural value.

In his analysis of its content, Thielicke considers classical and Christian ideas of justice. He finds classical theories such as Aristotle's fail satisfactorily to relate equality and difference. Instead, justice is variegated into different forms, such as arithmetic and distributive justice, without a unifying foundation. In Christian tradition, Thielicke finds that justice is a fundamental, divine attribute of a covenantal relation. It is quintessentially individualistic, and therefore is fundamentally distinguishable from the generality of law. The form of justice that relates to positive law is human justice (*iustitia terrena*), and it bears the characteristics of all human concepts that are framed and interpreted under conditions of everyday reality. At the same time, human justice must remain mindful of the relativity and finiteness of human law that seeks to realize it. In its failure to do so, it may be tempted to idolize law, or engage in fanatical pursuit of mundane justice. The role of human justice, for Thielicke, is to mediate and arbitrate within the sphere of reality, rather than project unrealistic ideals.

As a result, Thielicke sees justice as dialectical and marked by internal tensions. One is a tension illustrated by the definitions of justice and

---

77. Thielicke, *Ethik*, 3:324.

justness. Ideally, a just person is capable of discerning the ethical ramifications of the acts and omissions of herself and others. Such judgments transcend one's own value preferences and partial interests; they hint at the existence of a general, impartial order of value. Further, there is no unified order of justice, instead there are multiple orders of partial justice. Justice is inescapably perspectival and contextual; it is unavailable in purely objective form. It inhabits specific domains or spheres that often collide or overlap. Justice in the context of a commercial transaction will differ from justice in the context of family law or criminal law. Each sphere is partial in that its values and objectives are assessed in light of its particular circumstances and in light of the value preferences of that sphere. The valuing criteria may be formally identical, but their content will vary contextually. A just order consists of a holistic aggregate of partial, individual orders of value.

As an example of the perspectival character of justice, Thielicke mentions an example of a governmental agency responsible for cultural affairs. It views the rightness of its actions in light of its particular objective of promoting cultural activities. Its determination of the justness and appropriateness of its actions will at times conflict with those of another governmental agency that controls the funds for all governmental agencies. That agency will evaluate expenditures by the cultural agency according to economic metrics. It is responsible for overseeing expenditures by all government agencies. Tension results between justice understood from one perspective (the cultural agency) and from another (the finance agency). Thielicke's point is that there is always a potential tension among the ethical claims intrinsic to different spheres of activity and responsibility in which individuals act. He states, "This conflict among the partial forms of justice rules out any 'total' justice and entails that each separate sphere of justice will assert its claims of interest against other ones."[78] This characteristic also applies to law. "Law appears . . . only in perspectival, fragmented and distorted form, not as *the* law."[79] Given this situation, law must acknowledge the perspectival character of justice, and must aspire, procedurally and substantively, to transcend partiality in the direction of comprehensive fairness.

Justice enters into contact with law via its ethical dimension, and manifests itself in the pursuit of legal community. Law seeks the pragmatic, ordered coexistence of human beings through an *ordo convivendi*, while justice proceeds from the distinctiveness of the individual and coordinates it with that of other individuals. Thielicke identifies a tension in law generated by the "hiatus between normative and pragmatic determination . . . between

78. Thielicke, *Ethik*, 3:327.
79. Thielicke, *Ethik*, 3:329.

justice and purpose."[80] Justice is a transcendent "*tertium comparatonis*" that stands above and relativizes the particular interests of individuals. It reveals the contingency of positive law through its reflection of social and cultural circumstances. It is the norm of norms: the *norma normans*. Justice and law accordingly exist in relation to each other, but that relation is dialectical rather than hierarchical. Typically, justice manifests itself in law in the form of equity. Equity assists law in remedying its ethical shortcomings, but only within the possibilities of the present aeon: "Law is a part of a world that is not itself healthy (*heil*) but is enmeshed in self-contradiction."[81]

Admittedly, law in its pragmatism normally keeps its distance from the aspirations of justice. That does not mean, however, that the relation between law and justice should be slackened so that the relation becomes merely theoretical. Rather, questions of justice are implicit in all the functions of law: legislation, adjudication, compliance, and punishment. A more open acknowledgment of their existence in law could prompt greater awareness and scrutiny of them, and perhaps create possibilities for law's improvement. At the same time, Thielicke appropriately warns against the absolutization of justice. Law, he believes, will never be the means to absolute justice. The pursuit of it can only result in fanaticism; appropriate (*zweckmäßige*) pragmatism is its corrective.[82] Absolutes are consistently forced to yield to what Thielicke refers to as the "law of reality." Given this situation, every Christian ethic must be patterned on some version of the two kingdoms doctrine in that it differentiates between different modes of theological/ethical reality.[83]

Divine and Human Justice

As noted, Thielicke contends that justice as an attribute of a person or an institution is pluralistic and not unitary. An overarching, universally embraceable idea of justice is unavailable.[84] That is to say that Thielicke envisions justice primarily in the form of justness. Yet like other values, justness reflects the fragmented and disjointed circumstances of existence in the present aeon. This would seem to lead to a segmented and individualized concept of justice. But it seems that Thielicke is in fact seeking to emphasize that there is no Archimedean point from which justice can be determined.

80. Thielicke, *Ethik*, 3:299.
81. Thielicke, *Ethik*, 3:343.
82. Thielicke, *Ethik*, 3:309.
83. Thielicke, *Ethik*, 3:310.
84. Thielicke, *Ethik*, 3:327.

As a touchstone for understanding justice, Thielicke embraces what he terms "biblical justice." It is relational rather than perspectival; it exists *coram Deo*—before God. This places humans in a new divine relation, rooted in salvation history (*Heilsgeschichte*) and created through covenantal divine self-disclosure. Justice of this kind is not a matter of the fulfillment of legalistic decrees so much as "countersigning" of the divine covenant in response to divine initiative. It is personal, rather than institutionalized, instrumental justice. In contrast to human law, biblical justice manifests itself less as rational order and more as divinely established law. "What God does and so far as he does it, it is just. His own thoughts are the source and criteria of his legal assertions and enforcement."[85] This amounts to a divine command concept of justice.

Given the contrasts between them, the challenge is to bridge these contrasting understandings of justice. What, Thielicke asks, is the *tertium comparatonis* that relates them to each other? He believes any viable answer must distinguish between divine and human justice. Each functions on a different level. Divine justice is concerned with personal destiny in its trans-temporal significance. Human justice is expressed, imperfectly, in law as concerned with the relations of persons to each other. It is not eternal but relative and conditioned by time and circumstance. Justice must assume different forms because the human situation differs before and after the Fall and continues in the present aeon to be simultaneously redeemed and unredeemed. "From a theological perspective, the legal order is the ways and means God does justice to the human person, a person summoned to salvation, yet who in his earthly interactions is fallen."[86]

From this it follows that the ontic relation between divine justice and positive law is, at most, indirect. Positive law requires justice to guide development of procedural and substantive rights against the grain of self-interest. It is grounded in rationality and is subject to objective oversight. But this is the work of human justice. As noted, it is altogether different from divine justice, which is created by divine initiative through the covenant with human persons. Divine justice possesses ultimate insight into what is due to each person—precisely what human justice lacks: "The justice of divine judging does not manifest itself in the visible rationality of a legal order, which would be evident in and of itself."[87] The quality of divine justice is therefore entirely different from human justice; it is an expression of the

---

85. Thielicke, *Ethik*, 3:350.
86. Thielicke, *Ethik*, 3:375.
87. Thielicke, *Ethik*, 3:349.

divine self not bound by any objective order or obligation. The divine essence is justice itself.

Thielicke here posits a stark contrast between divine justice and human law: it is a relation of essential incongruence. The surd between them can only be affirmed in faith.[88] He wishes to avoid any idea of divine justice that would contradict or undermine the supremacy of grace and introduce eudaemonistic elements into it. It treats humans not as functional/economic actors but as relational persons; it is essentially covenantal rather than contractual or transactional.

As a result, the relation between divine justice and human law for Thielicke is equivocal. On one level, neither has anything in common, formally or structurally, with the other. If they are confused with each other, distortions result in the form of works-righteousness, theocracy, and enthusiasm.[89] At the same time, they are related in that both are concerned with human salvation, although in different ways. The respective competence of each must be acknowledged and respected. Divine justice is manifested in and through justification by faith, while mundane justice is concerned with the provisional, interim task of helping persons to coexist. Divine justice is animated by active, seeking love; human justice by effectual, preservative measures. In referring to *justicia terrana* as consisting of "emergency orders" and "orders of patience," such as law, Thielicke revises the notion of the orders of creation advocated by Althaus, Brunner and others to emphasize both human agency and divine solicitude.[90]

Despite these differences, both divine justice and positive law are concerned with rescuing humans from their predicament. Divine justice seeks this in the context of covenant and justification; positive law does so through the tolerable resolution of conflict and an appropriate distribution of benefits and burdens. In this respect, they share a "fundamental commonality."[91] Christians are challenged to observe both without confusing them. Even within a mundane legal order the love commandment has a place in acknowledging the transcendence of persons in face of positive law. A Christian judge, for example, must consider that litigants are not only disputants, but are also persons divinely loved and redeemed, and with whom God means well.[92] The practical consequence of this recognition is implicit and indirect. This does not relax the demands of law. Perhaps it motivates

---

88. Thielicke, *Ethik*, 3:350.
89. Thielicke, *Ethik*, 3:377.
90. See generally Althaus, *Divine Command*; Brunner, *Justice*.
91. Thielicke, *Ethik*, 3:377.
92. Thielicke, *Ethik*, 3:378.

caritive acts, reform of law or other such actions; Thielicke unfortunately does not tell us much about them. On this point, he seems to be describing an ethic of disposition more than anything else.

In short, positive law is a penultimate, relative institution, an instrument of preservation under fundamentally adverse circumstances. "It is charged with being a rescue service, and very relative, internally divided and incomplete, to be maintained as an interim order."[93] This exemplifies the character of law as compromise. It reflects the ambiguity of all mundane orders under conditions of the present aeon, in which divine commands are distorted by sin, and every expression of justice has a partial, incomplete quality.

Concluding Observations: Law as Concession

Thielicke's theology of law is marked by its dialectical character as well as its grounding of law in a classically Lutheran context. Its themes include the simultaneity of redeemed/unredeemed human existence, the central significance of divine grace and justification by faith, and the eschatological tension between present and future. Thielicke is particularly concerned to explicate the social/ethical function of positive law and its complex relation to morality. His interpretation is inflected by the contrast between the exteriority of law and the interiority of morality. In its external character, law is connected closely with the maintenance of order and the realization of proximate justice through the use of coercion, while morality is rooted in an interior, personal relation between self and God, and self in others. Thielicke's is a deeply theological vision, and reflects the traumatic exigencies of the postwar and Cold War contexts in which he wrote. Law's sober dialectics, its constraints and its susceptibility to subversion for political ends emphasize the importance of a theological frame for it in order to preserve it from ethical irrelevance. What is understated in Thielicke's reflections is law's capacity to accomplish acts of proximate justice that are intrinsically worthy even though they are the result of compromises between practical goals and the demands of absolute justice.

While Thielicke's notion of law as compromise endows it with a strong sense of realism, it prompts the question whether it over-emphasizes the pragmatic element. Does it underestimate law's ethical resources and discourage critique and reform of law, something so important for other writers? Thielicke's conviction is that law's pragmatism should be balanced against the demands of justice and morality. To balance normative and

---

93. Thielicke, *Ethik*, 3:379.

pragmatic elements as Thielicke attempts to do it requires concessions to pragmatism at the expense of ethical aspiration. Much of Thielicke's realism derives from his anthropology. It strongly, if not excessively, emphasizes human fallenness and the resulting provisionality of social institutions and arrangements. This leads Thielicke, unlike Pannenberg and Huber, to say little about the connection between law and love.

Thielicke's theology of law is primarily addressed to the reflections and actions of the Christian believer. Its theological aspects would therefore seem not to have much resonance with a secular audience. Yet such a categorical judgment is perhaps too peremptory. It certainly is the case that Thielicke holds that law must be theologically grounded, and its ethical significance only becomes fully apparent within a comprehensive vision of human life. But Thielicke's approach contain insights intelligible outside of a theological context. Two elements in Thielicke's analysis are particularly suggestive in this connection. First, though law as compromise assumes the provisional nature of *de lege lata* in that it allows for revision and development. Thielicke bases this theologically on the impetus of eschatology, but he also contends that law contains a tension between fixedness and evolution that keeps it open for improvement. Second, law must always be concerned with ethics and justice. While they are ultimately measured by the demands of divine justice, human beings must contend with the demands of practical reality in adapting and applying law. The improvement of law in the direction of greater justness can be a common cause between believers and fellow citizens, even though their motivations may be different.

VII

Wolfhart Pannenberg

Law as Mutuality and Reciprocity

Wolfhart Pannenberg (1928–2014) is considered by many to be one of the preeminent Protestant theologians of the latter half of the twentieth century. From 1968 until his retirement in 1994 he was Professor of Systematic Theology at the University of Munich; previously he taught in Mainz and Wuppertal in Germany. Pannenberg published prolifically, culminating with his three-volume *Systematic Theology* (1988–94). Many of his books and articles have appeared in English translation.[1] The breadth of Pannenberg's interests was vast. In addition to his concentration on the classical themes of theology, he explored other subjects from a theological perspective, among them sociology, science, nature, anthropology, politics and ethics. Pannenberg repeatedly addressed questions of law and jurisprudence, beginning with essays in the early 1960s and continuing up to a publication that appeared in 2004. For the most part, these writings consist of thematic essays, a form Pannenberg often used.[2] In addition to these essays, portions of Pannenberg's larger works treat law and jurisprudential themes, though often as subsidiary topics. His concern with law reflects his view that law is strongly tied to ethics, an area to which he returned after completing his *Systematic Theology*.[3] Taken together, Pannenberg's writings on law constitute a coherent legal theology, though one that has received limited

---

1. See the bibliography of Pannenberg's publications, including all English translations, through 2008 that appeared as an appendix to Pannenberg, "Intellectual Pilgrimage," 157.
2. See, e.g., Pannenberg, *Basic Questions*; *Beiträge zur Ethik*; *Beiträge zur Theologie*.
3. See, e.g., Pannenberg, *Grundlagen*.

attention, especially in Anglophone literature.[4] This is a consequence of the fact that many of Pannenberg's key essays on law have not been translated into English, aside from an important early essay.[5]

Elements of Pannenberg's Approach

Pannenberg approaches law as a theologian and not as a legal philosopher. His primary concern is not with jurisprudential theory for its own sake, but with law as a social institution with meaningful theological and ethical implications. At the same time, he seeks to critique contemporary notions of law by examining its roots in religious history and tradition, as well as its normative bases. Though Pannenberg addresses law from a Christian, and specifically Protestant, perspective, his approach is neither parochial nor sectarian. He emphasizes the rational accessibility and accountability of theology as he conceives it. His theology seeks to present a comprehensive view of reality, and he has long sought out, and participated in, inter-religious and secular dialogue on a wide range of topics including science, history, and metaphysics. Though recognizably Protestant and Lutheran, Pannenberg was quite active throughout his career in ecumenical activities.[6]

In several of his later writings on law, Pannenberg also examines the interaction of law and secularity. In particular, he addresses the impact of secularization on the interpretation of legal norms, and the consequences that secularization poses for the social experience of Christians as well as for adherents of other faith traditions. While his analyses relate to a German context, especially with respect to his analysis of the German Constitutional Court's jurisprudence regarding the individual right to self-determination contained in the German Basic Law (*Grundgesetz*), the substance of his reflections on these matters is applicable to other political-legal cultures as well.

A further characteristic of Pannenberg's theology of law is his attention to the historical context in which reflection on law occurs. In his foundational essay "On the Theology of Law" (1963), he notes the effects of World War II on attitudes in Germany toward law, prompting urgent

---

4. One of the few German analyses of Pannenberg's theology of law is Maihold, *Recht durch Liebe* (1994), a doctoral dissertation. Maihold's study, however, antedates several of Pannenberg's most important writings on the topic, which appeared after 2000. Also see Shingleton, "Mutuality and Recognition."

5. All translations of the German texts of Pannenberg's writings cited are my own.

6. He has also devoted attention to religious pluralism. See, e.g., Pannenberg, "Christliche Rechtsüberzeugungen," 256–66.

reconsideration of its basis. Pannenberg devotes considerable space in the essay to describing the status of contemporary discussions of theologies of law, closely examining and critiquing Barth, Brunner, and Wolf.[7]

The course of Pannenberg's thinking on law reflects a continuing interest in the anthropological dimension of law. In connection with ongoing debates of the 1970s in Germany about the place of theology in the secular university, Pannenberg became more deeply drawn to anthropology. Reflecting later on that period, he stated: "In dealing with the God of the Bible theology has to claim all reality—and first of all the human reality—to be the creation of God. To that end . . . it seemed necessary to claim to human reality as it is studied and presented by the secular disciplines and to try to show that is necessarily related to religion and to God."[8]

In addition to this interest in anthropology, Pannenberg is also a thoroughly historical thinker. He finds the biblical perspective to be pervaded with history. From it, "The world is seen in its totality as history."[9] But he argues that history cannot serve, by itself, as the starting point for an adequate understanding of law, because it "presupposes other, comparatively abstract and provisional aspects of mankind and human behavior in respect to man's basis in nature and to man's social relationships."[10] This leads him to push back farther, looking to sociology and anthropology to provide an "understanding of man that encompasses human nature in concrete events in the life of the individual."[11] His approach to law seeks to do justice to contrasting dimensions: general and concrete, historical and comprehensive, personal and social.

Pannenberg's concept of law arises out of, and is essentially shaped by, a convergence of several of his fundamental concerns. First, he is convinced that anthropology should serve as a point of departure for reflection on human and divine reality. He adduces several reasons for this position, but underlying them is Pannenberg's conviction that post-Enlightenment trends in philosophy and the social sciences have coalesced around an anthropological perspective.[12] Further, he contends that history and eschatology are indispensable for understanding reality as essentially whole and unified. Therefore, the data of anthropology (which for Pannenberg

7. Pannenberg, "Theology of Law," 23.
8. Pannenberg, "Intellectual Pilgrimage," 157.
9. Pannenberg, "Theology of Law," 34.
10. Pannenberg, "Theology of Law," 39.
11. Pannenberg, "Theology of Law," 39.
12. In the seventeenth century, Pannenberg writes, "In the place of religion, human nature became the basis of the social order in public culture" (Pannenberg, *Grundlagen*, 9).

includes biological, cultural and sociological elements) must be historically interpreted. They must be situated historically, and their insights must be viewed with respect to their interaction with historical developments. History is the dimension of becoming, and without it, anthropological findings remain abstract and static.

Law is not isolated from cultural developments. As noted, Pannenberg devotes considerable attention in his writings to secularization. He finds its impact to be culturally ambiguous, and sees it as particularly demoralizing for religion, and especially for Western Christianity.[13] Secularism also has impacted law by demonstrating that it is not an autonomous domain but one that participates in the historicity of all social institutions. Law is inherently reflective of the dynamics of broader social processes.

Eschatology is a significant theme in Pannenberg's theology, and for his theology of law as well. According to one commentator, relatively few attempts have been made to establish an eschatological-theological grounding of law; Pannenberg's is one of the few.[14] Law is interpreted from the perspective of the coming kingdom of God proleptically announced through Jesus Christ. This leads Pannenberg to avoid grounding law in natural law or the orders of creation but instead in its social context within the unfolding of history and its movement towards eschatological culmination.[15]

Finally, law bears directly on Pannenberg's concerns with ethics, or more precisely, with what he sees as the contemporary displacement of religion by ethics as the foundation of political community. The social status of law reflects this ethical focus. Given the erosion of ethical consensus in advanced North Atlantic societies, law is threatened with instrumentalization. Pannenberg wishes to retrieve and rehabilitate law's neglected dimensions, and this includes its relation to ethics.

The Importance of History

Of these four themes—anthropology, secularization, history and ethics—history has particular significance for Pannenberg. In his view, an adequate theological concept of history must be able to accommodate and account for historical development in its broadest sense, including contingency. History is only fully explained in light of the whole of reality; it is a continuum of contingent events that finds totality when seen in light of the biblical God:

---

13. Pannenberg's critique of secularism is summarized in his *Christianity and Secularism*.
14. Nordsieck, *Recht*, 72.
15. Nordsieck, *Recht*, 72.

"It has its unity only the form of God's history."[16] A theological approach to history does not draw on a "supernatural supply of materials, but it does place the phenomenon of existence in a different and broader framework than does any philosophy which asks its questions in the Greek manner."[17] Historically informed theology "is accessible to all in more comprehensive terms than it is possible for philosophy to attain on the basis of its Greek origins."[18] Pannenberg repeatedly contrasts Greek notions of cosmic order with a Hebraic understanding of history as dynamic and eschatological. In his view, law essentially and necessarily reflects and participates in historical processes. Therefore, historical approaches to the understanding of law are most adequate for grasping the complexity of law in light of its development. Pannenberg acknowledges the possibility of alternative accounts of law, such as positivism, which are based on an "independent subjective view of humanity."[19] But the understanding of history implied in such approaches is, in his view, less comprehensive than those informed by biblical perspectives.

Pannenberg's view of history is connected with other motifs that figure prominently in his theology, such as destiny, salvation and futurity. These are developed more explicitly in his larger theological works, and treated more allusively in his theology of law. Indeed, Pannenberg's analysis of law would have benefitted from a more sustained development of these themes alongside of the central themes of community and history. In any event, Pannenberg rejects the notion that his interpretation of law is relevant only for those who are sympathetic to his theology as a whole. He contends that his assertions about human history and its unity in a divine ground stand up to scrutiny when judged by the criterion of adequacy. Obviously, this claim depends on what Pannenberg means by adequacy.

Pannenberg formulates the criterion of adequacy in terms of the ability of a statement to "deal more adequately with anthropological phenomena than do other explanations."[20] By this, Pannenberg seems to mean that adequacy is a function of the ability to interpret data about, in this case, law. Theology must develop theories that account more satisfactorily for the historical nature of law than those found in the philosophy of law.[21] While

---

16. Pannenberg, "Theology of Law," 34.
17. Pannenberg, "Theology of Law," 34.
18. Pannenberg, "Theology of Law," 34.
19. Pannenberg, "Theology of Law," 35.
20. Pannenberg, "Theology of Law," 34.
21. Pannenberg, "Theology of Law," 34.

Pannenberg does not elaborate further on adequacy in this connection, it connotes, at a minimum, comprehensiveness, thoroughness and depth.

An Anthropological Orientation

As already noted, Pannenberg has embraced an anthropological starting point for his interpretation of human nature, and indeed for his theology as a whole. He describes this is as a response to the "philosophical concentration on the human person as subject of all experience" and the need for Christianity to assert "a sound claim to the universal validity . . . of the truth of its faith and message."[22] Some observers discern a continuous progression in Pannenberg's thought in a more comprehensively anthropological direction.[23] While his embrace of anthropology derives generally from his views of history, humanity and religion, Pannenberg also justifies his anthropological point of departure on grounds intrinsic to anthropology itself. His most systematic and explicit efforts to do so are contained in two volumes: *What is Man?*, which appeared in 1962, and a more extended volume published in 1985, *Anthropology in Theological Perspective*.[24] Two arguments advanced in those books deserve particular reference here: (1) the contemporary competence of anthropology for understanding humanity, and (2) the relevance of anthropology for the consideration of human law.

Pannenberg believes that anthropology has come to occupy central place in human self-interpretation. "We live in the age of anthropology." he declares.[25] He identifies three basic reasons for the rise of the anthropological perspective. First, modern philosophy and theology has turned from the natural world to humanity as the basis for conceiving God. To the extent it did not become atheistic or agnostic, philosophy showed increasing determination in conceiving God as a presupposition of human subjectivity and to that extent it thought of him in terms of humanity and not of the world.[26] Second, Pannenberg sees theology as compelled, after Marx and Feuerbach, to ground itself affirmatively and demonstrably lest it fall victim to the critique that it is merely a human projection. Further, theology must be intrinsically concerned with human history and society, and it must establish its truths in comprehensive terms. In so doing, it positions itself against notions of religion that view it as a matter of individual choice, belonging to

22. Pannenberg, *Anthropology*, 13, 15.
23. See, e.g., Wong, "Pannenberg's Thought," 382–402.
24. Pannenberg, *What Is Man?*; Pannenberg, *Anthropology*.
25. Pannenberg, *What Is Man?*, 1.
26. Pannenberg, *Anthropology*, 11.

the private sphere of autonomous individuals. For him, these assumptions fundamentally conflict with the biblical affirmation that God is the Creator of all reality.[27] Pannenberg's conviction that anthropology is an essential theme for contemporary theology pervades his theological program, and he has addresses it at length in the second volume of his *Systematic Theology*.[28]

Pannenberg cites two historical causes for the modern anthropocentric concentration. For one, the confessional wars of the seventeenth century led to the re-orientation of society and culture along political rather than religious lines; indeed, it led to the segmentation and privatization of religion altogether. Second, the rise of the physical sciences showed that nature could be understood without reference to God. This led, in turn, to the sense that nature was no longer a point of departure for the understanding of God.

Pannenberg sees contemporary anthropology as an empirically oriented discipline that is not only anthropocentric, but that also advances a view of the human subject as religiously detached. Unsurprisingly, he finds these assumptions unsatisfying. Pannenberg consequently argues in favor of a critical appropriation by theology of anthropology that uncovers the implicit religious themes inherent in human behavior and social life. Theology may not simply adopt anthropological explications, it must appropriate the human phenomenon described in anthropology. He writes, "The aim is to lay theological claim to the human phenomena in the anthropological disciplines. To this end, secular accounts are accepted as a provisional version of the objective reality, a version that needs to be expanded and deepened by showing that the anthropological datum itself contains a further and theologically relevant dimension."[29] This means that the anthropological data must be placed in a "different and broader framework" that employs more comprehensive, historical terms than philosophy derived from Greek origins.[30]

Pannenberg proceeds to relate anthropology to theology by seeking to articulate the theological implications of anthropological data. Two examples serve to illustrate this approach. According to social anthropologists such as Arnold Gehlen and Helmut Plessner, human beings are distinguished by an attitude of openness to the world (*Weltoffenheit*). This relates not only to the given world, but transcends any possible framework

---

27. Pannenberg develops this theme at length in Pannenberg, *Systematic Theology*, 2:1–161.

28. See generally, Pannenberg, *Systematic Theology*, 2:177–245.

29. Pannenberg, *Systematic Theology*, 2:19–20.

30. Pannenberg, "Theology of Law," 34.

derivable from the world. "Man seeks his nature beyond everything that he finds at hand, because he does not already have his nature and cannot find it in the world as it exists, either in nature or in culture."[31] For Pannenberg, this means that openness is intrinsically oriented to the future: the relationship between the two is symbiotic. Humans possess a certain constitutive openness because existence itself has a partial, fragmentary character; the future is fundamental in human experience because history is dependent on the completion of subsequent happenings for determination of the ultimate significance of every proximate occurrence. Pannenberg takes this a step further by connecting openness with transcendence toward the unbounded horizon of being. Openness points beyond the world to an unknown reality that holds out the possibility of fulfillment. This reality is given, by language, the name of God. Nevertheless, that naming is provisional and elusive: "What God is remains for the time being unknown."[32]

A second example of Pannenberg's reliance on anthropology is his interpretation of language. Just as openness leads human beings beyond any given notion of the world, at the same time it leads them to return to the experienced world. Language, he says, is "the first principal form of the human mastery over existence."[33] It enables humans to control the diversity of the perceptive world through creation of a notional world. Language makes conceptual thought possible, and also gives rise to imaginative thinking. In terms of significance, imagination is for humans what instinct is for animals. Not only does it engender creativity, but it also brings the contents of memory to light. Through these and other functions, language enables novelty through imagination and history through memory. Both of these capacities are key in Pannenberg's understanding of human existence. Novelty reflects the provisionality of each given situation; history traces its arc of unfolding in the future. In his interpretation of both these functions, openness and language, Pannenberg proceeds from fundamental, anthropologically attested abilities to elucidate their implicitly religious aspects. In *Anthropology in Theological Perspective*, Pannenberg seeks to demonstrate that humanness is inseparable from the religious thematic, as suggested by the biological characteristic of openness to the world and in the formation of personality and culture, including the foundations of law.[34]

31. Pannenberg, "Theology of Law," 41.
32. Pannenberg, "Theology of Law," 42.
33. Pannenberg, *What Is Man?*, 14–15.
34. Pannenberg states that he is concerned with fundamental-theological anthropology, rather than dogmatic theology. The former "turns its attention directly to the phenomena of human existence as investigated in human biology, psychology, cultural anthropology or sociology and examines the findings with an eye to implications that may be relevant to religion and theology" (Pannenberg, *Anthropology*, 21).

Pannenberg's anthropological approach also reflects his commitment to the possibility of comprehensive, universal truth. In several of his writings, Pannenberg argues for an understanding of truth as coherence.[35] To his mind, truth must present a comprehensive account of the whole of reality; he is opposed to the equation of truth with specialized knowledge of segments of reality.[36] Among other things, this means that he does not begin with a specific ethical tradition or doctrinal affirmation. This approach comes through clearly in his assessment of other contemporary theologies of law, such as those of Karl Barth, Emil Brunner and Erik Wolf. Their efforts are inadequate in Pannenberg's judgment because they proceed from, and are dependent upon, overt or covert theological presuppositions that are posited rather than rather than grounded in generally accessible phenomena. Of course, it bears asking whether Pannenberg's convictions about history do not also rest on theological premises.

Such presuppositions often contain limitations. In "On the Theology of Law," Pannenberg acknowledges Barth's appreciation of the "historical uniqueness of biblical thought" but criticizes him for his reliance on analogy, which results in "the loss of the historicity of the contents of law."[37] Barth's analogical efforts, Pannenberg contends, prevent him from finding access to "actual legal reality."[38] As for Brunner, Pannenberg finds his concept of law as ordinance deficient because ordinances are abstractions that do not reflect the realities of historicity and human sin.[39] Further, law as ordinance fails to provide a convincing alternative to positivism in that it rests on outdated metaphysical premises, particularly the supposition that values are immune from temporal change. "Historical thinking appears to have dissolved every absolute standard."[40] Consequently, for Pannenberg, the theological grounding of law in an order of creation ironically has a "strong tendency to positivism."[41] History must be restored in its depth and comprehensiveness. Through its study of the development of human cultures, anthropology can contribute to the retrieval of the historical dimension, provided it is not prejudiced by reductionist presumptions about historicity and religiosity.

35. See Pannenberg, "What Is Truth?"
36. Grenz, *Reason for Hope*, 38–40.
37. Pannenberg, "Theology of Law," 32.
38. Pannenberg, "Theology of Law," 33.
39. Pannenberg, "Theology of Law," 26–27.
40. Pannenberg, "Theology of Law," 24.
41. Pannenberg, "Theology of Law," 25.

Pannenberg's basing of theological reflection on law on anthropological data rather than theological premises gives it a historical-evolutionary character. This is consistent with his theology as a whole. Historical understanding without the benefit of anthropological observation is inadequate, and yields a vision of humanity and human behavior that is "comparatively abstract with respect to nature and social relationships."[42] It must be combined with an appreciation of the role of evolution in laws and societies. Anthropology and history must be brought together: "A theology of law is on its own ground only where the formulations of law are seen in historical perspective."[43]

As for Pannenberg's own conception of law, it is connected with a postwar movement in German jurisprudence known as the anthropological school of law. One of its leaders was Ernst-Joachim Lampe, a German legal philosopher and editor of a journal in which one of Pannenberg's important essays on law, "Recht und Religion," appeared.[44] Lampe developed an anthropologically based jurisprudence he called "genetic legal theory." According to that theory, legal systems result from an ongoing process of biological and cultural evolution, determined in large part by certain "anthropological constants." These constants are basic human needs that persist throughout the fluctuations of human history. In Lampe's words, "Every law, whether in the past, present or future, must be based on the essential characteristics of the human being and must arrange its norms accordingly."[45] In the judgment of James Herget, Lampe's theory presents an "almost natural law view, emphasizing the basic similarities exhibited by all persons and cultures."[46]

Pannenberg's affirmation of a pre-thematic religious orientation of human beings has drawn both questions and criticism. Some have contended that it reflects the importation of theological categories into the interpretation of empirical data. On the other hand, some have found significant correlations between the anthropological data and Pannenberg's interpretation of them.[47] His approach has also been endorsed by Martin Honecker, a prominent German theological ethicist.[48]

42. Pannenberg, "Intellectual Pilgrimage," 39.
43. Pannenberg, *Grundlagen*, 38.
44. Pannenberg, "Recht und Religion," 48–59.
45. Lampe, "Rechtsanthropologie Heute," 232.
46. Herget, *German Legal Philosophy*, 17.
47. Olson, "Pannenberg's Theological Anthropology," 161–69.
48. Honecker, *Grundriß*, 583. Honecker criticizes Pannenberg, however, in two respects: for his reliance on the law of the Hebrew Bible to establish a relation between divinity and law, and for his personalization of law through the concepts of recognition and mutuality, as discussed below.

Natural Law

Pannenberg's anthropological-developmental interpretation of law prompts the question of how he views natural law. His affinity for anthropological and historical perspectives leads him to be reserved about the contemporary plausibility of natural law. In Pannenberg's interpretation of the natural law tradition, it functioned in the biblical era as a source of legal norms that were an alternative to cultic law. It provided a basis for distinguishing between the essence of Jewish law and its non-essential accretions. In the development of early Christian thought, evolving interpretations led to a bifurcation into relative and absolute versions of natural law. Pannenberg agrees with Troeltsch's contention that relative natural law became a dogmatic cornerstone of early Christian social teaching, holding that natural law reflected the post-Adamic condition of fallen humanity. It modified stoic notions of primordial freedom by emphasizing the role of sin in human life. Relative natural law better accounted for institutionally imposed limitations on human freedom (such as slavery) than did stoicism with its notion of a Golden Age. In this respect, relative natural law was both a reflection of, and a remedy for, human sin.

Later, the confessional wars of the sixteenth century led to development of rationalized forms of natural law, exemplified in Calvin's notion of rationally derived divine law. The emergence of constitutional law theories helped to sever natural law from its confessional and religious foundations, although religion remained important for the legitimation of legal institutions. Eventually, natural law theories were undermined by the historical school of jurisprudence. In Pannenberg's view, the historical school contributed to the rise of historical relativism and eventually led to positivism. The postwar revival of natural law was largely a Catholic undertaking, though it had parallels in Protestant thought in the concept of the orders of creation.

While Pannenberg respects the historical importance of natural law, he nevertheless considers it to be essentially unavailable as a contemporary source or influence for positive law.[49] "One can hardly speak nowadays of natural law in a formulation that can claim transcultural validity."[50]

---

49. Hoon Woo has argued that there is a nomological dimension in Pannenberg's ethical thought, and that natural law "occupies an important place in Pannenberg's ethics" (Woo, "Natural Law," 348). It is true that Pannenberg refers to natural law as an enduring theme in ethics since it figures theologically in the relation of law and gospel. But it has limited significance for positive law. More important are the anthropological dimensions of human nature and sociality. Pannenberg sees mutuality as the common anthropological claim and natural law doctrines. As discussed above, this is an idea rather than a legal or ethical norm to which positive law can refer.

50. Pannenberg, "Christliche Rechtsüberzeugungen," 256.

Nevertheless, Pannenberg commends natural law's affirmation of human nature.[51] "[Natural law's] enduring element of truth," he writes, "may perhaps consist in the fact that [it] keeps alive the question of shared human nature. The core element of these conditions and of natural law itself is the principle of mutuality."[52] Before analyzing Pannenberg's notion of this principle, attention should first be directed to his understanding of how law relates to the cultural phenomena of custom and social practice.

Custom, Ethos, Law

Pannenberg places law within an anthropological continuum of practices and institutions that order communal life, ranging from custom to ethos to religion. Human communities require structures for their existence and for the interactions of its members. Those structures require, in turn, a modicum of order. In the earliest stages of social development, order was secured by custom congruent with cosmic order, as mediated through institutions such as a monarchy or a quasi-legislative person or body (*nomothetis*).[53] For Pannenberg, custom typically has the form of practices or customs (*Brauchtum*) that primarily protect social status and expectations rather than establish a hierarchy of values. As societies evolve, custom tends to degenerate, and other ordering institutions arise. This creates the need for more explicit norms to secure social stability and to protect the weaker from the stronger. The decline of custom thus gives rise to law, though obviously the boundary between the two is fluid. Initially, law as derivative from custom stood apart from ethics; Pannenberg contends that ethics first arose as a distinct category of reflection when law ceased to provide an immutable guide to human conduct. This reverses many commonly held notions of law as derivative of ethics.

In its inception, law, like custom, reflects a sense of cosmic order. As an example, Pannenberg cites Socrates' concept of *nomos*, which reflects cosmic *dike*, an overarching, pervasive order. In early Greek thought, *dike* reflected a divine distributive order, and human laws were to be aligned with that cosmic order. Eventually this notion was undermined by a realization of the mutability of human law in the Greek *polis*, which led to a sense that it was ultimately arbitrary, at least in comparison to immutable divine

---

51. Pannenberg, *Grundlagen*, 59.

52. The German term Pannenberg uses is "*Gegenseitigkeit*," which connotes both mutuality and reciprocity. Most English translations of Pannenberg's work render it as "mutuality" rather than "reciprocity," so I follow this usage.

53. Pannenberg, *Grundlagen*, 23.

principles, such as *physis*. Consequently, law originally reflected both human and divine origins. In the course of law's evolution, the cosmic aspect tended to weaken and gave rise to efforts to reinforce or replace law with other guides for conduct, such as those supplied by ethical principles.

While custom typically governs relations within more or less homogenous groups, law regulates relations between groups unassociated by heredity or familial affiliation.[54] While legal norms originated in custom, they are developed through the mediation of inter-group frictions, and refined through casuistic dispute resolution. "The explicit establishment of law (*Rechtsetzung*) had its basis in custom, from which the provisions of law largely draw their content, to the extent that they are not derived from the disposition of individual disputes not resolved by existing custom."[55] Though custom is wedded to social expectations, law transcends its origins in custom by generating norms that not only reflect custom but are also relevant for the unique circumstances of individual disputes. Pannenberg therefore sees custom as the primordial source of law, and this leads him to conclude that law is first concerned with the maintenance of social ordering structures, and only later comes to resemble a body of casuistically generated rules.

As noted above, Pannenberg finds the emergence of ethics to be prompted by growing suspicion about the historical foundations and forms of human law. In his interpretation, the Socratic tradition sharply questioned the relationship between the beautiful and the just on one hand, and law and custom on the other. Ethics has continued to scrutinize the relation between law and custom. "Ethical argumentation aims at reestablishing the claims to validity of law and custom, while at the same time reforming its basis in the contents of what is intrinsically good for human beings and human society."[56]

Accordingly, Pannenberg sees both law and custom as sources of structure and as essential for human community. "Every community, if it is to endure, requires a firm structure, and ordering of life by definite mutual duties of its members toward one another."[57] However, consistent with his method of explicating the theological implications of anthropological data, he sees law as not only concerned with the maintenance of social order but also with the expression of a community's sense of its destiny. "Human

---

54. Pannenberg, *Grundlagen*, 23.
55. Pannenberg, *Grundlagen*, 23.
56. Pannenberg, *Grundlagen*, 26.
57. Pannenberg, *Grundlagen*, 39.

nature and destiny are expressed in various provisional forms through the formation of concrete societies."[58]

The connection between law and destiny gives Pannenberg's notion of law an eschatological turn; as already noted, he is a strongly eschatologically oriented thinker. He locates the roots of eschatology in biblical sources. He also finds it metaphysically grounded in a Hegelian understanding of history as evidencing a trajectory possessing an internal developmental dynamic culminating in the future. Destiny and futurity belong together for Pannenberg, and both cohere in the foundational characteristic of human openness, since no provisional ordering of human community is conclusive and final. Further, destiny is ultimately an integrative, cumulative horizon, because history entails a promise of comprehensive meaning that is only knowable at the conclusion of historical occurrences. "Only the final outcome of all that occurs will finally reveal the true meaning of individual figures and events in the course of history, reveal, that is, what they really involved."[59] While Pannenberg's interpretation of the relationships between custom, law and ethics seems somewhat schematic, he clearly emphasizes by those relationships (1) the historically conditioned character of law, and (2) the impetus they provide for the creation and deepening of community, not only as a result of extrinsic necessity, but as an expression of the destiny of individuals and societies to seek identity in a comprehensive sense of reality.

Pannenberg's argument for law's significance in maintaining the cohesiveness of society raises a question: How does law contribute to community? The answer to this leads to the heart of his theology of law, namely, his notion of law as the institutionalization of the human phenomena of recognition, benevolence and mutuality.

Recognition, Benevolence, and Mutuality

Pannenberg's project of the theological explication of anthropological themes is particularly evident in his theory of the genesis of law and legal norms. In his view, these norms derive from basic social acts of inter-personal recognition. Recognition, in turn, prompts benevolent acts, and culminates in forms of interaction characterized by mutuality. He contends that these anthropologically attested activities are fundamental for the social foundation of law. Based on his reading of Malinowski, Levi-Strauss, Gehlen and other social scientists, Pannenberg contends that this triad of inter-personal

58. Pannenberg, "Theology of Law," 45.
59. Pannenberg, "Theology of Law," 44.

actions underlies all legal norms, and it relates them structurally to love. Further, he argues on the basis of anthropological evidence that mutuality manifests itself as a ubiquitous social practice, discernible in geographically diverse cultures with different religious-social characteristics. Mutuality is expressed in and through acts of recognition and benevolence. Collectively, they give social relations a fundamentally reciprocal structure, and provide stability and durability, which is necessary for all legal relations.

While these notions—mutuality, recognition and benevolence—are key in Pannenberg's writings on law, regrettably he does not systematically relate them to each other. One interpretation of their relationship is to see recognition as a first-order action that prompts a second-order, unilateral response, benevolence, extended to the person recognized. Both of these culminate in mutuality, a third-order action in which the two preceding acts are reciprocated. Mutuality moves beyond the subject-oriented actions of recognition and benevolence to create a relationship of inter-personal mutuality. On this view, recognition precedes mutuality, anticipates it, and creates its possibility, although Pannenberg does not explicitly describe their relationship in terms of antecedent and consequence.

Recognition

For Pannenberg, recognition is a social/ anthropological activity with an implicitly moral dimension. Fundamentally, it consists in the act of acknowledgement of another person's social role and status, and ultimately, of her/his personhood. It combines perception of another's existence and social position with an affirmation of shared humanness. Pannenberg's notion of recognition reflects a Hegelian strand in his thought, derived from Hegel's view of human relationships. He cites approvingly Hegel's assertion that "Mutual recognition is the foundation of all true human relationships."[60] Pannenberg qualifies Hegel's claim, however, by contending that typically roles, not persons, are the objects of recognition. In actual social practice, recognition is status-oriented, meaning that persons are recognized in their roles with their respective social status. The meaning of roles is determined by social customs (e.g., parent, consumer, friend), but as custom becomes conventionalized, its roles acquire a more fluid character. Though role-based recognition is limited in this way, it nevertheless contributes to the establishment of common ground for social existence.

---

60. Quoted in Pannenberg, *Grundlagen*, 86. Also see Pannenberg, "Theology of Law," 53.

What is the source of recognition? Anthropologically speaking, it is rooted in the basic human trait of exocentricity. Human needs impel individuals to social interaction, and the satisfaction of needs is best secured cooperatively rather than unilaterally. But recognition also has an ethical dimension that expresses love in the form of fundamental respect. "The basic act of love is respect for one another."[61] Pannenberg argues that recognition constitutes the structural connection between law and love. Without some such connection, the theological dimension of law would either remain implicit, or lack a basis altogether.

The connection between law and love is first evident when "all legal connections are understood as grounded in recognition, and namely prior to the recognition of legal norms, in the mutual recognition of the persons involved as regards their roles . . . and their related status."[62] Recognition also involves social trust: "Recognition of others is not possible without a more or less limited amount of benevolence and trust, and such mutual recognition is necessary in all legal relations in which persons interact with each other as bearers of specific roles."[63] Therefore, it is not limited to the social role occupied by another, but leads beyond that to acknowledgment of the other's humanness: "Recognition as an accepting of the other in his role and in his status at the same time as a human being always lies at the basis of legal norms that regulate such relations."[64] The mutual act of recognition by the members of the community constitutes community: "In reality every form of human community . . . depends on the mutual recognition of its members."[65]

In some contexts, Pannenberg associates recognition with the essence of law itself. "Law primarily involves the shaping of social life that is established by the mutual recognition of the participants and that has a claim to faithful preservation."[66] Law, as noted, is concerned with the creation and maintenance of community. This contrasts with more individualistic notions of the relation of the individual and society in which self-interest is primary. Pannenberg unfortunately does not further elaborate on the suggestion that the content of law is traceable to recognition. It appears to follow from, at least in part, his view that membership in a community entails a certain entitlement to treatment consistent with the fundamental dignity

61. Pannenberg, *Grundlagen*, 85.
62. Pannenberg, "Rechtsbegründung," 323–24.
63. Pannenberg, *Grundlagen*, 90.
64. Pannenberg, *Grundlagen*, 91.
65. Pannenberg, "Theology of Law," 53.
66. Pannenberg, *What Is Man?*, 102.

of being a person. "Recognition creates or establishes for one's fellows a particular position in corporate life along with myself and others."[67] Recognition thus anchors a reciprocal standard of fair treatment of other persons. It is manifested in legal norms that preserve and institutionalize recognition.[68]

Further, recognition is grounded most adequately in love. To the extent recognition is fundamentally an acknowledgment of the existence and personhood of another, it is an act of love. Pannenberg argues against the notion of love as the "sentimental isolation of its emotional elements and an isolated emphasis on its drive for reunification."[69] He rejects the supposed opposition between the internality of love and the externality of legal norms found, for example, in Tolstoy and Sohm. Instead, Pannenberg proposes that love be seen as the underlying motivation for law. He writes: "Love not only exceeds the bounds of existing legal norms through its unconditionality. It is also the motive for new forms of law, and *vice versa* permits law to be seen as an expression of love."[70] He acknowledges that law often appears as anything other than this kind of expression, but he also contends that this reflects law's alienation from its ethical roots.[71] To the extent that law is motivated by sources other than love, its character as just law (*gerechtes Recht*) becomes questionable. The basis for this contention is, apparently, love's creative capacity, without which law can become stultified.

Here love and law relate most fundamentally. "A [connection between law and the concept of love] has only been established when all legal relations are understood as being grounded in the act of *recognition* that occurs prior to the recognition of any legal norms, and this underlying mutual recognition is of the persons involved in the light of their roles and associated status."[72]

Pannenberg also associates recognition with the notion of the conduct of life (*Lebensführung*). This refers to the comprehensive task of ethical orientation that confronts every individual.[73] It manifests a basic ethical outlook, and forms the frame for individual ethical acts. In contrast to custom

---

67. Pannenberg, *Grundlagen*, 91.

68. This view of the role of recognition in law has also been embraced by Trutz Rendtorff, who asserts, "Law gives a binding form to the mutual recognition of those involved in the actions of community and those affected by the community" (Rendtorff, *Ethics*, 2:86 [translation altered]).

69. Pannenberg, "Rechtsbegründung," 336.

70. Pannenberg, "Rechtsbegründung," 335.

71. Pannenberg, "Rechtsbegründung," 335.

72. Pannenberg, "Rechtsbegründung," 336.

73. Pannenberg, *Grundlagen*, 20. Pannenberg cites Rendtorff as having focused on this concept in an ethical context.

and ethos, though, it lacks any given content. At a minimum, however, it is other directed—it primarily relates to others yet in doing so it affirms that life is related to life.[74]

Is recognition obligatory? Pannenberg does not say so, but he implies that it is since community is ultimately impossible without it. Social institutions, practices and arrangements are insufficient to secure an enduring basis for community without some kind of relation among its members that underlies that community. For him, that foundation is not self-interest but its opposite: the other-regarding acknowledgment of fellow members of community.

Recognition is implicit in legal relationships. Because recognition can be an active expression of love, and since love motivates the formation of law, recognition resultingly contributes to the establishment of law. Pannenberg suggests that it is the linchpin connecting law and love: "Love creates law through the act of recognition."[75] Recognition is therefore a key concept in Pannenberg's thinking on law, establishing a "structural" connection between law and love.[76] It is questionable, however, whether this concept of that relationship adequately addresses the customary assumption that they are opposed to each other. Pannenberg rejects other attempts to posit an affirmative relationship between law and love, such as in the thought of Erik Wolf, because they are unable to demonstrate a necessary relation; he finds them to rely on positivistic assertions. Does he avoid the same problem? Recognition, for him, is a "structural element of love."[77] This is evident, he contends, in the fact that recognition acknowledges the "enduring rights of the other and his otherness."[78] But how does this come to be expressed? It may remain an interior phenomenon within the recognizer. Law may give expression to this act, but then again it may not, depending on one's attitude. If not, law would not involve an ethical acknowledgement of personhood but a pragmatic pursuit of individual ends. Pannenberg would likely find that to be an alienated form of law, but this possibility calls into question whether his view of the relationship between love and law is, in fact, as necessary as he claims.

While Pannenberg's notion of social relations as recognition-based has a certain ethical appeal, it would seem to require a more elaborated

74. Pannenberg, *Grundlagen*, 20.

75. Pannenberg, *What Is Man?*, 99. The English translation of this passage misleadingly translates the German original "Recht"—a singular noun—as "rights," a plural noun.

76. See generally, Pannenberg, "Rechtsbegründung," 335–36.

77. Pannenberg, "Rechtsbegründung," 336.

78. Pannenberg, "Rechtsbegründung," 336.

justification than he provides. Religiously based communities are grounded in a shared commitment to a common historical tradition and moral vision, all contributing to distinctive forms of social integration. Recognition as contributory, if not constitutive, for such interactions is certainly a plausible notion. But in secularized societies, interactions are driven by other motives, such as economic self-interest and gratification of psychological needs. Pannenberg would likely acknowledge their presence, but would nevertheless contend that reciprocity, widely attested by anthropological data, underlies individual and socially specific motives for interaction.

Benevolence

Recognition is one component of mutuality; benevolence is another. For Pannenberg, benevolence is the essence of the ethical life. "Concrete morality," Pannenberg writes, "as the overcoming of the barriers of egotistical self-interest springs from another source, namely from the impulse of benevolence towards others."[79] Benevolence is intrinsically directed to other persons and, to some extent, other creatures as well. It does not necessarily imply reciprocity; it is more fundamentally an act of unilateral dedication (*Zuwendung*) that includes an element of spontaneity. In this respect, benevolence as an inter-personal act is distinguishable from friendship, which Aristotle defines as mutual benevolence.[80] But given the mutability of human relations, benevolence lacks durability. Durable relationships require, and must provide for, reciprocity. "Without reciprocity, no durable relationships arise between people."[81] Recognition is also embodied in legal norms that govern such relations. Nevertheless, regardless of its nature and duration, a relationship requires an element of benevolence in the form of recognition of the other party corresponding to his or her function and role.

Pannenberg does not sufficiently describe the essence of benevolence. What form does it have in a legal setting—something akin to good faith and fair dealing? Is it refraining from harm to others and their property? He does not say. Based on what he does suggest, benevolence seems to be an internal, motivational attitude, one that strengthens the sense of obligation and fills legal lacunae with a spirit of fairness and compliance. It expresses, in short, the spirit of equity.

How does benevolence relate to law? Here, Pannenberg's exposition remains rather general. He contends that (1) benevolence is not inherently

79. Pannenberg, *Grundlagen*, 77.
80. Pannenberg, *Grundlagen*, 88.
81. Pannenberg, *Grundlagen*, 89.

reciprocal, and that (2) relationships require a degree of reciprocity in order to be durable. But it is not clear how benevolence contributes to durability. Durability, he states, does not require benevolence; many relations possess a certain degree of durability as a result of external circumstance (family, workplace, neighborhood).

The answer is perhaps to be found in Pannenberg's distinction between "personal" and "impersonal" benevolence. In friendship, benevolence is directed to the person of another, and since personhood entails trans-temporal continuity, such relations require durability. In the context of non-personal, legal relations, durability is also necessary, but these relations do not concern a person, rather the role carried out by that person. Benevolence is nevertheless necessary in both contexts. This is because Pannenberg links benevolence and recognition: "Recognition of the other is not possible without a more or less limited amount of trust and benevolence."[82]

Mutuality

Mutuality is fundamental in Pannenberg's understanding of law and ethics. As noted above, while both recognition and benevolence may be unilaterally expressed, they are more enduring and complete when they are reciprocated. In his words: "Every system of social relationships and every concrete form of community rests on . . . acts of recognition which are always dependent on a certain mutuality."[83] Referring to Bronislaw Malinowski's theories, Pannenberg sees mutuality as an independent foundation of law, and as separate from religion. But it is religion that establishes law's obligatory character.[84]

Pannenberg also finds mutuality to be thematically implicit in natural law. In his interpretation of that tradition, he finds it to prescribe principles conducive for social coexistence, with mutuality as its central value.[85] Its classic formulation is the Golden Rule; it is also expressed in the injunctions against inflicting harm and the obligation to honor commitments.[86] In contrast, Pannenberg sees the ideas of freedom and equality in Stoic formulations of natural law as relating only indirectly to mutuality. "Freedom and equality are conditions of mutuality, but do not contain the basic

---

82. Pannenberg, *Grundlagen*, 90.
83. Pannenberg, *Grundlagen*, 99.
84. Pannenberg, "Religion als Ursprung," 77.
85. Pannenberg, *Grundlagen*, 58.
86. Other religious scholars have noted the ubiquity of the Golden Rule in various religious/moral traditions. See Küng, *Global Responsibility*.

anthropological data of relatedness and dependence on others. Notions of freedom and equality in natural law can be described as conditions of mutuality, but they do not, in themselves, contain the anthropological basic data of relatedness and dependence on others."[87]

Pannenberg connects mutuality with both love and law through the act of recognition. "Recognition," writes Pannenberg, is "a fundamental structural moment of love that acknowledges the being of another and affirms his individuality. That is shown in the tendency toward mutuality that is involved in every act of recognition."[88]

Mutuality is equally present in the context of inequality. "Justice is the application of mutuality under the conditions of inequality of individuals."[89] Mutual recognition does not require equality; it can occur between unequally situated persons. "The act of recognition combines moments of inequality and specialness that are the direct object of recognition, and equality that is established through the reciprocity of recognition, even when it is not itself the object of such recognition."[90] This somewhat opaque formulation suggests that it is the *act* of recognition that gives rise to mutuality rather than the *status* of the participants. Mutual recognition constitutes a kind of social exchange that affirms an element of commonness within difference. Pannenberg's presentation here would have been better served by a more extended development of this theme since it relates to the pivotal concept of mutuality, and in turn, to the basis of legal normativity.

What are the implications for Pannenberg's theological/anthropological project of proposing mutuality and recognition as foundational for law? There appear to be at least two. First, law prototypically concerns various kinds of relational activity of persons. Whether directed to the roles exercised by individuals or their dignity as persons, mutuality as a practice of giving and receiving necessarily orients members of a community toward each other. While mutuality is an activity of persons, such as occurs in contractual relations, it is not limited to the personal realm. It can also inhere in one's attitude toward the property of another.

Second, legal relations have an irreducible moral element. Mutuality reflects the exocentric nature of human selfhood. Mutuality and recognition are both kinds of moral activity. While they lack the prescriptive content of the Golden Rule, they are nevertheless other-regarding and stand counter to excessive self-regard. In finding the content of mutuality to consist of

87. Pannenberg, *Grundlagen*, 59.
88. Pannenberg, "Rechtsbegründung," 336.
89. Pannenberg, *Grundlagen*, 59.
90. Pannenberg, *Grundlagen*, 59.

recognition, Pannenberg contends that an element of ethical acknowledgment and affirmation is reciprocally conveyed in legal acts. This is different from seeing law as essentially the assertion of self-interest, for it includes acceptance of the other as a member of a legal community.

One can ask, though, whether Pannenberg overemphasizes the role of mutuality in law. In Anglo-American law, implied obligations such as the duty of good faith are counterbalanced by respect for party autonomy. This illustrates a tendency in Pannenberg's theology of law to mingle prescriptive and descriptive elements, sometimes openly, sometimes implicitly. While Pannenberg sees contemporary forms of recognition in complex societies as primarily concerned with roles and not with the persons behind them, it is difficult to see how recognition nevertheless constitutes an acknowledgement of personhood. Though Pannenberg notes the dehumanizing consequences of role-based recognition, he contends that benevolence, love or a shared sense of humanity—or all of them—can be present in the recognition of roles. Perhaps he believes that this follows from certain moral presuppositions of law that presume the personhood behind each role player. In that case, law preserves the moral substance that contemporary life corrodes.

Pannenberg's anthropological grounding of law in the social practice of mutual recognition has a certain appeal. But how does it account for certain functions of law, such as legal prohibition, deterrence, or punishment? Pannenberg cites the *lex talionis* as an example of reciprocity-based penal law, but it is an ancient norm that does not figure in contemporary criminal jurisprudence. Further, does mutual recognition do justice to the fact that legal conditions are often imposed unilaterally through adhesion by one party on another? Corporations, which are legal, not natural persons, are among the most vigorous legal actors. How does recognition apply to such non-personal legal actors?

Perhaps Pannenberg would respond that these questions reflect the contemporary tendency to emphasize status excessively, in some form or other, over personhood in legal transactions. Roles are inevitably reflective of economic status, rather than moral value. If status and role are seen as fundamental social realities, then adhesive (unilaterally determined) transactions will tend to predominate. The party with superior resources will prevail over the one with fewer. Theoretically, recognition that points to the persons behind the roles is morally better because it promotes communal integrity as a worthy value alongside individual autonomy. Pannenberg's thinking here has a communitarian flavor—with a difference. For him, community is an eschatological as well as an historical reality. It exists as promise as well as current fact. To the extent moral import is diminished, law becomes hollowed-out and can degenerate into convention, unable to enlist voluntary compliance and prompting evasion and circumvention.

Law and Love

As already noted, Pannenberg sees love as closely connected with law; indeed, it partly constitutes it. This is a consequence of his concept of recognition and benevolence. Through the act of recognition, love acknowledges the other in his/her social role or personhood; indeed it creates the foundation of community altogether: "Recognition creates or establishes for one's fellow man a particular position in corporate life, along with myself and others."[91] Love aspires toward durability and permanence. It seeks structures to preserve what is created through the act of recognition, including legal structures. In this connection, Pannenberg refers to Adolf Schlatter, an influential German theologian of the early twentieth century who contended that love is the basis of legal relations. Schlatter emphasized an intrinsic demand of love for permanence in the relation of persons to each other.

Pannenberg derives love's importance for law from scripture as well as from common moral experience. In the New Testament, love is a new law that intensifies the imperative toward personal wholeness. In this demand, law is continually challenged to adapt to changing circumstances, as demonstrated by the history of Israel. Pannenberg finds the biblical roots of love and law in the concept of covenant in the Hebrew Bible. Covenant, rather than any notion of cosmic order reflected in creation, typifies law. That love can be expressed as law as in the Decalogue, and subsequently in Jesus's commandment of love of God and neighbor is not oxymoronic, for love can take the form of dynamic law. Pannenberg insists that the relation between law and love cannot rest on solidarity and fairness alone, for they have no necessary connection to love. Instead, he contends that recognition constitutes the connection between law and love. A universally valid connection between the two only exists "when all legal relations are understood as based in the act of recognition of the persons involved in view of their roles ('being as') and related status which is antecedent to, and underlies, the recognition of legal norms."[92]

For Pannenberg, the traditional separation, if not opposition, of love and law has yielded unwelcome consequences. These include the association of love with inwardness, the separation of legality and morality, and the notion of human beings as separable into inner and outer dimensions.

91. Pannenberg, *What Is Man?*, 99.
92. Pannenberg, "Rechtsbegründung," 336.

Pannenberg considers these manifestations of the separation of law and religion as inconsistent with the fundamental contention, found in Jesus's teachings, that love is the central content of law.[93] Love's contribution to law, for Pannenberg, lies not only in relativizing legal norms, but also in providing motivation for their continual renovation. "Love becomes not only a motive for a new form of law, in reverse fashion it allows law to be an expression of love, so that one can speak not only of a motivation-based connection between the two, but of a structural connection as well."[94] Pannenberg also refers approvingly to Harold Berman's contention that the separation of law and religion is based on a prejudicial perception of law as a system of rules that loses sight of law's role in the process of social ordering.[95]

In Pannenberg's broad conception of it, law is more than a body of positive enactments concerned with social and economic order. Both law and love are concerned with the creation and preservation of inter-personal relationships. Obviously, law and love are not the same, as is evident in the difference between friendship and other personal relations, including legal relations. But their contrasts should not obscure their common essence of mutual recognition and benevolence. Love often requires the structure of law to secure its durability. Pannenberg contends "a durable form of human coexistence always has legal character."[96] In this sense, love serves as a basis of law.

Pannenberg's association of love and recognition is consistent with the significance of recognition in his theology of law as a whole. It reflects a communal emphasis in Pannenberg's thought, one in which identity and destiny are seen as collectively influenced. This is not to diminish their significance for individual persons, only to acknowledge that, like history itself, they are concerned with a comprehensive understanding of reality that transcends yet encompasses individuals.

Concluding Observations: Law and the Shaping of Society

In his writings on law, Pannenberg is concerned to determine in what ways law contributes to the creation and preservation of humane societies. Further, he asks how the evolution of the law both contributes to and deals with the religious and ethical tensions inherent in contemporary social

93. Pannenberg, "Rechtsbegründung," 335.
94. Pannenberg, "Rechtsbegründung," 335.
95. Pannenberg, "Rechtsbegründung," 335.
96. Pannenberg, "Rechtsbegründung," 91.

existence. Pannenberg also questions the relatively insulated status of law as a specialized and technical realm of rules and regulations in order to show its connection to religion and its significance for society and culture generally. His willingness to locate and interpret law within an ethical-religious framework bears out his conviction that theology and religion must be concerned with the whole of reality. Pannenberg's concept of law is a protest against its purported autonomy. Obviously, this vision runs counter to liberal understandings of law and disregards the Rawlsian demarcation of public and private reason. It stands in contrast to social contract theories of society, with their emphasis on autonomous individuals acting on the basis of self-interest. For Pannenberg, those understandings are untenable in the long run to the extent they are premised on deficient notions of community, on reductive and privatized notion of religious commitment, and on minimalist views of the relation between morality and society.

A second contribution of Pannenberg's theology of law lies in his critique is of instrumental notions of law. Pannenberg would endorse Terry Eagleton's claim that God is a perpetual critique of instrumental reason.[97] While he would agree that law serves social purposes and therefore has certain instrumental uses, it is far from simply being a set of traffic rules for social life. That view overlooks law's role in the constitution of social life and in the moral orientation of community, resulting in truncated understandings of what law is, and what it means, morally and religiously.

Pannenberg's framing of the question in this manner reveals how central the category of history is for his project. For him, law is essentially protean, constantly adaptive and evolutionary, and anything but a static corpus of rules and principles produced by legislation and adjudication. At the same time, it possesses a certain degree of coherence. This derives from, on the one hand, the comprehensive reality known in religious traditions as God; on the other hand, it reflects the unity of history in that divine reality. Historical change, to his mind, disqualifies every abstract, timeless theory of what law is, particularly what he calls 'cosmic' theories rooted in the classical Greek tradition. For Pannenberg, these are ahistorical attempts to define the essence of phenomena that must remain provisional in light of the future.

A comprehensive evaluation of this position would require an assessment of Pannenberg's theology as a whole—a larger undertaking than can be attempted here. The focus has been on his thesis that law is essentially grounded in the mutual recognition of persons as legal subjects. Based on his interpretation of recognition, this results in a deeply moral vision of law based on the anthropological interpretation of social interaction as

---

97. Eagleton, *Reason, Faith*, 10.

constituting primordial acts of acknowledgment ratifying the status of persons as members of a community. The act of recognition, in Pannenberg's view, is intrinsic to personhood; it is not a byproduct of membership in an ethnic or cultic *Gemeinschaft*.

Despite its appeal, Pannenberg's theory of recognition does not explain adequately the nature of legal obligation. How does it cause laws to be binding? In and of itself, recognition of another does not indicate how self-interest is to be balanced with regard for the interests of the other. After all, one can nevertheless prefer one's own goals over the needs of others, while acknowledging at the same time that those needs exist. It appears that Pannenberg overburdens the concept of recognition. As Ralf Dreier argues, the concept of recognition is unable to support the structural connection between law and love. Recognition, he contends, can be based on indifference, fear and opportunism as well as love.[98] Pannenberg might respond by asserting that recognition would lack durability if based only on negative motives. He contends that the anthropological characteristic of openness to the world for him is, by itself, inadequate to generate the elements of law: "The empty thought of the openness of humans is unable to lead by itself to the formation of any content for the reality of law."[99] It is love, he implies, that supplies that content.

This emphasis on the relation of love and law has drawn criticism. Huber criticizes Pannenberg's position by contending that the biblical commandment to love God and one's neighbor transcends the horizon of human law in that it envisions a divine-human relationship that "cannot be captured in the image of symmetrical mutuality."[100] While Honecker, like Pannenberg, embraces an anthropological approach to law, he also objects to the connection of law and love. "Anthropological access to law does not occur directly by means of the personal relationship of love. Law is to be connected to justice and not to love."[101] Dreier, speaking from a legal perspective, criticizes Pannenberg for moving away from an anthropological emphasis on the relation of law and religion to a concentration on the structural relation of law and religion.[102]

The centrality of love in Pannenberg's vision reflects his conviction that societies can endure only if they are based on some consensus regarding

---

98. Dreier, "Entwicklungen," 27.
99. Pannenberg, *Grundlagen*, 55.
100. Huber, "Recht im Horizont," 1052–53.
101. Honecker, *Sozialethik*, 583.
102. Dreier, "Entwicklungen," 28.

fundamental values.[103] A common religious foundation traditionally supplied this consensus for what Pannenberg terms "pragmatic" reasons. This is no longer an available option in pluralistic societies. Instead, it has been replaced often by unreflective tolerance that is indifferent to contending worldviews and skeptical of the possibility of mediating among them. But how does love remedy this situation? It is not clear that it can. It may be a foundational value for a religious community, but not for contemporary social life, at least not in same way. Yet Pannenberg does not condition love on social context. It is simply not clear how love can fulfil this social role, even if mediated by recognition. In short, there appears to be a disjunction between the anthropological/historical and the prescriptive/constructive aspects of his interpretation of law. Both aspects inform the other, but do so without any intrinsic necessity.

In one sense, Pannenberg's theology of law is fundamentally an attempt to answer the question: what holds a society together? Pannenberg sees law as having a significant role in constituting and maintaining human society. Rather than a technical apparatus predominantly shaped by judicial, legislative or economic influences, law provides moral import to the shaping of human society. His vision is compelling in many respects, but its ultimate persuasiveness is qualified by the discontinuities that remain unresolved. Mutuality, recognition, benevolence: all are at work in the functioning of law, but they do not account for the whole of legal experience. Stable precedent, appropriate constitutional principles, procedural fairness and accountable and reliable adjudicatory procedures are also important to the proper functioning and social acceptance of law. Pannenberg's theology of law is commendable for its deeply moral vision, but it less than fully accounts for law in its complexity.

---

103. See generally, Pannenberg, "Christliche Rechtsüberzeugung."

VIII

Wolfgang Huber

Law as an Instrument of Preferential Justice

Wolfgang Huber is one of the most well-known living theologians, church leaders and public intellectuals in Germany. After an academic career as a professor of theology and ethics in Marburg and Heidelberg, Huber (born 1942) served as a Bishop of Berlin-Brandenburg (1994–2009), as well as Chair of the Council of the Evangelical Church in Germany (EKD) (2003–2009), the governing body of the Protestant church in Germany. His father, Ernst Rudolph Huber, a law professor who had been a student of Carl Schmitt, had supported the Nazi regime through his academic work.[1] His father's troubling past, according to several commentators, played a role in Huber's interest in the intersections of theology, ethics, and law.

In 1996, Huber published a substantial volume on law, ethics and theology, *Gerechtigkeit und Recht: Grundlinien einer christliche Rechtsethik* (*Justice in Law: Baselines of a Christian Ethic of Law*), now in its third edition.[2] It stands as one of the principal contemporary works on the ethics of law from a Christian perspective. *Gerechtigkeit* is a comprehensive and ambitious work, noteworthy for its engagement with biblical and theological sources as well as with contemporary German and Anglo-American jurisprudence. In the book, Huber urges a view of law linking law, justice and love in a social-communicative context as an alternative to positivism and natural

---

1. Regarding Huber's biography and paternal relationship, see generally, Nolte, "Theologen," 23. A biography of Huber was published in 2016. See Gessler, *Wolfgang Huber*.

2. Huber, *Gerechtigkeit*. Unfortunately, it has not appeared in English. All references are to the first edition (1996), and all translations from it—and from all other German-language sources in this chapter—are mine.

law. In 2016, Huber published a lengthy chapter on the ethics of law in a volume on Protestant ethics.[3] In it, Huber devotes his attention primarily to the ethical, rather than the theological, dimensions of law, even though he speaks in terms of a theological ethics of law. There he writes, "The theological ethics of law does not present itself with a claim to produce a theological grounding of mundane law. Rather it understands law as a part of mundane reality and a task for human structuring."[4] This seems to signal a change in emphasis in his approach to law. This notwithstanding, the focus here is on his earlier book, *Gerechtigkeit und Recht*, as his most comprehensive analysis of law.

Huber sees his project against a background of indifference towards law in modern Protestant ethics. In his view, the last comprehensive treatment of law from a Christian perspective before the publication of his book was Brunner's *Justice and the Social Order* (1943). Although significant work on theology and law appeared in the immediate postwar period from Erik Wolf and others, it had little lasting effect in the political/legal arena—Huber speaks of its "peculiar inconsequentiality."[5] As the era of reconstruction drew to a close, theological attention shifted to more abstract discussions of law as a social institution and other political themes, leaving law again largely ignored. Contemporary theology, Huber insists, must renew its concern with law. It must examine the presuppositions and consequences of law in light of the "reality of the world in the horizon of the universality of God."[6] Within this horizon, "the interaction with reality is determined by the hope of comprehensive justice."[7]

For Huber, interaction between law and theology not only benefits theology; it is also necessary for law. It stands, in his view, before a series of challenges. While law is a pervasive social reality, intruding into areas of life previously beyond its ambit, it has become increasingly "hollowed out," morally attenuated, and increasingly legalistic and technical. It has been progressively relinquishing its fundamental function—facilitating the exercise of freedom. These developments should not prompt rejection of law but should lead to deeper questioning about its relation to justice. The question of the relation of law and justice is the fundamental theme of his book.[8] "Justice in its inalienably eschatological character forms the horizon

---

3. Huber, "Rechtsethik."
4. Huber, "Rechtsethik," 137.
5. Huber, *Gerechtigkeit*, 15.
6. Huber, *Gerechtigkeit*, 17.
7. Huber, *Gerechtigkeit*, 17.
8. Huber, *Gerechtigkeit*, 26.

of law."[9] And law gives expression to justice; the relation between the two is fundamental for his thinking.

Huber helpfully elaborates on the central themes of his book in a reply to a critical review of it by Hans-Martin Pawlowski, a jurist. In response to Pawlowski's doubts about the legitimacy of that project, Huber contends that theological reflection on law is essential for understanding its historical evolution in the West. Even though positive law has evolved to become independent of theological or ecclesiastical oversight, this process of secularization was itself encouraged by the Reformation. Notwithstanding its secular character, law continues to bear traces of its historical affiliation with Christian influences and it can only be fully understood in light of that historical background. Above and beyond this historical legacy, law is an ethically important institution. In his view, Christian ethical perspectives can and should contribute to discussions of law's ethical dimension.

The reviewer further contends that theological discussion of law is out of place given the religious neutrality of the modern state. Huber rejects a concept of neutrality that flatly prohibits any reference to religious/ethical considerations in connection with law. Neutrality does not mean exclusivity in favor of a secularist worldview; that is tantamount to the state favoring one worldview over others. Instead, the role of the state is to determine whether "consequences of one or the other position are consistent with basic rights and other cornerstones of our legal system."[10] Reformed traditions respect the secularity of law and its modern grounding in reason and in autonomous, human self-legislation. Huber reflects a traditional Protestant respect for the status and integrity of positive law. But he is equally emphatic that religious and ethical perspectives may productively be brought to bear on law without sacralizing it. This requires a critical and constructive approach.

Consequently, in *Gerechtigkeit*, Huber advocates both a "critical *theory* of law" and a "critical *theology* of law."[11] The two undertakings interact yet remain distinct. The first is dedicated to overcoming the opposition between positivism and natural law by means of a theory of legal principles. Huber here draws upon the work of Alexy and Dworkin. In their respective views, law consists not only of rules but principles that guide the articulation of legal rules.[12] In contrast, a critical theology of law seeks correspondences between "the rescuing acts of justice of God [and] the liberating events in which justice has been achieved under the provisional conditions of human

---

9. Huber, "Rechtsethik," 26.
10. Huber, "Parteiliche Rezension," 438.
11. Huber, "Parteiliche Rezension," 440.
12. See generally Shingleton, "Law, Principle, and the Global Ethic," 46–48.

history."[13] It attempts to overcome the antinomy between the Lutheran two kingdoms doctrine and *Eigengesetzlichkeit* as the autonomous right of social and political spheres of life. Instead of pursuing the "deductive derivation of legal statements from theological premises," Huber's critical theology of law is concerned with the "critical correlation between the analysis of legal problems and reflection on principles of anthropology and ethics, leading to insights that benefit legal culture."[14] Both of these undertakings are pursued, hand-in-hand, in *Gerechtigkeit*. Further, Huber wishes to overcome traditional conceptions of law unduly modeled on criminal law that emphasize compliance and punishment or liberal notions of law as concerned primarily with rights and self-interest in favor of a conception of law centered on social recognition. A comment Huber makes regarding Erik Wolf's theology of law applies to Huber's own position as well: "The legal community is more important than legal competition."[15]

Based on his "critical theology of law," Huber proposes development of an ethics of law (*Rechtsethik*).[16] This is centrally concerned with the relation between law and ethics, with the theological element indirectly informing ethical understanding. For Huber, the law-ethics relation is problematical, and is no longer self-evident.[17] In his understanding, the relation between them is properly focused on the concept of justice: Huber terms it "the key to an ethics of law."[18] An ethics of law is concerned with reconciliation of a duty of compliance with law with a duty to improve it. In a review of Huber's book, Hartmut Kreβ notes the tensions between these duties: "It must be a challenge for every ethics of law to work out the necessity of loyalty and compliance with law and, at the same time work towards further development of law in a humane, free and just direction."[19] For Huber, these two tasks are to be informed by an understanding of law's provisional character, with due regard given to the eschatological awareness of the Christian community.

The close relation of "ethics" and "theology" is revealing; Huber's prescriptive vision of positive law is at once theologically framed and ethically motivated. A critical theology of law is a form of public theology, which

13. Huber, *Gerechtigkeit*, 167.
14. Huber, "Parteiliche Rezension," 440.
15. Huber, *Gerechtigkeit*, 207.
16. Although the German term is singular, the plural form ("ethics of law") is used here as more in keeping with customary English usage, as in "medical ethics" or "professional ethics."
17. Huber, "Rechtsethik," 128.
18. Huber, "Parteiliche Rezension," 437.
19. Kreβ, "Sonne der Gerechtigkeit," 236.

Huber defines as the effort to interpret the theological relevance of questions of social life in its institutional forms and to investigate the contribution of Christian faith to the structuring of human community.[20] Public theology employs generally comprehensible, non-sectarian language, and engages in communication with other disciplines.[21] It is bound by imperatives of openness and transparency.[22]

Huber is less than specific, however, about the connection between a critical theology of law and an ethics of law. At times, the two appear to be aligned; at other points they are held apart with little interaction. He contends that the contribution of a critical theology of law to a critical theory of it can be modeled on the critical-constructive relation between eschatology and teleology.[23] Teleology is concerned with relative purposes understood within the context of human action, while eschatology interprets the divine promise for nature and history as fulfilled in divine action. Justice can be understood both eschatologically and teleologically: its teleological meaning is embodied in law, and its eschatological aspect lies in the continual evolution of law towards greater recognition of the needs of the most disadvantaged members of society. Huber suggests that an eschatological dimension can be brought to bear on law by means of correspondences between the eschatological and teleological. It is not clear what these correspondences would look like, nor is it evident why these correspondences would be compelling for those who lack appreciation for eschatology.

A more promising alternative for connecting critical theology/critical theory may be through ethics. A critical theology of law obviously bears upon an ethics of law if the latter is to be theologically informed. Huber speaks from time to time of a theologically grounded ethics of law.[24] At the same time, such a theology must concern itself with the "basic dimensions" of an ethics of law, namely, legal loyalty and reform.[25] It deals with the development of criteria that ethics applies in its critical and constructive capacities. This is Huber's principal interest, and consequently the ethical aspect predominates over the theological in his approach. This produces an understanding of law shaped by biblical perspectives, yet attentive to its context in contemporary culture.

20. Huber, *Gerechtigkeit*, 14.
21. Huber, *Gerechtigkeit*, 14.
22. Huber, *Gerechtigkeit*, 14.
23. Huber, *Gerechtigkeit*, 168.
24. Huber, *Gerechtigkeit*, 146.
25. Huber, *Gerechtigkeit*, 148.

As noted above, Huber believes that contemporary reflection on law should no longer be concerned with an attempt to provide a grounding for law. He believes that pursuit of a theological grounding of law has become a sterile exercise. Debates in German theological circles about the theological foundation of law manifest in his view "provincial self-satisfaction," and are marked by a rehashing of worn-out arguments and a repetitive reliance on traditional sources.[26] Here, he would seem to have in mind mid-century debates about Christocentric law and the orders of creation. Accordingly, Huber is largely disinterested in general theological grounding of law like Pannenberg's attempt, except to the extent that it bears on the relation of law and ethics.[27] Instead, he combines the theological and the ethical, with primary emphasis given to the ethical element.[28]

Huber identifies three traditional *foci* in the theology of law: (a) the theological foundations of law, (b) the relation of ethics and law, and (c) the connection between state and church—the traditional field of church law, which customarily has received the most attention. Instead, Huber is concerned with theological considerations to the extent they help to generate ethical principles with which law must be concerned—fairness, freedom and equitable treatment of the disadvantaged.

While he rejects the project of a theological grounding of law, a key question for Huber is the possibility of a normative grounding of law.[29] For him, this involves the question of law's validity (*Geltung*), construed socially, legally and materially/substantively. Huber concludes that: (1) law is best seen as a social-communicative activity; (2) law and morality (ethics) are related through primary and secondary rules of obligation, and (3) law should be responsive to the requirements of justice.

The principal constructive elements of Huber's theology of law include the following theses: (1) neither positivism nor natural law furnish a tenable basis, contemporarily, for law; (2) law is the result of a communicative process of social orientation; (3) law is inseparable, although distinguishable, from ethics, for without an ethical orientation law deteriorates into an ideological instrument for the pursuit of proximate ends; (4) justice, eschatologically understood, is essential for law; (5) law institutionalizes the performance of recognition of the members of the legal community; (6) law is related to love in an intrinsic way. Huber bases these contentions on various sources, such as Habermas's communicative ethics and Rawls's

---

26. Huber, *Gerechtigkeit*, 18.
27. Huber, *Gerechtigkeit*, 205.
28. Compare this with the approach in Kreß, *Ethik der Rechtsordnung*.
29. Huber, *Gerechtigkeit*, 49.

notion of justice as fairness, as well as on scriptural passages and theological arguments.

Beyond Positivism and Natural Law

Positivism

Huber sees every theory of law as confronted with a basic question: How is law different from coercive force, on the one hand, and from morality on the other? Sociological theory, for the most part, tends to see coercion as a defining characteristic of law, as in Weber's conception of law. This perspective downplays the normativity of law. Positivism views the positing of law through recognized and defined processes as constituting the essential characteristic of law, rather than its compulsory nature or its moral validity. Natural law theories emphasize the normativity of law at the expense of its coercive aspect and its procedural modes of enactment.

The modern predominance of positivist theories of law leads Huber to scrutinize closely several of them in *Gerechtigkeit*. He criticizes John Austin's jurisprudence for its cramped notion of law as the compulsory command of a sovereign. It disregards the role of law in facilitating certain voluntary actions, such as entering into a contract or marrying. In this respect, Austin's theory is underdetermined since law is not only concerned with compelling certain behavior. Nevertheless, Austin's analytic approach and his elimination of any theological or ethical influence in defining law continues to influence positivist theories of law.

Huber also criticizes modern positivism in his critique of Hans Kelsen. Kelsen proposed a basic norm (*Grundnorm*) as the ultimate ground of positive law. The basic norm is not ethical but legal in nature; as such, law is normative but not ethical. Its normativity is hypothetical and transcendental, (in a Kantian sense of being located beyond the empirical realm), rather than ethical and prescriptive. While Austin's emphasis on the coercive character of law is dismissed by Kelsen, his separation of law and morality is retained and combined with ethical relativism. The separation of law and morality is consistent with, and reflective of, contemporary pluralism. Acceptance of law is underwritten by its universality which results from its placement in a normative hierarchy. The result is a view of law that emphasizes the process of its positing rather than its content and relates that positing to an internal hierarchy of norms that endow law with a certain kind of legitimacy. "The legitimacy of law does not follow from its ethical grounding but from procedure."[30]

Though Huber rejects these positivist theories, his rejection is qualified.[31] He respects the distinction between the significance of the positivity of law (its legality), and its morality (its legitimacy). These concepts are distinguishable but not separable. This view places Huber in the vicinity of some form of inclusive positivism. Through communicative participation in public discourse about law (as discussed below), moral perspectives are introduced and promoted without the universalistic claims of natural law. Huber accordingly proposes a revision of Kelsen's basic norm in which legal deduction (from the basic norm to subsidiary law) is replaced by a relation to moral principles and by a concept of social recognition.[32] While Huber diverges from Kelsen with respect to the basis of legal norms, this does not contradict his acceptance of Kelsen's notion of law as a normative legal order. Rather, it is possible that two differing, non-exclusive characteristics of law coexist, one of law as a social-political institution, and the other of law as an instrument of justice.[33]

Unlike several of the writers considered in these pages, Huber does not hold positivism responsible for the extreme injustices of the Nazi regime. In his view, ideological distortion of law, rather than positivism, was the cause of the subversion of law during the Third Reich. Rather than its historical legacy, it is the amorality of positivism that Huber finds objectionable. His critique of positivism is based on its failure to acknowledge the moral validity and legitimacy of law. "Legal positivism reaches its limits where a statute and its application has lost its connection to the substantive validity of law."[34] In other words, positivism fails to show how law is different from other means of coercion. But if law is law by virtue of the manner of its enactment (H. L. A. Hart's primary rules as prescribed in accord with his

---

30. Huber, *Gerechtigkeit*, 76. Michael Moxter views Huber as embracing a "postpositivist" conception of law that follows Kelsen's concept of normativity to an extent. While Huber finds Kelsen's fictive basic norm to be problematic in that it assumes what is to be proven, he favors, according to Moxter, a "reflective" theory of law that neither wholly dismisses nor embraces positivism. It consists, instead, of "self-critical reflection" on law's legitimacy. See Moxter, "Recht und kommunikative Freiheit," 121.

31. Huber, *Gerechtigkeit*, 99.

32. Huber, *Gerechtigkeit*, 79.

33. Moxter contends, as I understand his interpretation, that Huber's revision of Kelsen undermines his acceptance, limited though it may be, of positivism's emphasis on the significance of procedural enactment for determining law. For Moxter, Huber ends up affirming an ethical teleology of law like that of Gustav Radbruch: law's meaning is to serve justice. See Moxter, "Recht und kommunikative Freiheit," 123.

34. Huber, *Gerechtigkeit*, 83.

secondary rules), or if its normative character is ultimately dependent upon a non-ethical basic norm, then why are they not, at least arguably, plausible theories of law? For Huber, they are not because they fail to account for law's need for validity and legitimacy.

The importance of validity and legitimacy in law can be seen in Huber's endorsement of the Radbruch Formula. A prominent German legal scholar, Gustav Radbruch, believed that the Nazi experience had so undermined and perverted law that it surrendered its character as law and became an instrument of terror. At some point, the distortion became so significant that one must say that law has ceases to be law. After the war, Radbruch proposed a formula to determine when law surrenders its legitimacy. In "cases where the discrepancy between the positive law and justice reaches a level so unbearable that the statute has to make way for justice because it has to be considered "erroneous law," law ceases to be law."[35] While Radbruch looked to natural law for guidance in determining when this boundary is crossed, Huber is skeptical of the viability of natural law; he appeals instead to social discourse and communicative activity as furnishing evolving criteria of the legitimacy. He shares the affirmation underlying Radbruch's formula that the essence of law is to serve justice, and accordingly Huber emphasizes the importance of substantive validity as well as legal validity in constituting the legitimacy of law.

Natural Law

Huber devotes relatively little attention to natural law, believing it to be unavailable as a contemporary option. Cultural diversity and the historical development of legal norms raise questions about the presuppositions of natural law, but Huber's dismissal reflects his belief that law and morality must not be merged. Theology, ethics and law must reflect pluralistic circumstances, as well as demonstrate fundamental respect for individual freedom and autonomy. Consequently, law and ethics must remain distinct. He writes: "Every engagement with law within the horizon of Protestant theology has an interest in the abiding difference between legality and morality, and between law and ethics."[36] This does not mean that law should be divorced from religion and ethics. To the contrary, law must remain open for engagement with them. "The question of the ethical presuppositions of law is as unavoidable as the question of the legal consequences of ethical

---

35. Huber, *Gerechtigkeit*, 83.
36. Huber, *Gerechtigkeit*, 16.

demands."[37] This does not, however, require an embrace of natural law. Such an embrace would be unavailing, in his eyes, because "the era of natural law is over."[38] One may ask, though, whether Huber's dismissal is too categorical. Law and morality, as Kreß notes, are not conjoined in all forms of natural law. Perhaps Huber's thinking will come to reconsider this rejection.

Law as a Social-Communicative Activity

For Huber, law is an institutional mode of communicative activity that occurs within a social context. It is not concerned primarily with individual rights and their assertion for private ends. Huber understands individuality and sociality as two sides of the same reality.[39] Fred Dallmayr notes that "for Huber, it is important to recognize that individual moral action is always embedded in social contexts and especially in the institutions of human interaction."[40] An understanding of law as an expression of communicative freedom is influential in Huber's ethics of law. Through this notion of freedom, Huber means that humans achieve and fulfill freedom through communicative interaction with each other, an activity that law facilitates and promotes.

Law assumes the equality of social participants; law helps to establish and preserve the social solidarity of the legal community. This is necessary because of the tension in personhood between individualization and sociality. "Law is essentially institutionalized in order to balance the human will to self-assertion with human sociality."[41] The legal rules governing these interactions must themselves attain a minimum of social recognition, meaning they must establish legal procedures that are predictable, reliable and morally justified, qualities that are both descriptive and normative.

Law is a significant part of a broad social spectrum of interpersonal interaction. In essence, it is a communicative and coordinating kind of activity, and as such, it promotes human sociality. Obviously, this is far removed from understandings of law as essentially concerned with sanctions, social order, and compliance. It also contrasts with Kant's view of law as regulating

37. Huber, *Gerechtigkeit*, 16.

38. Huber, *Gerechtigkeit*, 16. For a critique of Huber's rejection of natural law, see Kreß, "Review," 236–37. As Kreß notes, rationalist versions of natural law, such as that of Pufendorf, also contributed to the development of the modern distinction between law and morality.

39. Huber, *Gerechtigkeit*, 172.

40. Dallmayr, "Huber," 149.

41. Dallmayr, "Huber," 53.

individual freedom for the sake of the freedom of other individuals. In Huber's view, Hegel's effort to relate reason and reality is more satisfactory than Kantian theory in that it posits that ethics and law become a "tangible unit" in which institutions are "the reality of ethical life."[42]

The concept of law as communicative action has two distinguishable parts. First, it involves public discourse and discussion. This occurs in various fora and forms, such as in political debates and legal proceedings as well as in informal social encounters. Second, it requires the coordination of individual actions through communication; this is achieved through the orienting function of law that provides directives for conduct so that agents may coordinate their actions. This orienting function produces a degree of regularity and predictability. Both involve interpersonal interaction. An understanding of law as communicative action is based on a consensual theory of knowledge in which truth is determined by a consensus of all persons who participate in argumentation in an ideal speech situation.[43] The first aspect emphasizes the verbal, discursive interaction of individuals in and through the exchange of expressive activity. The coordination of activities by means of communicative action involves (1) strategic actions (goal-oriented actions involving at least two actors) and (2) communicative actions (understandings among multiple actors achieved through verbal communication). Since it comprises both of these kinds of communicative activity, law is an "essential, constituent condition of social action."[44]

Underlying the concept of communicative activity is Huber's notion of communicative freedom, a central idea in his thought. Freedom is a foundational Huberian concept, and like personhood, it must be understood both socially and individually. Freedom is not realized in the actions of isolated agents but in the context of interaction with others. Through communicative interaction, Huber writes, "Freedom realizes itself in society and in mutual communication, in communion and communication; that is why it can be called 'communicative freedom.'"[45] Moxter contends that this understanding of freedom is inspired by Hegel's contention that "a person alone cannot be free."[46] This idea lends itself to law, which encompasses forms of social interaction governed by prescribed rules and procedures. Obviously,

---

42. Huber, "Communicative Freedom," 43.

43. See generally, Herget, *German Legal Philosophy*, 46–47. Nolte states that Huber's interest in the concept of communicative freedom dates to the late 1970s. See Nolte, "Theologen," 31–32; Huber, "Freiheit und Institution."

44. Huber, *Gerechtigkeit*, 51.

45. Huber, *Folgen*, 118. It has been translated in Huber, "Freedom and Institution," 46.

46. Moxter, "Kommunikative Freiheit," 114.

the freedom that law helps to secure is external in nature. But it has deeper roots—both theological and philosophical. Further, Moxter traces Huber's concept of freedom to Luther's understanding of freedom as liberation for devotion to others.[47] This suggests that Huber's idea of justification has a social dimension.[48] Philosophically, it reflects the influence of a Hegelian view of freedom as increased through intersubjective interaction (positive freedom) as compared to the assertion of the autonomy of the self against competing selves (negative freedom). Law helps to structure social interaction such that it creates concrete opportunities for the expansion of freedom.

In addition to being a form of communicative activity, law is also an institution. In Huber's understanding, the institutional character of law as an institution does not primarily connote either an assemblage of procedures and rules for the enforcement of behavioral norms, or a judicial system staffed with expert practitioners, but an array of interactional social practices for resolving conflict and protecting vital interests of the members of a political community. It both requires and promotes freedom. The communicative nature of law, with its iterations of claim and response, assertion and counter-assertion, enhances law's democratic potential and facilitates the rational and humane handling of disputes, transactions and violations of law.

Unfortunately, neither *Gerechtigkeit* nor subsequent writings explicate in detail the relation between law and communicative action.[49] Some of his other writings describe its significance, but do not say much about law.[50] In describing the relation, Huber tends to refer generally to the work of Habermas and Alexy. But communication is clearly an ethically significant activity for Huber, and by connecting it with law, he emphasizes the linkage between the individual and the social. Communication is a form of human interaction that coordinates individual action and aspires toward a degree of consensus. Law provides a framework of rules and norms for this interaction. By facilitating this interaction, law (1) promotes individual and social well-being by resolving disputes, facilitating transactions, and ordering affairs, and (2) provides a positive impetus for its ongoing reform and improvement.

---

47. Moxter, "Kommunikative Freiheit," 114.

48. Huber writes, "Only at the time when the social structure of justification was observed could the concept of law in the doctrine of justification become thematic again" (Huber, "Recht im Horizont," 1047).

49. The index to *Gerechtigkeit und Recht* lists only two pages referring to law and communicative action in a book of 480 pages.

50. For example, the essay "Freiheit und Institution," 123, only briefly mentions law.

The Validity of Law

Huber's understanding of law places particular emphasis on the validity (*Geltung*) of law. Validity is a tripartite concept for him, consisting of social, legal as well as intrinsic, substantive (*inhaltliche*) validity. Social validity has to do with the enforcement of law and with the means used to effect compliance. Legal validity is related to the means and procedures through which law becomes acknowledged as law. Substantive validity deals with the ability of legal rules to be grounded according to "evident" criteria of justice.[51] Each of these kinds of validity combines descriptive and prescriptive elements.

This understanding of validity expands it beyond a focus on its legal application and transcends the positivist concentration on the enactment and recognition of laws. Its justification also rests on extra-legal grounds—on its social and ethical quality. As such, social and substantive validity raise the question of law's autonomy by subjecting law's status to extra-legal considerations. In particular, substantive validity is a, if not the, principal concern of an ethics of law in that it addresses the ethical quality of law. Huber writes: "A theological ethics of law, which inquires about the internal legitimacy of law, cannot limit itself to pressing ethical demands on law; it instead has to perceive the ethical quality of law itself."[52]

Huber views each of these forms of validity in terms of recognition. Validity under each of these aspects depends on how well it protects and permits the pursuit of recognition as a basic social activity. He sees law as rules specifically concerned with recognition in that "the content of those rules produced by previously agreed and applied procedures of a constituted social entity . . . serves to enable and protect relations of reciprocal recognition."[53] So, for Huber, recognition is the consequence of the social, communicative practices that law facilitates. Law's ethical quality depends on its ability to serve this function. "In its ethical meaning, law is a construct of actionable rules and duties that form the frame for mutual recognition and therefore for reciprocity and cooperation."[54]

Does this tripartite concept of validity—and particularly the facet of substantive validity—overly moralize law? Not all law is subject to all three kinds of validity. Some law (recall Thielicke's traffic laws) possesses little or no intrinsic validity, except in an attenuated sense; they are essentially rules of coordination to ensure proper functioning of a social order. Of the three

---

51. Huber, *Gerechtigkeit*, 48.
52. Huber, "Legitimes Recht," 226.
53. Huber, *Gerechtigkeit*, 54.
54. Huber, "Legitimes Recht," 226.

kinds of validity, the substantive kind will be the most contested. Certain laws would seem to be socially and legally valid (in Huber's meaning) without possessing substantive validity.

Law and Recognition

The communicative interaction of law inherently involves recognition. Huber writes, "Law, in so far as it enables social activity in its strategic and communicative aspects, is based on the principle of mutual recognition."[55] The parallel here with Pannenberg is noteworthy, though Huber appeals to Habermas' social communication theory rather than to social/anthropological data.[56] Law facilitates communicative interaction among persons consisting of strategic and communicative elements. Strategic activity involves goal-directed actions that take the decisions and actions of others into account; communicative activity implicates linguistically conveyed understanding between persons.[57] This yields an understanding of law as a process of developing alternative options for action, and as a prohibition of other options through sanctions. As such, it contributes to the shaping of social activity. Social actors seek recognition through their actions; by this, Huber seems to suggest that the pursuit of reciprocal recognition is a significant motivation in social action. "In the principle [of mutual recognition] the structural core of all law can be discerned."[58]

Recognition is relational, and for Huber relations among persons include an element of fellow-appreciation that bears the simulacra of love. In fact, Huber comes close to equating recognition and love: "Love not only allows recognition of the dignity of the one or the other without compulsion, rather helps him or her to develop that and it does so unilaterally, without being dependent on a response. Love therefore opens up relations of reciprocal recognition in the form of non-obligatory unilateral action."[59] At the same time, love is related to justice, and justice can and must shape and adapt love in its social applications. This is an unsentimental understanding of love that extends it beyond close personal relationships to include more tangential social interactions. Like Pannenberg, Huber sees love as a constituent element in social, and therefore legal, existence. This conception of

---

55. Huber, *Gerechtigkeit*, 51.

56. Huber, *Gerechtigkeit*, 51. Huber here cites the work of Charles Taylor with regard to the significance of recognition.

57. Huber, *Gerechtigkeit*, 51.

58. Huber, *Gerechtigkeit*, 51.

59. Huber, *Gerechtigkeit*, 54.

love has a certain plausibility, but is also susceptible to exaggeration. Is love in this conception actually an element in adversarial legal disputes? Perhaps love is, in fact, more essentially related to justice than to law.

Law must provide for the desire for recognition, for it constitutes the substance of law. Recognition cannot be legally compelled; its roots run deeper than law. Recognition reflects human behavior, it is promoted by love and protected by law. But law can create the conditions for recognition. This interpretation is, like Pannenberg's, a social-anthropological notion of law in that the fundamental social activities that constitute law are continuous with activities that take place in other social fora—all involve a pursuit of recognition. In this sense, law is continuous with non-legal kinds of human activity. This does not diminish law but integrates it into a broader spectrum of social activity. Huber resists the reduction of law to an autonomous realm administered by privileged technicians concerned with adjudication and the enforcement of laws and regulations through sanctions.

While the concept of recognition is derived from different premises by Pannenberg and Huber, there is no reason why both conceptions cannot be complementary. For Pannenberg, recognition is a broad-based social practice that values fellow persons and is reflected in law. In contrast, for Huber recognition has a stronger political aspect—it arises in the communicative process. But the one does not exclude the other: persons engage in a vast range of social interactions that calls for reciprocal recognition. The significance of recognition is that it expands a rights-centric concept of law in a communitarian direction. While recognition in this sense is uncommon in Anglophone jurisprudence, it can productively broaden and enrich understanding of the social nature of law. Seen in the context of recognition, law becomes more relational, counteracting what Huber terms the "subjectivizing" of law.[60] This is not to say that rights are peripheral to law, only that they are exercised in an interactional context. What difference, then, does recognition make? It expresses a sense of shared humanity of those with whom one deals, above and beyond transactional interactions.

Law and Love

As with other writers considered here, a fundamental task for Huber is to define the relation between law and love. Both law and love declare "that human beings can recognize each other in freedom, but do so in different ways."[61] This is an sober yet accommodating notion of both love and law; it

60. Huber, *Gerechtigkeit*, 140.
61. Huber, *Gerechtigkeit*, 140.

avoids any suggestion that law and justice are antithetical to love. In reality, they stand in need of each other. Love acknowledges the dignity of fellow persons through unilateral actions of recognition without insistence on reciprocity. Law also conveys recognition: the principle of reciprocal recognition is the "hard kernel of all law."[62] At the same time, it uses compulsion to promote solidarity among individuals by resisting egocentric attempts to benefit at the expense of the common good. "True law is known by its promotion of acts of solidarity and in setting limits to acts against solidarity."[63]

Huber believes that recognition implies the existence of a connection between law and love. This is the focal point for a theological analysis of law: "For the sake of this connection and only for this connection is theology obligated to participate in discussion about the concept and validity of law."[64] For him, the tripartite concept of validity opposes any categorical opposition of law and love. Instead, law can and must give expression to the biblical notion of love—of God, of neighbor and of itself. "Such a basic orientation must be expressed in the structure of law."[65]

The concept of recognition also creates common ground between love and law—"recognition of the other and by the other in love is the basis of mutual recognition that is the theme of law."[66] Law represents an institutionalized form of recognition, while love creatively expresses recognition in personal interactions; they are complementary and not identical.

Against traditional notions of the opposition of love and law (Sohm), Huber finds a motivational and structural connection between love and law: both affirm the solidarity of humans with each other. Law facilitates solidarity-promoting activity by governing the individual pursuit of recognition. It serves to fulfill the solidarity that love helps to create.[67]

Despite their relation, love and law remain distinct. Love incorporates and transcends mutuality—in the direction of sacrificial and unreciprocated action. Therefore, the nature of recognition differs according to context—whether in love or justice, and Huber faults Pannenberg for underappreciating this. For Huber, love encompasses both love of God and neighbor. It is the interpretive horizon for all ethical and legal reflection. Love surely includes recognition of others, freely and generously extended, but law does

---

62. Huber, *Gerechtigkeit*, 51.
63. Huber, *Gerechtigkeit*, 53.
64. Huber, *Gerechtigkeit*, 55.
65. Huber, *Gerechtigkeit*, 55.
66. Huber, *Gerechtigkeit*, 209.
67. In this context, Huber endorses Erik Wolf's interpretation of the neighbor relation as the ground and center of law. See Huber, *Gerechtigkeit*, 208.

not aspire so highly. Voluntary, uncompelled acts of recognition are not usually thought of as characteristics of legal activity. But law does aim at creating a social environment in which reciprocal acts of recognition can occur, as well as at preventing abusive assertions of self-interest. In this respect, law is indeed concerned with recognition.

As Huber sees it, love is uncoerced and largely unconcerned with the specification of rights and duties. In contrast, law is concerned with the limitation of conflict generated by contending claims to recognition. In this respect, law is deeply engaged with the problematics of human sociality.[68] Its regulation of the pursuit of recognition promotes solidarity in that it protects communal interests within the continuous competition in the assertion of legal rights.[69] Love envisions community as the culmination of social existence; law contributes to the possibility of community by contributing to the creation and maintenance of its foundation.

Is some form of social solidarity a goal of law? As noted, Huber contends that law values the interests of the legal community over competition about rights.[70] This suggests that it relates to more than discrete, transactional interactions and the assertion of individual rights, important as they may be. It also has to do with providing structures for interactions among strangers and the coordination of their activities. These contribute to the creation and maintenance of community. To isolate love from law threatens to reduce law to regulating the excesses of individual conduct while ignoring the dimension of sociality.

At the same time, Huber warns against any kind of subsumption of law and love by each other, a danger to which he finds Pannenberg subject, given his close linkage of the two. Pannenberg's approach threatens the legalization of love and the "amorization" of law. Huber finds their relation to be structural rather than substantive: "All legal relations are concerned with human relations; they are measured according to whether they give structure to relations as enabling mutual human solidarity."[71] Can Huber's criticism of Pannenberg be applied to his own position? He implicitly distinguishes between two kinds or contexts of recognition. In a legal context, recognition is typically mutual. In the context of love, recognition transcends the reciprocity of recognition customary in a legal context. "Love

---

68. Huber, *Gerechtigkeit*, 207.

69. Huber, *Gerechtigkeit*, 207.

70. "One of the historical indicia of law . . . is that it regulates competition about legal positions in such a way that legal community is recognized as having precedence over competition involving legal rights" (Huber, *Gerechtigkeit*, 207).

71. Huber, *Gerechtigkeit*, 208.

includes mutuality, but is not limited to it."[72] Love possesses a transcendent impulse. For both Pannenberg and Huber, reliance on recognition as a link between law and love appears to, at least theoretically, risk some degree of confusion between them. But Huber's distinction between them is sharper than Pannenberg's—love goes beyond law, while law enables love to perform its work.

The Relation of Law and Morality/Ethics

In distinguishing between the reciprocal expectations of law and the unilateral actions of love, Huber raises a question of the relation between law and morality. That relation, Huber contends, is one of alternating effect (*Wechselwirkung*).[73] The two domains are distinct yet interdependent. They are not definable in terms of binary alternatives such as internal/external or motive/act, rather they form what might be called overlapping layers.

Originally, religion, law, and morality constituted an undifferentiated continuum. Legal requirements were embodied in what Huber calls primary rules of obligation. Ultimately, they were grounded in religion.[74] With increasing cultural complexity, primary rules became harder to define and enforce. Eventually, additional rules—secondary rules—were needed to define primary rules. These rules by necessity also dealt with the validity and enforcement of primary rules.[75] Modern legal systems, Huber believes, emerged out of the primordial continuum of cultural/legal/moral practices and have become progressively distinguished from morality. In many contemporary understandings, morality serves as a kind of normative penumbra to law—effective only outside its perimeters. But morality affects the readiness of citizens to respect and obey the law, and in this respect is legally relevant. As examples, Huber refers to the resistance activity of Dietrich Bonhoeffer and others in the Second World War. Morality also figures in aspects of law in that it bears on motive and intent. Intent, for example, can be shaped by conscience, which has a moral dimension. In short, law and morality continue to interact.

---

72. Huber, *Gerechtigkeit*, 209.

73. Huber, *Gerechtigkeit*, 67.

74. This contrasts with Pannenberg's notion of the relationship of law and religion. See chapter 7 above.

75. Huber defines four kinds of secondary rules: (1) rules identifying primary roles, (2) rules for amendments, (3) rules for determining violations of primary rules, and (4) rules for sanctions. See Huber, *Gerechtigkeit*, 62–63.

The relation of law and morality is not, however, symmetrical. While law depends on morality, the converse is not true. They exist on different levels of action and decision making, and their overlap is implicit and indirect. In relation to law, morality bears on attitude and motivation. Law primarily deals with conduct. Huber, following Kant, finds this distinction important, though insufficiently nuanced. While Kant insisted that law is concerned with external action and not internal motive, Huber finds that law is concerned to some extent with both. It is dependent on certain moral assumptions, such as the moral insight of citizens.[76] Furthermore, the separation of law and morality protects freedom of conscience and the autonomy of individuals. This, together with the pluralism that autonomy entails, requires that law not be subsumed by morality.

Nevertheless, morality (as concerned with the right) is influential for law, for it motivates acceptance of law by supporting its legitimacy.[77] "It is in no ways a matter of indifference what motives are at work in people's affirmation of a legal order; and it would be a risk to law, difficult to calculate, if all members of the legal community . . . only approve of [law] for external rather than internal reasons."[78] For its part, law often serves to define the sphere of moral action. Law defines when, for example, promise-keeping is required, and when it is not. It addresses the situational obligations of truth, loyalty, and fairness. For Huber, law and morality may not be separated without diminishing each of them.

In what way do theology and ethics (as concerned with the good) interact with law? They do so primarily on the level of legal principle rather than statutory enactment. Following Alexy and Dworkin, Huber distinguishes between principles and rules within law. A theology/ethics of law is concerned with principles. Huber likens them to presuppositions upon which legal rules are based: "A critical theory of law . . . examines law, as it is, with a view to those principles that it contains and that unfold in the course of its development."[79] Law is not self-supporting. "The validity of law itself is dependent on pre-legal conditions."[80] Principles are part of those presuppositions. Collectively, principles form a constitution—like foundation for legal community. They qualify themselves for this function by facilitating the reciprocal exchange of recognition: "Law aims at the enabling of mutual

---

76. Huber, *Gerechtigkeit*, 65.

77. In a later book on ethics, Huber defines morality as concerned with the question of the right, and ethics with the question of the good. See Huber, *Ethics*, 9.

78. Huber, *Gerechtigkeit*, 65.

79. Huber, *Gerechtigkeit*, 167.

80. Huber, *Gerechtigkeit*, 65.

recognition."[81] As already noted, recognition is the moral fulcrum of law for Huber, and by promoting recognition, principles serve to establish the internal validity of law. As principle-based, law combines positivism's desire to avoid the moralization of law with natural law's concern that law possess a minimum of "material correctness."[82]

In addition to principles, Huber also finds norms to be legally important. He defines law as a "system of norms established according to an established procedure, that is by and large socially effective, and possesses a minimum of ethical justifiability."[83] This conception combines elements of positivism and natural law, while preserving a difference between law and morality. While he distinguishes between norms and principles, Huber believes that principles are elements of the legal environment by which enacted law is guided and to which it aspires.[84] He seems to suggest that principles transcend norms and orient them.

The principle–rule distinction Huber develops is another example of his underlying pursuit of an adequate articulation of the relation between law and morality. Rules are fitted to circumstances, and produce predictable legal consequences. In contrast, principles are optimization imperatives (*Optimierungsgebote*) that generate different results under varying circumstances.[85] Their optimality is circumstance-dependent and therefore require judgment and discretion in their interpretation and application. Principles are orientational and critical; this, along with their historical character, differentiates principles from norms of natural law. Principles include basic, constitutional-level values, such as democratic participation, due process, and the rule of law. They all have "unmistakable indirect moral content."[86] The nature of principles and their role in law exclude, for Huber, any hard version of positivism. Indeed, the concept of principle seeks to avoid the deficiencies of both positivism and natural law.[87]

Certain principles exist in constitutions while others are not directly posited. If implicit, how are they identified? One possible source is ethical declarations such as the initial Universal Convention on Human Rights, and the Global Ethic developed by Hans Küng.[88] Even broadly accepted state-

81. Huber, *Gerechtigkeit*, 52.
82. Huber, *Gerechtigkeit*, 102.
83. Huber, *Gerechtigkeit*, 102.
84. Huber, *Gerechtigkeit*, 101.
85. Huber, *Gerechtigkeit*, 100.
86. Huber, *Gerechtigkeit*, 101.
87. Huber, *Gerechtigkeit*, 102.
88. See Küng, *Global Responsibility*. Huber also speaks of the need for a concept of world citizenship based on responsibility. See Huber, *Ethics*, 87–96.

ments of principles, however, are subject to reservations from a pluralistic perspective. Huber refers approvingly to Barth's use of analogy as a means of developing principles from, for example, scriptural sources. Following Heinrich Bedford-Strohm, he derives a preferential option for the disadvantaged from biblical sources. Huber locates the concept of principle in the critical theory of law, and as such it serves as a bridge between ethics and secular jurisprudence.

Huber's appeal to principles has been contested. One critic contends that Huber misunderstands the interpretative, rather than prescriptive, role of principles and norms in constitutional interpretation.[89] Indeed, the nature and function of principles in law is controversial.[90] They have been challenged as being external to law. Yet they may be seen as expressive of the text and spirit of posited law. Obviously, principles are not directly transposable into legal rules. Nevertheless, they can serve a meaningful role in the development of law by exerting paranetic pressure on it and by facilitating the interpretive synthesis of relevant legal precedents, as in Dworkin's theories. At a minimum, principles underscore the importance of law's corrigibility as well as its need for ethical guidance.

Law and Justice

Justice is the conceptual linchpin of Huber's ethics of law, providing an indispensable ethical impulse for the preservation and improvement of law. Further, it furnishes a prescriptive vocabulary for viewing law as an institution concerned with social order but also expressive of moral imagination. Huber's concept of justice is eschatological, social, and functional. A significant characteristic of Huber's ethics of law is an attempt to balance opposing concepts, and justice serves to balance contending or conflicting values—freedom and equality, individuality and community, and preservation and reform. In addition to its social character and its rights-creating capacity, justice is concerned with equality and fairness. Huber conceives of these values in an egalitarian sense that affirms the equal dignity and equality of life chances for individuals while also appropriately recognizing individual achievement.

Law is anchored by justice, and justice depends on law for its actualization. Justice and law exist symbiotically. Every theory of justice, Huber contends, must address two challenges: (1) reconciliation of the disparity

---

89. Jannssen, "Abschied," 4. Jannssen raises other questions as well, such as about the epistemological basis of principles.

90. See Shingleton, "Law, Principle, and the Global Ethic," 49.

between the promise of justice and the shortcomings of its historical realization, and (2) definition of the relation between freedom and equality.[91] Eschatology is relevant to the first question, as explained below. Law bears on the second question. Huber states that "Law is to be understood as the instrument with whose help the tension between freedom and equality is to be minimized."[92] But this tension is enduring, and therefore law must always be concerned with it. Justice is egalitarian in its concern for fairness, its acknowledgment of legitimate individual achievement, and its disapproval of unjustifiable individual advantage. At the same time, it is solicitous of those who suffer want and deprivation.

Huber urges a combination of elements of Aristotelian justice with a biblical notion of justice.[93] To his mind, the Aristotelian concept of justice is indispensable but incomplete. For one thing, in its contemporary versions, it underplays or even obscures the connection between law and justice, and does so despite its conception of *iustitia legalis* and its emphasis on procedural fairness, obedience to law and concern for the common good. If seen as a virtue, justice can give rise to individualistic distortions. While Huber affirms the emphasis on equality and the common good in the Aristotelian tradition of justice, he rejects some contemporary interpretations of Aristotelian justice because they tend to over-emphasize the element of *iustitia communtativa* with its focus on transactional fairness. This distributive emphasis has been seen as particularly valuing legal stability and legal compliance, but it has also been used to justify ideologically the ethical significance of transactional activity, symbolized by the market. Instead, Huber favors a biblically oriented notion combining interpersonal, corrective justice with a preference for the excluded, marginalized and weak. He also proposes a contributive form of justice that advocates equality in chances for active participation by persons in political affairs and other matters of common concern. Huber's understanding of justice seeks to accommodate both classical and biblical perspectives.

Biblically informed justice stands in contrast to classical notions of justice by expressing both promise and goal, understood in communal terms. It is essentially concerned with just action and the expression of mercy; it is manifest in *sedaqa* and acts of justification. Further, it corresponds, in human acts of mercy and reciprocity, to divine, covenantal acts of mercy and promise. Huber terms this connective justice, and sees it as expressing

91. Huber, *Gerechtigkeit*, 174.
92. Huber, *Gerechtigkeit*, 178.
93. For the sake of clarity, Huber's hybrid notion of justice is referred to as "biblically informed justice."

a preferential option for those who lack justice.[94] This preference mirrors the concern of divine justice for the marginalized and excluded. Human sin distorts human justice, which is only saved by divine justification. Biblically informed justice, for Huber, is critical, prophetic, and partial to the disadvantaged. Modern Aristotelian conceptions of justice have overshadowed biblical justice in contemporary understandings, and Huber argues that a critical theology of law must emphasize the importance of the latter. "Justice is one of the biblical concepts in which theological, political, religious and social perspectives are directly connected with each other. Accordingly, a critical theology of law must assert a preference for the biblical understanding of law against dominance of the Aristotelian concept of justice."[95]

Another source of the content of justice is human rights. Huber finds them to be the most important criterion of justice in modernity.[96] Human rights help to define the legitimacy of law. He declares that the contemporary significance of human rights makes the connection between law and morality obvious, in contrast to a positivist separation of them.[97] For him, there is a close correspondence between human rights and the biblical theory of justice, and he proposes a quasi-Barthian method of analogy to illustrate the interaction between them. For example, Huber finds a correspondence between a secular understanding of human autonomy and Christian anthropology, manifested in their common endorsement of the values of freedom, equality and joint participation (*Teilhabe*).[98] Human rights are for him an important aggregation of evolving norms for assessing the legitimacy of the legal order from the perspective of justice.[99] They are grounded in the concept of human dignity that, in modern understanding, is rooted in freedom and in the rational capacity of human beings. Huber insists that the basis of human rights and human dignity must be formulated inclusively and openly.[100] While Huber values a Christian understanding of human rights and dignity for its transcendent grounding of human selfhood and as a basis for distinguishing between a person and her deeds, he admits that it cannot be an exclusive or even the dominant foundation for human rights and dignity in a pluralistic era. The ultimate significance of human rights and human

---

94. See Huber, *Ethics*, 57, where he attributes the term "connective justice" to Jan Assmann.

95. Huber, *Gerechtigkeit*, 166.

96. Huber, *Gerechtigkeit*, 180.

97. Huber, *Violence*, 140.

98. Huber, *Violence*, 266.

99. Huber, *Violence*, 216.

100. Huber, "Rechtsethik," 156.

dignity for law lies not only in their role in compelling it to restrict power when it threatens human dignity, but also in setting limits to law itself.[101]

Huber envisions that the concept of justice in a critical theology of law must be teleological, historical and functional. He urges that eschatology (as concerned with divine promise) and teleology (as concerned with purposes and ends) be brought into contact. Connecting them addresses the challenge of balancing freedom and equality, promise and realization. This notion of eschatological justice relates in a complex way to law, for it is neither equivalent to, nor separate from it.[102] It is the criterion of law, not its source.[103] Justice will always be imperfectly realized in law and appropriately so, for it aims at an ideal, transhistorical reconciliation of freedom and equality. In contrast, law seeks an incremental reduction in the tension between them, rather than in their harmonization. The legitimacy of law essentially depends on its contribution to the realization of justice.[104] This is a progressive process: "The eschatological orientation of theological thought about justice contains an affinity to gradualist considerations that concentrate on the question of how additional justice can be realized under given circumstances."[105]

In addition to the eschatological dimension of justice, Huber identifies a teleological relation between justice and law. This dimension expresses itself through a concern with the legitimacy of law. Legitimacy is relevant for law on three levels: in the relation between justice and individual laws, in the relation between justice and the legal system as a whole, and in the execution of law. However, Huber does not spell out how an eschatological perspective aligns with law's teleological orientation. It is also unclear whether eschatological justice is only meaningful for and within faith communities. If, as Huber suggests, eschatology encompasses teleology, then it should manifest itself, in some way, in law's teleological nature.

In his theological concept of justice, Huber seeks to balance freedom and equality. He rejects Brunner's orders of creation for their failure to take into account sufficiently the impact of sin. Barth's Christocentric personalism, he believes, must be expanded to include nature and history in light of their ultimate, eschatological fulfillment.[106] Justice must also address the tension between freedom and equality on the one hand, and merit and need

101. Huber, "Rechtsethik," 157.
102. Huber, *Gerechtigkeit*, 180.
103. Huber, *Gerechtigkeit*, 198.
104. Huber, *Gerechtigkeit*, 179.
105. Huber, "Rechtsethik," 162.
106. Huber, *Gerechtigkeit*, 170.

on the other. Such a harmonization is promised in the eschatological future.[107] Eschatology complements, critically and constructively, teleological notions of justice with their focus on persons, processes, and things.

Further, Huber sees the vocation of justice primarily as contributing to the legitimacy of law rather than in maintaining social order. The contrast between Huber and Thielicke on this point is revealing. Huber has moved beyond a concentration on the preservative, stabilizing function of law in traditional two kingdoms thought in the direction of a dynamic understanding of law as a means of furthering justice. For him, law is less concerned with the conundrums of distributive justice than with a multifaceted notion of justice incorporating eschatological as well as Aristotelian elements of justice. This gives justice a transcendent role in relation to law. Anything less would be reductionist. "Justice cannot simply be identified with law as it is; it is much more the case that the difference between justice and law is ineluctable."[108] Given the discursive character of justice, its application to specific legal actions will depend on communicative discourse drawing on various elements, such as human rights.

Huber's notion of a biblically oriented concept of justice, and particularly his incorporation of eschatology into it, prompts two concerns. First, Kreβ criticizes Huber's eschatological emphasis for its failure to recognize adequately the transcendent nature of eschatology. "Eschatology transcends . . . the categories of human action and society's operational capacity."[109] Huber would perhaps reply that, while eschatology does contain a transcendent dimension, it nevertheless retains mundane relevance.

Second, how do these biblical and eschatological elements mesh with the pluralistic premise? Huber asserts that "the theological interpretation of God's final future calls forth correspondences in the teleological interpretation of historical processes."[110] These correspondences can be introduced into the teleological analysis and critique of legal systems.[111] Yet it is unclear how this is to occur. Presumably, it can take place through vigorous articulation of the preferential option for the poor as an expression, provisionally and penultimately, of eschatological hope. While eschatology may be an unusual and even alien element in contemporary discussions of justice, it addresses aspects with which every concept of justice must deal, such as the disparity between the promise of justice and its historical realization,

107. Huber, *Gerechtigkeit*, 170.
108. Huber, *Gerechtigkeit*, 180.
109. Kreβ, "Review," 236.
110. Huber, *Gerechtigkeit*, 168.
111. Huber, *Gerechtigkeit*, 168.

and the relation between freedom and equality.¹¹² For Huber, contemporary theories of liberal justice are unsatisfying because of their rejection of eschatological hope as utopian. This diminishes their critical power. That rejection also has the effect of tending, by default, to favor individual freedom at the expense of equality. Huber seeks balance in the concept of justice, and he believes that eschatologically informed justice is a more adequate means to achieve this.

How, though, is a biblically informed concept of justice to be promoted in positive law? Huber rejects attempts either to isolate contemporary legal systems from, or align them directly with, biblical notions of justice. He believes correspondences (*Entsprechungen*) can correlate Christian understandings of law and justice and secular ones without theocratic overtones. Correspondences seem, in Huber's usage, to be similar to analogies. For guidance, Huber looks to Barth's association of justification and law in "Rechtfertigung und Recht." He declares the Barthian method to be a point of departure for a critical theology of law provided that it is understood as referring to all law, not only ecclesial law.¹¹³ Justification is the central act of divine concern and salvation for the world and human beings in and through the person of Christ. It is both exclusive (as embodied in Jesus Christ) and universal (as transcending any exclusivist limitation). This leads Huber to Barth's concentric circles. For him, they symbolize the identity and difference of the faith community and the civil community. Both aspects must be affirmed: difference, expressed through the faith community's own status as an exemplar of eschatologically fulfilled community, and identity, signified through the faith community's prophetic engagement in the civil community. This includes loyalty to the legal system as well as commitment for its reform.

Huber places considerable reliance on correspondences and on Barth's "formula" relating justification and law. What supports this reliance? Huber acknowledges that religious pluralism is pervasive in Western societies, and he affirms freedom of religious belief as necessary for protection of the distinction between law and morality. But the ethical dimension of Huber's idea of justice is clearly biblical in character and origin. Is this problematic? Huber might argue that elements of biblical justice have parallels in secular theory, such as in Rawls's theory of justice and its concern for the least well off. This would warrant a place for biblical justice in public discourse.

But what additional contribution does biblical justice make, either substantively or motivationally, to those located only in the outer concentric

---

112. Huber, *Gerechtigkeit*, 174.
113. Huber, *Gerechtigkeit*, 142.

circle? The importance of community, of loyalty to law and concern for its improvement—these are appreciable even in the absence of correspondences between justification and divine justice. If correspondences add little to the understanding of these matters, it is not clear why and how they would engage those outside the faith community.

A further question concerns the role of faith perspectives in the promotion of justice through law. Huber proposes Christian co-responsibility (*Mitverantwortung*) for law based on a non-ideological view of law and the state.[114] In *Gerechtigkeit*, Huber does not elaborate on how this co-responsibility is expressed, but it would seem to manifest itself in concern for specific causes, such as the protection of human rights. He returns to this theme in a subsequent essay, "Recht als Beruf."[115] There, Huber argues in favor of broad-based involvement by laypersons on behalf of the improvement of law. "Everyone has a relation to law; those who expressly give account of this relation to law have a vocation in the law."[116] In speaking of cooperative responsibility for law, Huber suggests that faith communities and their members should join in efforts with others for the sake of the betterment of law. Motivating beliefs might be expressed, but only in the context of cooperation, not in efforts to sacralize law.

Concluding Observations

In *Gerechtigkeit und Recht*, Huber contends for a bifurcated approach to law—in the form of a critical theory and a critical theology of law. The first essentially deals with jurisprudential themes internal to law, including its philosophical bases, normativity and substantive content. In contrast, a critical theology of law is concerned with the nature and content of justice, its relation to law, as well as the legal significance of human dignity and human rights. It approaches these themes from a Christian perspective, but one that is receptive to other perspectives. The critical theory of law conforms to the requirements of Rawls's idea of public reason; the critical theology does not.

This approach raises several questions, some already mentioned. What is the relation between the critical theory and critical theology? Huber speaks of a "fruitful interaction" between them. Yet the concepts, references, and principal themes of each, though related, differ. How does theology affect theory, and vice versa? Certain topics, such as principle, justice, and

---

114. Huber, *Gerechtigkeit*, 146.

115. The title is an allusion to Max Weber's lectures titled "Politics as a Vocation" (1917) and "Science as a Vocation" (1919).

116. Huber, "Recht als Beruf," 46.

human rights, relate to both of the undertakings. While these topics certainly have a place in both critical theory and critical theology, their content is context-dependent. This presents interpretive challenges.

Further, how is a critical theology of law expressed—and to whom? Under contemporary circumstances, theological/ethical perspectives have an indirect and distanced role in positive law. Huber accepts this and looks to Barth's "Rechtfertigung und Recht" in response.[117] Jesus Christ is the center point of the circles of the Christian community and the civil community. Huber contends that a temporal (eschatological) dimension must be added to Barth's concentric circles. Until the time of eschatological fulfillment, the Christian community must serve as an example by devoting itself to its liturgical and caritive activities.[118] This can involve concern for mundane law in the form of Christian co-responsibility for law based on a "strictly functional view of law."[119] In light of this, a critical theology of law would seem to be primarily suited to faith communities. Any significance it may have for a secular audience would be secondary.

Obviously, Huber is principally concerned with the theoretical aspects of a Christian ethics of law. But given that law is a social/political institution, engagement with it requires more than theoretical reflection. Huber identifies specific areas of law that call for critical attention and action, including human rights and equality, environmental law, criminal law, and immigration. His proposals for these areas are not only intended for faith communities, for law does not belong only to them. Justice is a conceptual thread that runs through these specific areas, indeed through all areas of law as he sees it. As noted, a critical theology of law is centrally concerned with justice, and he understands justice eschatologically. But eschatology rests on theological presuppositions. The question, then, is how adequately justice can also be understood in non-eschatological terms. Huber's idea of justice as a preference for the disadvantaged seems to express such an understanding, but it would need the support of some notion of how this is socially beneficial. This raises the question whether the critical theory and critical theology are essentially different perspectival aspects of a common undertaking.

A further question concerns Huber's concept of law as social-communicative activity. This emphasizes law's discursive nature, but does it map well on the practices of law? Can law essentially be understood as a seeking

---

117. "Both [biblical justice and secular law] do not allow themselves to be related to each other through a cognitive model of legitimizing identification" (Huber, *Gerechtigkeit*, 140).

118. Huber, *Gerechtigkeit*, 143.

119. Huber, *Gerechtigkeit*, 146.

of consensus or compromise? Law's procedures are more obviously premised on the persistence of disputation and conflict. Further, it bears asking whether the quality of discourse about law does not diminish its legitimacy. The view of law of at least one social critic in the United States presents a darker picture, one that portrays it as a social/political battleground.[120] In any event, further elaboration of the notion of law as communicative discourse would be helpful.

Another question concerns Huber's concept of recognition, which plays a key role in his ethics of law. Recognition has a legal aspect that fundamentally presupposes the equality of persons before the law.[121] But recognition also has a moral aspect that is more expansive. It affirms an essential equality despite empirical differences among persons. These two aspects reflect Dreier's distinction between the legal and moral types of recognition. When Huber speaks of recognition, is he referring to both kinds? Only legal recognition? If so, is that sufficient? If the former, how is moral recognition expressed in law?

Huber speaks of the relation of morality and law as one of reciprocal dependence. Morality, he contends, is a presupposition of the validity of law. In turn, law is an empirical presupposition of moral consciousness and practice.[122] How does pluralism affect the relation between morality and law as Huber conceives it? It would seem that as morality becomes less socially homogenous and more pluralistic, morality's role in helping to establish the validity of law becomes more complicated if not compromised. The politicization of law also can undermine law's validity. The role of morality in supporting the validity of law is evolving, and this suggests that the relation between morality and law is evolving as well.

Finally, Huber's critical theory and theology is notable for its commitment to law and its commitment to law's improvement. These activities are not only available to legal professionals but to laypersons as well. Lay engagement may take various forms, including judicial submissions, efforts to increase access to justice, citizen participation in legislative activity, and, as Huber discusses, civil disobedience. Participation in these and other activities involving the law by persons with differing comprehensive perspectives is congruent with the pluralistic premise assuming appropriate regard for law's procedures, authorities, and reasoning. Here, Huber's ethics of law is particularly impressive for its broad-based commitment to democratic involvement with law as an essential political and social institution.

---

120. Hunter, "Law as Common Good."
121. Huber, *Gerechtigkeit*, 51.
122. Huber, *Gerechtigkeit*, 66.

IX

Postscript: Hartmut Kreß

The Ethics of the Legal Order

Since the publication of Huber's book, a number of theological/ethical reflections on positive law have appeared in the Germanophone sphere.[1] One of the most impressive of the recent publications is *Ethik der Rechtsordung* (2012) by Hartmut Kreß. Kreß, a professor of social ethics on the Protestant theological faculty in Bonn, presents an incisive analysis of contemporary law from an ethical perspective, with particular reference to Germany. While he assesses the writings on law of several of the authors discussed above (among them Barth), Kreß moves beyond traditional theological interpretations and situates law squarely in a cultural context characterized by secularism and pluralism. Of course, many of the writers considered here also acknowledge the secular and pluralistic context of modern law, but none of them emphasizes the impact of pluralism as thoroughly as Kreß does. In this respect, his analysis represents a culmination of sorts, or at least a significant milestone, in the theological/ethical reflections on law considered in this book.

To illustrate Kreß's approach and argument, a brief summary of three of Kreß's major themes follows: his conception of law as a cultural good, his understanding of the relation of law and ethics, and his conception of human dignity in relation to law. While he deals with many other aspects of law in his extensive and provocative ethical analysis of the legal order in Germany,

---

1. In addition to Kreß's book, see Kistner, *Rechtstheologie* (2017); Plathow, *Liebe und Recht* (2018); Herms, *Politik und Recht im Pluralismus* (2008); Welker, "Moral, Recht, und Ethos" (2002); Moxter, "Der Mensch im Recht" (2008). These are a few; there are obviously others.

his treatment of these three topics displays the thrust of his approach and suggests one direction future ethical reflection on law may take.

Law and Culture

Contemporary law, Kreß believes, must be considered in its cultural setting. In Germany and other developed societies, the prevailing cultural context is secular and pluralist. "They are not adventitious circumstances that incidentally affect law; they fundamentally shape it. This is a result of law's status as a cultural concept and cultural good."[2] Law is neither autonomous nor immune from cultural developments; it is part of culture.[3] Conceived in this way, law becomes less predominantly a political institution (though it remains that) and more a social-cultural "artifact."[4] From this perspective, law is historical, is concerned with values, and interacts with other cultural domains such as science, education, economy and art. This leads Kreß to propose broadening the traditional modes of legal interpretation (textual, logical, historical, normative and teleological) to include a *comparative* approach analyzing law and its cultural setting. Since law is a component of culture, and since cultures express contrasting value systems, comparative perspectives can illuminate how law is structured and administered in diverse cultural settings. It can explore the historical and cultural bases of law, and seek to understand how its contents have been shaped by these factors.

Kreß contends that seeing law's character as a cultural good facilitates such comparative, cross-cultural scrutiny. For example, he refers to healthcare, medical ethics, questions of contraception and legal definitions of death as topics that can productively be explored in a comparative manner. Comparison can also be directed internally within a legal system. It involves consideration of the differing experiences of groups within a society, and the contrasting impacts of their engagement of law. Not only do such comparative explorations enrich understandings of law, they also help to address what Kreß sees as the seeming paradox of the simultaneous erosion of legal legitimacy and increasing pervasiveness of law in social life. (Germany is his frame of reference.) Comparative insights can enrich discourse about one's own legal system, especially in light of the relativizing effects of pluralism. This is a positive benefit of pluralism.

2. Kreß quotes Radbruch in support of this assertion: "The concept of law is a cultural concept" (Kreß, *Ethik der Rechtsordnung*, 15).

3. Other ethicists also have adopted this approach. For example, Martin Honecker contends, "Law is an expression of culture in a form of its appearance" (Honecker, *Grundriß*, 567).

4. Kreß, *Ethik der Rechtsordnung*, 49.

But what does it mean, exactly, to interpret law as a cultural good? It means to view law in light of cultural presuppositions and constraints, as reflecting cultural inclinations and aversions towards certain values. Legal culture reflects its surrounding culture. As Roger Cotterell suggests, "The idea of legal culture entails that law (as rules, practices, institutions, doctrine, etc.) should be treated as embedded in a broader culture of some kind."[5] Cotterell refers to culture as "some kind of complex totality of meaning and experience."[6] As a consequence, when law is viewed from a cultural perspective, it is seen as encompassing more than rules, doctrines and procedures.

Considering law as a cultural manifestation has two further consequences. First, a cultural perspective on law relativizes law's purported autonomy and critical distance from its surrounding culture. Instead, it is continuous with, and reflective of, that culture. Seeing law as a cultural good renders it more available for critique and recommendations for reform by those outside of the professional sub-culture of law. This serves to expand the public forum for discourse about law. Social and political values are no longer extraneous, *per se*, to law, but form part of the cultural matrix that frames and impinges on law, and that law in turn affects. Second, comparative analyses aid law's development by prompting critical reflection on it. This is particularly profitable for the field of constitutional law. In some legal systems, such as the United States, constitutions are deeply revered and are difficult to amend, making judicial interpretation an important means for further development of that body of law, and others as well. For its part, that mode of interpretation is subject to public influence.

Kreß's conception of law as a cultural good has certain implications that open up law for critique and interrogation, such as that advanced by the Law and Society movement in the United States.[7] It raises questions about access to justice and the social effects of law on marginal populations as part of public debate about minimum social entitlements. In times of political polarization, it challenges the politicization of justice and the co-optation of the legal system for partisan purposes. And it prompts reflection on the importance of democratic participation in the development of law.[8]

---

5. Cotterell, "Comparative Law," 710.

6. Cotterell, "Comparative Law," 710.

7. See generally Calavita, *Law and Society*.

8. A recent study argues that broad public participation by lay persons and interest groups outside of traditional legal circles has had a significant effect on the development of constitutional law in the United States. See Cole, *Engines of Liberty*.

Law, Morality and Ethics

A second topic Kreß examines is the relation of law and ethics. In Kreß's definition, ethics consists of theoretical reflection on morality. Morality, in turn, is the personal ethos of an individual, and includes the customs, norms, or rules deemed valid in a society that contribute to the integrity of human life and action.[9] Often, the relationship between law and ethics is blandly described as involving neither their separation nor identity. Kreß sees a dialectical relation between them.

For him, the separation of law and ethics in modern reflection is irreversible—they are categorically different. While he contends that law is generally concerned with external behavior and ethics with internal convictions and motivations, in reality the boundary between them is porous. Law seeks to secure the greatest possible degree of freedom and space for personal decisions; it thereby supports morality by helping to secure the capacities that are necessary for authentic ethical existence. Kreß refers to this as the "facilitation of individual ethical responsibility as a purpose of law."[10] The promotion of individual agency and responsibility is not simply an incidental side effect but is an essential part of law. In a pluralistic era, he believes it is both appropriate and necessary for law to support such autonomy. While he does not specifically refer to discourse ethics, Kreß's view of law is consistent with it in that law is expressed in, and it facilitates and coordinates, the discursive and other social interactions of individuals.

Law and ethics are also connected through the concept of justice. Justice prevents law from being a self-referential system. To a degree, law must reflect the prevailing ethical standards of the society. It cannot be excessively in tension with those standards. "In so far as the legal order seizes on the dynamics of the development of moral standards and the advance of ethical expertise and civil society, the state becomes the notary of changes in values."[11] To be sure, the ethos of a pluralistic society is not easily definable due to its syncretic and corrigible nature. But as a general principle, laws become outmoded and are ignored if they are overtaken by changes in social mores and standards.

The support law renders to morality does not alter the fact of their fundamental separation. Kreß speaks of their "non-identity."[12] Their relation is premised on this non-identity. Separation preserves the critical and

---

9. Kreß, *Ethik der Rechtsordnung*, 59.
10. Kreß, *Ethik der Rechtsordnung*, 75.
11. Kreß, *Ethik der Rechtsordnung*, 73.
12. Kreß, *Ethik der Rechtsordnung*, 67.

constructive capacity of ethics, as captured by Radbruch's formula delineating correct law from incorrect law. A law may be facially neutral yet yield inhumane consequences. At times, law may be incapable of supporting morality, either due to the absence of law, or the presence of constraints on its effectiveness.[13] At those times, morality in the form of personal action must enter the breach. Kreβ cites climate change as an example of a situation in which law appears inadequate to address potentially catastrophic harm. Obviously, law can and does regulate many kinds of activity harmful to the environment. But law cannot regulate all the various kinds of individual behavior that contribute to the problem. Kreβ writes: "As important as law and statutes are—the basic presupposition of social partnership (*Konvivanz*) is the ethics of citizens lived out on a daily basis, their personal ways of behavior and the moral convictions ("virtues") up to civil disobedience."[14] Law cannot replace personal morality, nor can it capably satisfy all or even most of its demands.

Finally, Kreβ poses the question whether law serves a moral-pedagogical function. For him, it is too restrictive to conceive of law solely in terms of the regulation of external behavior. Legal norms and rules affect, though indirectly, the moral convictions of citizens. "Progress in ethical knowledge and changes in humane social values are aided by concurrent initiatives of legal policy."[15] He cautions, however, that the pedagogical possibilities of law are limited. Law should restrict itself to promoting tolerance and the self-responsibility of individual citizens, allowing each of them to incorporate morally significant aspects of law into their personal worldviews. To expect more than this from law is to invite legal paternalism.

Therefore, law, morality, and ethics should neither be separated nor combined. They are distinct and different domains, yet are concerned with individual and collective actions. Their relation is complex and nuanced and not simple and univocal. Comparative analyses of law demonstrate the spectrum of possible relations between the legal, moral and ethical spheres. Comparative law is a long-established legal discipline, but comparative study of both law and ethics in their interactions would be an illuminating step beyond traditional understandings of their relation.

---

13. He refers, as an example, to the inability of asylum-seekers in Germany to enjoy a secure right to medical care as a result of applicable legislation. Kreβ, *Ethik der Rechtsordnung*, 69.

14. Kreβ, *Ethik der Rechtsordnung*, 70.

15. Kreβ, *Ethik der Rechtsordnung*, 80.

Human Dignity

A third theme of particular note in Kreβ's ethics of the legal order is the role of human dignity in law. Like Huber, Kreβ sees it occupying a central place in contemporary understandings of law.

Human dignity, in Kreβ's view, is one of the fundamental concepts of ethical and legal culture.[16] Although Huber acknowledges the importance of human dignity, his focus in *Gerechtigkeit* lies more on human rights. He considers them to be, along with basic rights, the "critical measuring rod for analyzing positive law and for its future development."[17] (Basic rights (*Grundrechte*) are individual constitutional rights.[18]) Human rights are frequently seen as derived from, and rooted in, human dignity, but Huber insists they should be grounded more openly and inclusively, and not linked to a single source. As noted, he sees the significance of human dignity for law in the limitation of governmental power through law, as well as in the limitation of law against its own excesses.[19]

In contrast to Huber, Kreβ focuses on the concept of human dignity in itself and as the basis of fundamental individual rights. He terms it a leading normative concept of legal culture, one with a high moral claim."[20] It is both a basic right in and of itself, as well as a conceptual foundation for other constitutional rights. At the same time, Kreβ points out vulnerabilities in the concept, including its vagueness, susceptibility to rhetorical inflation and vulnerability to trivialization. Moreover, the interpretation of human dignity rests on subjective or social perspectives that are time-conditioned and potentially ideological.[21] Undoubtedly, the dignity concept can be used to obscure legal rights rather than to clarify them. Kreβ therefore argues in favor of a notion of human dignity that is rationally grounded, historically rooted, and capable of interpretive refinement. He is critical of the interpretation of human dignity advanced by some modern Protestant theologians, such as Barth and Thielicke, because of their grudging acceptance of it on theological grounds as well as their culturally relative conceptions of it.[22] Kreβ prefers an interpretation of human dignity that allows various

---

16. Kreβ, *Ethik der Rechtsordnung*, 117.
17. Huber, *Gerechtigkeit*, 225.
18. Creifeld, *Rechtswörterbuch*, 605.
19. Huber, "Rechtsethik," 157.
20. Kreβ, *Ethik der Rechtsordnung*, 117.
21. Kreβ, *Ethik der Rechtsordnung*, 119.
22. As an example, Kreβ cites Barth's denunciation of homosexuality as contrary to the divine image, which Barth conceived on the relational model of man-woman, instead of in terms of personal rights. See Kreβ, *Ethik der Rechtsordnung*, 145–46.

justifications to one dependent on a single metaphysical premise. Foundational openness is pluralistically advantageous, for it gives human dignity an integrative capability, one that allows various perspectives to intersect, interact and coalesce.

Kreß's discussion of human dignity clearly reflects the legal-cultural context in which he writes. The concept of dignity is specifically incorporated in the quasi-constitutional German Basic Law and has foundational significance for German constitutional interpretation.[23] Dignity does not have an equivalent status in the domestic law of most Anglophone legal cultures, though it figures in international treaties, conventions, and individual statutes, and therefore has attained a footing in US law. Nevertheless, it is important to appreciate that the cultural/legal context affects interpretation of the dignity concept.

Do theology or ethics properly play a role in the interpretation of human dignity? Kreß prefers a rational, historical and interpretive approach over what he considers the particularism of religious traditions. This is understandable to an extent in view of the constricted and distorted understandings of human dignity that can be found within those traditions. But not all religious interpretations present these deficiencies. Huber prefers to see religious accounts of human dignity as perspectival enhancements rather than particularist constrictions.[24] Further, he emphasizes the contribution of theological understandings of justification and of human self-transcendence as enhancing the spectrum of meanings of the human dignity.[25] Nevertheless, Kreß's insistence on pluralistic, rational and publicly comprehensible groundings of human dignity seems both reasonable and desirable. Though one might suppose his approach to be too restrictive, Kreß likely sees it as enhancing the intelligibility and plausibility of human dignity as a criterion for positive law. One can imagine, though, how Karl Barth might view Kreß's notion of dignity. Perhaps he would complain that excluding theological doctrines such as justification and sinfulness from the interpretation of legal concepts diminishes the concept by rendering it superficial. This, he might possibly contend, shows that pluralism generates more constricted understandings of dignity rather than more open and inclusive ones. Kreß might possibly respond that contemporary discourse about law—a cultural good—must nevertheless be impartial towards all worldviews, religious or otherwise, even if elements of law lack the thickness of meaning they may

---

23. Kommers and Miller write, "Germany's new constitutionalism has placed human dignity at the core of its value system" (Kommers and Miller, *Constitutional Jurisprudence of Germany*, 44).

24. Huber, "Rechtsethik," 157.

25. Huber, "Rechtsethik," 157.

have in a particular religious tradition. Obviously, pluralism cannot plausibly mean either abandonment of one's own perspectives or disregard of the discursive context in which they are expressed. But it must remain inclusive and accessible for different worldviews.

A Path Forward

Kreβ's *Ethik der Rechtsordnung* deals with many other topics than those discussed here. A constant motif of the book is the contemporary inadequacy of traditional understandings of the relation of law and religion. In the words of one reviewer, "Kreβ's consistent cultural-historical perspective leads to a critical farewell to customary theological and ecclesiastical rhetoric."[26] In this respect, Kreβ's work represents a certain disengagement with the traditional theological modes of interaction with positive law discussed in the preceding chapters in favor of a concentration on the ethical potential of law. This is not to suggest, however, that theological interpretations of law have been abandoned in continental Protestantism. That would be incorrect. Michael Welker, for one, is a forceful advocate of such a mode of reflection.[27] But at least one branch of the tradition is taking a significantly different direction.

On first impression, Kreβ's ethics of the legal order appears, from a theological perspective, to have a pronounced secularist orientation. This reflects undoubtedly the particular characteristics of the German legal situation in which institutional churches have a particular legal status. But his emphasis on toleration, justice and, human rights as ethical concerns of law stands as an example of an understanding of law that strives to be adequate for a secularist and pluralist era.

It is difficult to imagine positions farther removed from each other than Kreβ's *Ethik der Rechtordnung* and Barth's "Rechtfertigung und Recht." In a sense, these two writings mark off an arc that the theology and ethics of law has taken over the course of almost a century, from the early decades of the last century to the present day. One can believe, however, that both Kreβ and Barth, as well as all the other writers considered in this book, would agree that positive law should receive more attention from Protestant ethicists and theologians. Their reflections provides resources for that work.

---

26. Von Scheliha, "Review," 295.
27. See his recent essay, Welker, "What Could Christian Theology Offer?"

X

Toward a Conclusion

The previous chapters represent critical soundings of the reflections of eight Protestant thinkers on positive law. These explorations have been both expository and critical, sympathetic where possible and skeptical where necessary. This is the point to engage in some tentative stock-taking and to attempt to discern some directions for future inquiry.

The texts considered display a certain trajectory. It ranges from more theological interpretations of positive law to more ethical ones, from the grounding of law to its critique, from soteriology to justice. It is increasingly self-critical in questioning its own assumptions. It is a trajectory shaped by the evolution of theological thought generally, as well as by political and social upheavals. Traditionally, a central question animating the theological reflections of Barth, Brunner and Ellul about law concerned the connection between divine and human law. The focus in Huber and Kreβ, in contrast, is more directly on human law itself. How does it measure up to criteria of justice and love? How is it—and should it be—shaped by pluralism and secularism?

Most of the writers affirm some kind of relation between positive law and a religious or ethical order of value. Significant divergences arise in how that relation is conceived. Some authors speak in terms of divine justice as the source and ground of human law and against which human law is measured and found lacking. Others do not refer principally to divine law but instead to certain values as benchmarks for mundane law such as love or justice. They are usually but not necessarily of theistic origin. For some writers, this theistic foundation is understood Christologically; others relate it to the divine first person. In both cases, human accounts of positive law are inadequate if they fail to acknowledge a need for legitimacy and moral authority in law. The authors generally dismiss positivism as a comprehensive and exhaustive account of law, though some accept elements of it. For example, positivism's account of the origin and nature of human law is considered more or less persuasive to an extent for Huber, though he rejects hard forms of positivism and the separation thesis.[1] Most writers are dismissive of natural law on theological grounds, although several (such as Brunner and Kreβ) affirm some concept of universal rights and structures of value in all forms of human culture. Recent scholarship suggests that this traditional aversion to natural law is under reconsideration.[2]

The differing conceptions of the relation of divine and human law lead to divergent understandings of how theology/ethics relate to positive law. The alternatives advanced by the authors can be grouped as follows:

1. A theological grounding of positive law in which the normativity of positive law, and to some extent its substantive content, that consists of a relation of direct dependence on divine law and justice. Barth, Brunner, Ellul, and Thielicke represent this position, each in his own way.

2. An ethics of law, rather than a theological grounding, as a means of mediation of religious and ethical insights regarding the nature and role of positive law. Huber and Kreβ advocate this approach.

3. An interpretive approach in which the anthropological character of law is identified and interpreted theologically in order to uncover their theological and ethical implications. In particular, Pannenberg approaches law in this way (though he also proposes a theological grounding of law as well), and then applies theological categories to that data in order to arrive at foundational conclusions.

Each of these interpretative approaches implies a certain relation between theological categories or ethical values and positive law. A grounding of law presupposes that positive law has a derivative relationship to divine law and is dependent on a religious foundation. This places human law under divine oversight—a conception of law remote from contemporary understandings. This kind of approach presents a problem in a pluralistic context; it is more appropriate and relevant within a faith communities. An ethics of law is concerned less with the genesis and basis of law and more with its ethical quality and consequences. It does not occupy itself primarily with the relation of human law and divine law but with its ethical character. Of course, the norms employed in an ethics of law must be warranted in some way, and theological considerations enter the picture in that regard.

---

1. Huber speaks of a "post-positivist" understanding of law that preserves the positivist separation of legality and morality (Huber, *Gerechtigkeit*, 84).

2. See generally vanDrunen, *Natural Law*; Grabill, *Natural Law*.

An anthropological approach places law within a context of human social behavior and relates it to forms of social interaction that are, in turn, interpreted in light of human religiosity.[3] These two approaches—ethical and anthropological—seem to be more resonant for contemporary sensibilities.

The following are some of the significant topics treated by each of the eight authors. On some of them a high degree of consensus exists, on others, there is a diversity of opinion.

An Expansive Understanding of Law

All of the authors assume, some more explicitly than others, that law should be viewed broadly and expansively, not merely as an institutional apparatus for securing order and enforcing it through sanctions. Law is more than a collection of technical regulations and coercive rules; it is a social and political institution and an ensemble of practices that pervade social life. The consequences of this conception are twofold: law is valued as a partially autonomous sphere to be protected and developed; it is also a realm of ethical action. It opens theoretical and practical possibilities for engagement beyond participation in legislative and adjudicative processes.

The Contextualization of Law

If, as Reinhold Niebuhr contends, "Religion is a sense of the absolute," then law exists as an element of a larger whole.[4] It is situated within a broader context and is conditioned by it. This contextualization makes law's rationale and purpose part of a larger rationale and purpose; it renders its significance and meaning part of a broader context of significance and meaning. The opposite of contextualization is insularity and autonomy, in the sense of self-directing independence from external circumstances. Indeed, law's autonomy endows it with an enigmatic quality.[5] None of the writers accept an understanding of law as wholly autonomous. But the degree of autonomy they acknowledge varies; this is evident from the range of attitudes towards positivism. Several reject it as a conception of law that must be overcome. Others tolerate or even embrace autonomy to some extent. When viewed affirmatively, positivism may for example be seen as allowing some place

---

3. This is essentially the approach followed by Pannenberg; it is obviously not the only one.

4. Niebuhr, *Moral Man*, 52.

5. "It is indeed the unique feature of the Western legal tradition that it is fundamentally enigmatic" (Goodrich, "Law and Critical Theory," 5360).

for morality. This perspective has precedents in Protestant, and particularly Reformed, tradition.

Each writer situates law within a theological/ethical framework broader than an exclusively jurisprudential/philosophical one. It also places it within a cultural and social setting. Contextualization also affirms that law has ethical and theological significance within and for that cultural setting. Among its tasks, law establishes the terms of participation in public affairs by persons, prescribes rules of fairness in private transactions, distributes goods and burdens, and provides for the resolution of conflicts. In its constitutional form, law concerns the fundamental aspirations of a political community. These are economic and political activities, but they are also ethically and theologically significant.

Differences exist in how the authors conceive of contextualization. For Barth, the Christological center is the contextualizing principle; for Brunner, it is the orders of creation under divine authority; for Pannenberg, it is the universal horizon of history as a revelation of the divine self. Each accentuates different theological elements: for Barth these include reconciliation and Christology; for Pannenberg, love and eschatology.

Different historical and political circumstances also affect a writer's particular contextualization of law. In his later writings, Brunner portrays human law at standing at low ebb, undermined and discredited by Nazism. Positive law had become enfeebled, and divine law is its anchor. Similarly, Ellul holds that the *ius divinum* frames positive law. Thielicke's notion of law as an institution of compromise, was developed in the shadow of the Cold War, and expresses a sense of urgency and provisionality in viewing law as an emergency order of maintenance.[6] It also reflects a strong sense of human infirmity and ethical tension created by existence within conflicting normative domains of work, personal life, religious life, associations and political orders. Pannenberg's vision of law, in contrast, is less sharply dialectical, and looks to the findings of the social sciences for the origins of law. Law is seen as the institutionalization of foundational social practices, legitimized and transformed through the agencies of religion and ethics into an eschatologically-oriented anticipation of communal destiny. Huber similarly views law as a foundational social institution, but emphasizes the role of ethical critique within a field of continuous communicative discourse and construal. It advances law, increases social justice, protects human rights and the natural environment. All of the authors acknowledge not only law's social and political functions, but also its role as a vital component of social life and an

---

6. The section on the theology of law in Thielicke's *Theologische Ethik* contains an excursus on Soviet law that is predictably negative. See Thielicke, *Ethik*, 3:315–20.

expression of a community's ethical orientation. This gives law religious and ethical significance beyond its importance for the maintenance of human community. While these contextualizations of law are meaningful primarily for those in faith communities, they encourage commitment by all citizens to law and its improvement.

Law and Legitimacy

Another important aspect of law all the writers emphasize is legitimacy. This is interpreted by most in terms of some kind of moral acceptability. Huber refers to validity as well as legitimacy. For him, it has various forms: social, legal, substantive. Legitimacy is a contested notion in analytic jurisprudence. But the authors here all affirm that legitimacy includes more than the manner of creation of law. It also encompasses its substantive provisions and administration. For some, the *ius divinum* is the criterion for the content of positive law (Brunner, Ellul); for others, it is congruence with justice or some other value (Thielicke). Like contextualization, legitimacy provides an entrée for the introduction of theological and ethical considerations into law.

The importance of legitimacy in law underlies reservations about positivism. Positivism can account for legal compliance and obedience, but not, without more, for respect for law. The sources of law according to positivism—both governmental and political organs—are imperfect human institutions. Legitimacy requires that law possess some intrinsic justness and authority. For some writers, this authority is religiously-based, and for others it depends on an ethical criterion or value.

Justice and Law

Each of the eight authors asserts a relation between justice and law. The significance of that relation depends on the foundational concepts on which each relies, including the concept of justice. While many relate human justice to divine justice, they conceive of that relation in different ways. For Barth, Ellul, and Wolf, human justice derives from, and is dependent upon, divine justice and righteousness. For Huber and Kreß, human justice is less dependent on a transcendent theological point of reference and more reflective of the ethical values of society and concern for those least well off.

Obviously, justice has a plethora of meanings. Martin Honecker contends that justice is, in fact, "not a norm, not a usable measuring rod, not a condition, and is also not a pure ideal. Instead, it is a model, an orientation for human action."[7] This variability in the meaning of justice is evident in the contrast between theological/ethical conceptions of justice and legal ones. Legal justice is conceived by some in procedural terms as fair and impartial processes of litigation and adjudication.[8] Substantive aspects of justice are also relevant, often understood in relation to fundamental constitutional principles such as the rule of law, equal protection, and due process. With few exceptions, discussions in mainstream jurisprudential literature regarding legal justice do not reference or acknowledge theological conceptions of justice. Even legal justice itself has a modest role in many jurisprudential texts. John Bell notes that "lawyers and legal philosophers have not been overly preoccupied with the question 'What is justice?'"[9] Some have challenged this attitude. Robin West argues that "these questions—the demands of justice, the ideals we have or should have for law, or the nature of the 'good' that a good law exhibits and a bad law lacks—should be the defining questions of jurisprudence."[10]

Contemporary secular jurisprudence tends to define justice in distributive terms.[11] Several of the writers here, above all Brunner, follow this path. In contrast, Barth is not particularly interested in distributive justice. He envisions justice as modeled on divine justice, in which justice and mercy are united, and particular concern directed to the poor and helpless. As we saw, Huber conceives of justice in a quadripartite manner (distributive, communtative, connective, participatory) and as essentially concerned with the common good. The variety of contexts and relations in which justice plays a role requires a multidimensional conception of it. Theological and ethical reflection on positive law draws on multiple aspects of justice, and therefore requires justice to be a pliable concept.

Justice serves law through critique. Some points of its critique concern equal access to law, the politicization and misuse of law, concern for the socially marginalized, insistence on democratic accountability, and humaneness in criminal justice and punishment. Several writers have limited confidence in the ability of human law to advance justice. This may reflect an acute sense of realism for some; for others it reflects the innate sinfulness of human nature. For Huber and Kreß, justice is vital for positive law

---

7. Honecker, *Auf der Suche*, 273.

8. A classic statement of this view is Fuller, *Morality of Law*.

9. Bell, "Justice and the Law," 114.

10. West, *Normative Jurisprudence*, 2.

11. "Nowadays, first thoughts about justice are primarily centered around issues of distribution and on expectations of "social" justice, either in the sense of equal distribution or of a distribution that corresponds to the perspective needs" (Höffe, "Justice," 110).

because it challenges it to better itself in the direction of greater human welfare, inclusivity and freedom. Justice is a key desideratum of a contemporary ethics of law, and it is one of its foundational elements.

Reservations about Natural Law

As we have seen, most of the authors express a range of reservations about natural law. Some display a degree of hostility to it (Thielicke); others concede some validity to it while still maintaining a generally dismissive stance (Barth). Only Brunner embraces natural law broadly, though he is critical of some traditional conceptions. While not unanimous in the intensity of their rejection, most writers see, at most, limited prospects for natural law. The recent revival of interest in natural law in Protestant circles may prompt reconsideration of traditional attitudes toward natural law. Should that occur, theological and ethical reflection on law would have a role to play.

A Theology of Law versus an Ethics of Law?

The trend towards an ethics of law among the more recent writers in this book does not entail abandonment of a theology of law. Indeed, interest in theologies of law in the Germanophone sphere has continued.[12] Certainly, a contemporary legal theology will be different than it was in the past. Society, church, and law have each undergone enormous change since, for example, Barth's ethics lectures of 1929. A theology of law is no longer viable if it requires cultural deference to the doctrines of a predominant faith tradition.[13]

Theological reflection on law can be meaningful and relevant in faith communities in their understandings of law and appreciation of the need for the improvement of law. Within these communal contexts, legal theologies remain valuable resources for the contextualizing law, defending it against excessive politicization, and relating it to foundational values of faith traditions. For example, Jeffrey Hammond advocates development of Protestant jurisprudence in the form of "Protestant legal theory." He defines that as the "active, searching, humble, theologically oriented, biblically focused

---

12. Recent publications include Kistner, *Rechtstheologie*; also see McIlroy, "Theology and Legal Theory."

13. As Martin Marty has noted, "All fabrics of value systems, all advocacies of virtues, all claims for moralities tend to be 'relative' to those in other cultures and do not seem to be easily available for lawmakers beyond sectors of particular believing communities" (Marty, "Religious Foundations of Law," 312).

theorizing about the nature, purposes, functions, orientations, and consequences of law as a discipline."[14] It is also "the quest for theoretical answers to theological questions that arise as law manifests itself in many forms as law interacts with human choices and actions of all kinds."[15]

In the public realm, an ethics of law is a particularly appropriate basis for bringing perspectives of belief and value to bear on law. Ethical engagement with law involves reciprocal exploration of the domains of both faith and law. An ethics of law is more concerned with understanding intersections between these two human modes of knowledge, belief and practice than with subordination of one to the other. Ethics and theology are also concerned with many of the goods with which law is concerned: community, dignity, autonomy, equality and fairness. Unless one accepts a rigid idea of sector morality insistent on the ethical autonomy of different spheres of life (workplace, personal life, politics, international relations, etc.), ethics and law must interact to some extent.

In this understanding of the roles of an ethics of law and a theology of law, it is unnecessary to choose between them. They have distinct roles in differing contexts. Both have a place in the public realm as well as within faith communities, but their vocabularies and content vary.

Implications for North America

Modern Protestant theologies of law have largely been a continental, and particularly German, undertaking. Obviously, North America presents a different cultural context. Law has different cultural characteristics in Germany and the United States. Gerhard Robbers summarizes one difference from a German perspective: "Law in the USA serves primarily as an instrument, as a weapon, for the enforcement of one's own individual interests. In Germany, law serves primarily the cohesiveness and burden-sharing of the community."[16] This difference has various causes, including contrasting conceptions of the relation of the individual to the state and society and different social understandings of law, as well as varying notions of how law

---

14. Hammond, "Protestant Legal Theory?," 89.

15. Hammond, "Protestant Legal Theory?," 89. Hammond acknowledges that, conceived in this way, Protestant legal theory is a "marginal approach to legal theory" that is essentially confessional, though subject to the rigor of academic theology and academic jurisprudence.

16. Robbers, "Woran das Recht," 35. The rights-centered orientation of American law has also been noted by American writers: "Americans appear more oriented toward self-interest and less toward community well-being that many other peoples in the world" (Jacob, "Law and Courts," 26).

and religion relate to each other.[17] It also reflects differences internal to the German and American legal orders, with their different systems of litigation and contrasting costs and burdensomeness.

These cultural differences would seem to limit the relevance of continental theologies and ethics of law for an American setting. Yet continental and American cultures and legal systems confront many common questions and imperatives, including: the relation of politics and law, the nature of legal normativity and validity, the interaction of justice and law, democratic participation in legal matters, the effect of technology on law, and the necessity of the improvement of law. But two characteristics of the American situation would appear to inhibit any theology/ethics of law: its traditional understanding of the relation of religion and the state (including law), and the role of theology in the public square. This raises a question of the plausibility of theological/ethical reflection on law in the public realm.

Theology, Ethics, Law, and the Public Square

A significant challenge for a theology/ethics of law in a North American context is the justification of theological/ethical language in the public realm. To enter into the debate about public reason and religion in the public square would lead too far afield; nevertheless, it cannot be sidestepped completely. A few thoughts follow.

Is theological engagement with law plausible in a pluralistic cultural context? A negative answer is unsatisfying for two reasons. First, law has deep historical continuities as well as structural similarities with religion. As Harold Berman observes, certain legal concepts such as equity, fault and promise in legal institutions such as marriage cannot be fully understood without their religious foundations.[18] To be sure, legal doctrines are developed and construed according to legal canons of interpretation. But that interpretation will be richer and more resonant to the extent that it regards its historical dimensions. As Huber asserts: "The development of European and American legal systems cannot be explained without the influence of Christian legal thought."[19] This is not to deny the secularity of contemporary law, only to underscore an important influence in law's evolution.

Second, many legal concepts possess a normative dimension. For example, the contractual duty of good faith deals with elements of fairness

17. See generally Jacobs, "Law and Courts."
18. For other examples, see Berman, "Christian Sources of General Contract Law."
19. Huber, "Parteiliche Rezension," 434. The work of Berman, Witte, and Alexander on this point is indispensable.

and the prevention of manipulative conduct. Aristotelian understandings of fairness and proportionality contained in the concept of communitative justice remain a vital part of the heritage of the law of contracts.[20] Though it may profess neutrality toward ultimate values, contemporary law is not without its own normativity. The difference between legal and religious domains is not a difference between normativity and non-normativity, but between different varieties of normativity. According to James Davison Hunter, "The distinction between law and religion as separate spheres of discourse is overstated because, by necessity, both are infused with normativity; both are inextricably addressing questions of the common good."[21] While the ethics of religious traditions are overtly value-oriented (though not necessarily unambiguously), the secular character of law, in Hunter's view, conceals its normativity "within a *habitus* or systems of dispositions, tendencies, and inclinations" that are sustained by "immense plausibility structures."[22] The shared characteristic of normativity invites interaction between law and religion as distinct yet not disjunctive normative systems. These normativities inform and interrogate each other in light of their intrinsic values.

This suggests that theological and ethical engagement with law is neither irrelevant nor inappropriate when law interprets its own history (which it constantly does) or when it must wrestle with matters of ethical significance. The interactions between law and theology question assumptions about the autonomy of law and the purported normative neutrality of the public realm. This does not mean that a theology or ethics of law should provide decisional criteria for law; of course, they should not. But it also means that they may critically scrutinize law and its functioning.

Obviously, religious/ethical perspectives can be expressed in various ways in public discourse. They can be offered in a direct and unmediated manner, as axiomatic propositions based on revelation, scripture, or ecclesial authority, and presented as authoritative and binding. For law, this mode of expression is untenable. It violates what Rawls terms the "duty of civility" that requires positions in the public square to be advanced without appeal to non-public reasons.[23] The scope of this duty is debatable, but if it applies to any public activity, it is certainly applicable to law. Alternatively, one could simply refrain from any public expression of religious or ethical convictions and embrace whatever secular position that approximates one's

---

20. See Berman, "Christian Sources," 138–41; McCauliff, "Historical Perspective."
21. Hunter, "Law, Religion, and the Common Good," 1077.
22. Hunter, "Law, Religion, and the Common Good," 1071–72.
23. Rawls, *Political Liberalism*, 218.

religious/ethical views. This would result in self-censorship of expression of one's deep values. This seems currently to be a common practice in the United States regarding law.[24]

As a third alternative, one could advance reasonably comprehensible principles ("secondary" or "second-order" principles) derived from and informed by principles expressive of one's worldview ("primary" or "first-order" principles). "Principle" is used here in the sense of that proposed by Ronald Dworkin: "a standard that is to be observed, not because it will advance or secure an economic, political, or social situation deemed desirable, but because it is a requirement of justice or fairness or some other dimension of morality."[25] Theological-ethical assertions, as primary, first-order principles could engender second-order views about law, intelligible in themselves, that would stand in tiered relation to first-order principles.[26]

Second-order principles would be inspired by and indirectly reflect first-order principles without explicit inclusion of their theological or metaphysical groundings. Though secondary principles lack the fullness and depth of their primary counterparts, they can nevertheless express values embedded in them. This tiered relation between primary and secondary principles envisions their interaction as involving extrapolation rather than translation. Extrapolation is a form of derivation, while translation aims at producing equivalents. An extrapolated principle would not be expressed in comprehensive or absolute terms, nor would it appeal to scripture or revelation for authority. Instead, it would reflect, indirectly, a congruent concern or value. An example of a first-order principle could be the concept of creation as the physical habitat of all forms of life divinely entrusted to human stewardship; a second-order principle based on it could be an obligation to protect and conserve the physical environment for the welfare of all lifeforms—a goal that benefits both the environment and all forms of life, and that is consistent with, without express mention, a divinely imposed obligation to do the same.

Some would dispute that theology and ethics can be meaningfully be separated and would also resist the notion that theological ideas can be translated into ethical ones without a loss of substance. This is a legitimate

---

24. In a review of a book on Christian legal theory, William Stuntz remarks that "in America's legal conversation, Christianity is an unwelcome guest." As a result, in the realm of law and legal theory, "Christian voices are nearly silent" (Stuntz, "Christian Legal Theory," 1707).

25. Dworkin, *Taking Rights Seriously*, 22.

26. See Shingleton, "Law, Principle, and the Global Ethic," 43–64. In that essay, I alternately referred to primary principles as "metaprinciples." For the sake of simplicity, I adhere here to "primary principles" or "first-order principles."

concern, but it is not fatal. Secondary principles will ideally convey something of importance to its primary principle in generally accessible terms. It can allude to a first-order principle at the same time as standing on its own. Within a faith community, first-order and second-order principles would coexist without separation.

In this construct, Barth's Christological view of law, Elull's concept of law as covenant and Erik Wolf's notion of biblically-guided law would qualify as primary, first-order principles in that they are grounded in, and expressed in the vocabulary of, fundamental theological assertions. Huber's legal ethic of preferential concern for the disadvantaged, though scripturally-based, could be viewed as a second-order principle arguably justifiable on consequentialist grounds, similar to Rawls's second principle of justice—the difference principle.[27]

According to this theory, justice could be either a primary or secondary principle. As we have seen, theologians such as Brunner and Ellul contend that human justice can only be adequately understood in relation to divine justice. Obviously, though, many people speak of justice without reference to any divine basis or template for it. Aristotle referred to the general, legal form of justice as corresponding and practicing universal virtue in dealing with others. For him, "what we do as a result of practicing virtue in general are those very actions which conform to law."[28] Kreß proposes an understanding of justice without explicit theological reference; nevertheless it has foundational significance for the legal order in that a principal responsibility of that order is to preserve and stabilize justice.[29] Justice is broadly meaningful and evocative. It will have special resonance in communal contexts to the extent that it is theologically grounded. If it is not, it will nevertheless be meaningful and will support respect for principles such as fairness, equity, impartiality, and equality.

This two-tiered model of principles has affinities to what Heinrich Bedford-Strohm refers to as bilinguality. By this, he means that "public theology needs both theological and reason-based language."[30] It requires a capacity for translation and for expressive parallelism. Like a bilingual text, each principle has an integrity of its own and in relation to the other

---

27. That principle states that the social and economic inequalities should be arranged so that they are to the greatest benefit of the least advantaged, and are attached to positions and offices open to all on fair and equal terms. See Rawls, *Theory of Justice*, 302.

28. Aristotle, *Nicomachean Ethics*, 144.

29. Kreß, *Ethik der Rechtsordnung*, 210.

30. Bedford-Strohm, "Public Theology and Political Ethics," 283.

principle.[31] Both of the concepts of tiered principles and bilinguality are implicitly discursive and communicative. They reflect an understanding of faith groupings and political societies as linguistic communities.[32] In the context of public engagement with positive law, they suggest that such engagement will consist essentially in discourse and deliberation rather than consensus. As Arif Jamal contends, "We will have to embrace a greater and more raucous polyphony them liberalism may have imagined."[33] Instead of banal and trivial openness, this public discourse requires a robust and vigorous openness of each toward her counterpart, amounting to what Habermas calls a "complementary learning process."[34] Given the current cultural climate in the United States, this presents a considerable civic challenge. But it is not impossible.

What other kinds of second-order principles would be supported by the critical temper of Protestant attitudes toward positive law? Other candidate principles include equality, fairness, equal access to law and democratic participation in the improvement of law. The principles would scrutinize distortions and subversions of law, whether due to economic influence or political manipulation, limitation on access to justice, excessive legalization and under-legalization.[35] These principles could be anchored in first-order principles of human personhood, love, or neighborliness that are meaningful in faith communities. The second-order principles could intersect with secular counterpart principles on the "common ground" of justice.[36]

It is important that theological/ethical reflections on positive law should be presented in way that dispels apprehensions about proselytism. This is not merely a tactical consideration: several of the writers here affirm

31. Of course, the concept of primary-secondary principles includes a hierarchical relation that bilinguality does not. But translation has a certain hierarchy of its own in that one text proceeds from the other; in this sense the latter is derived from the original.

32. Regarding the cultural-linguistic character of faith communities, see Lindbeck, *Nature of Doctrine*, 32–33, where he refers to religion as a communal phenomenon that "comprises a vocabulary of discursive and non-discursive symbols together with a distinctive logic or grammar in terms of which this vocabulary can be meaningfully deployed."

33. Jamal, "Addressing Religious Plurality," 345.

34. Habermas, "Secularization," 47.

35. Brunner rightly asserts that the failure to regulate activities that require regulation is as much a violation of justice as excessive regulation. "The legal system of the country can become unjust ... through what it fails to regulate" (Brunner, *Justice*, 211).

36. It is perhaps with regard to justice that religious and secular thought most directly engage. In Brunner's view, Justice "is a topic where Christian and non-Christian thinking meet, where they have a common ground without being identical" (Brunner, *Civilization*, 2:108).

that positive law can be an arena of encounter between Christians and non-Christians. Ideally, the interaction of theology, ethics and law can be beneficial for each of them. For each has insights that can be valuable for the other.

Confronting Common Quandaries

Despite contrasts in legal culture between German and American legal systems, they face an array of common social, political, technological and environmental challenges. They include climate change, genetic engineering, abortion, assisted suicide and others. Dealing with them requires the expertise of various disciplines, including law and ethics. Huber and Kreß both devote significant attention to identifying ethical challenges for which an ethics of law is relevant. Comparative insights on these matters are often valuable, and the experiences of one legal system can be quite helpful for another. Though they are reflect culturally influences, ethical perspectives are not bounded by political boundaries in the way law is, they transcend them. An ethics of law can and should be relevant across legal systems, at least in offering comparative insights about problems common to all societies. In this sense, an ethics of law as seriously elaborated by writers such as Huber and Kreß, both writing in a German context, can have relevance for a North American context.

Implications for Contemporary Theological and Ethical Reflection on Law

To return to the question of the relevance of theologies or ethics of law for North America, how can they be useful in a political society so different from those of continental Europe? What, if any, elements of the theologies and ethics of law treated in this book are appropriate and useful for a North American context? The following possibilities come to mind.

First, the contextualization of law entailed by these theologies and ethics of law here would be relevant for an American setting. Alienation from law, excessive legalization and erosion of the legitimacy and authority of law are also observable in the United States. Contextualization would not eliminate these problems, but it would contribute to a broader and more affirmative understanding of law that, in turn, could help address them. It offers a more constructive view of law's possibilities than minimalist alternatives in which law is essentially a compendium of rules and regulations, administered by an insular cohort of legal technicians, primarily concerned with the orderly functioning of society.

Second, these theologies and ethics of law resist the political manipulation and exploitation of law. If law is seen less as a substitute for social morality or as an instrument of political power, if it is related to scriptural and prophetic traditions and to foundational social practices, then it becomes more mindful of its aspirational vocation as the moral conscience and imagination of a political community. If, instead of being weaponized as an instrument for partisan purposes and becoming a more democratically legitimated sphere for preserving and enhancing just and orderly social organization, fairly arbitrating between conflicting visions of a good society, then both law and society will benefit. This positive role for law is also supported by the contextualization of law. A contextualized concept of law would heighten appreciation of various aspects of its higher vocation: promotion of tolerance (Kreβ), realizable justice (Thielicke), protection of human dignity (Huber), securing of human rights (Ellul), and promoting recognition of others (Pannenberg). Obviously, a change in how one understands law will certainly not banish politics from it, nor will it fundamentally alter law's relation to violence or its capacity for injustice. But it would, hopefully, enhance appreciation of law's ethical significance beyond its practical utility.

Third, these continental reflections on law are relevant in encouraging broad-based citizen engagement with law. This is a *desideratum* for American legal culture as it is for every other one. Such engagement would enrich the collective moral imagination and enlarge the vocabulary for the critique and improvement of law. Civic engagement can also counter partisan misuse of law and strengthen its legitimacy. It will not only be manifest in efforts to alter the letter of the law as to affect its spirit. It would be more in the form of what James Davison Hunter refers to as "faithful presence."[37] This is both ambitious and modest. It is ambitious in entailing involvement in the seemingly arcane sphere of law; it is modest in not seeking dramatic change but steady improvement. As Zachary Calo phrases it, it will not be a matter of attempting to capture law for the good but of being present in it.[38]

Within the context of this engagement, particular attention would be directed to the notion of justice particularly in the form of legal justice. Ralf Dreier defines legal justice as a property of law "through which a generally consensus-capable order for compensation and for the distribution of goods

37. Hunter, *To Change the World*, 243–48.

38. He states further "Faithful presence in law is thus less about transforming law than in imagining and embodying its meaning made anew" (Calo, "Faithful Presence and Theological Jurisprudence," 1089).

and duties is preserved and established."³⁹ This reflects the distributionist emphasis in many contemporary conceptions of justice. While this is an important element of justice, it is not the whole of it. Citizens can and should participate in the continuous task of determining what a fuller sense of justice—including legal justice—should be for a given time and place. With its strong interest in fairness, equality and equity, legal justice both undergirds and leavens law. Yet, it is oftentimes difficult to reconcile the daily operation of the law with the demands of a worthy idea of legal justice.

In sum, these implications suggest that these theologies and ethics of law have something to offer for the contemporary American legal environment. They reflect what Huber describes as a Christian co-responsibility for law that involves critical loyalty to the legal order.[40] But this is not only a Christian or religious task but a pluralistically civic one. It may involve questions of jurisprudential interest. One key theme of contemporary jurisprudence is the legitimation of law. Unless law's legitimacy is to be based on coercion alone, it must have some kind of normative grounding. As Andrei Marmor contends: "In every legal system, we reach a point where some account must be given, in nonlegal terms, to explain what grants certain actions and events the legal significance they have."[41] The legal significance of which Marmor speaks has an irreducibly normative aspect. Among other things, it involves respect for law, a duty of qualified obedience to law, and appreciation of the importance of law for ordered social existence.

But co-responsibility for law need not, and in many cases will not, involve abstract jurisprudential matters. Instead, it will more often consist of practical activities that increase the justness of political arrangements, commercial activity, human rights, and the functioning of the legal system itself. It could involve, for example, participation in litigation through *amicus curae* submissions. As Ruben Garcia has argued, litigation and the judiciary play important roles in defining the contours of a deliberative democracy. Citizen participation in legislation and litigation are forms of speech and petition to which the courts should give appropriate consideration. They serve to broaden the transparency and democratic legitimacy of a judicial system.[42] They also provide a means for public input regarding the develop-

---

39. Dreier, "Justice—Law," 113.

40. See Huber, *Gerechtigkeit*, 140; "Recht als Beruf," 39, where Huber contends that all who are concerned with responsibility for common life must concern themselves with law as a basic characteristic of human coexistence. See also Pannenberg, "Christliche Rechtsüberzeugungen," 265–66.

41. Marmor, *Philosophy of Law*, 49.

42. Garcia, "Democratic Theory of Amicus Advocacy," 315–57.

ment of the law.[43] To be sure, such engagement must respect contemporary pluralistic circumstances, but this is a qualification, not an invalidation.

Obviously, in none of these activities should theology or ethics seek to sacralize law. They have something to say about the legitimacy of law, what it requires, and how it relates to desirable political visions and notions of the common good. Their contributions in most cases should be offered "bilingually" through second-order principles such as justice, human dignity and human rights. Appreciation of these principles within faith communities will draw on first-order, theologically informed principles. But they will also be meaningful in a secular context when formulated in a vernacular of shared historical experiences, rational intelligibility and concern for human rights and values.

The marginalization and neglect of positive law in theological and ethical reflection is as undesirable from a North American perspective as it is from a continental one. The relation of law to its social and ethical context, its applicability beyond nations and states, its role in informing the understanding of political community, its character as a theologically significant form of social interaction: these are themes that invite further exploration. Engagement with them is worthwhile given law's prominence and importance in contemporary societies. Theological and ethical reflection can play a modest yet meaningful role in that engagement. Accordingly, the reflections of these Protestant theologians and ethicists on positive law are not only historically instructive but also are prolegomena for future thought and action.

---

43. An example of use of amicus submissions by a noted Christian ethicist is Stanley Hauerwas, who has been a party to several amicus briefs. See Inazu, "Stanley Hauerwas and the Law," in 5.

Bibliography

Adams, James L. "Law and the Religious Spirit: Rudolph Sohm." In *On Being Human Religiously: Selected Essays on Religion and Society*, edited by Max L. Stackhouse, 188–206. Boston: Beacon, 1976.
Alexander, Frank S. "Beyond Positivism." In *The Weightier Matters of the Law: Essays on Law and Religion; A Tribute to Harold Berman*, edited by John Witte Jr. and Frank S. Alexander, 251–84. Atlanta: Scholars, 1988.
———. "The Validity and Function of Law: The Reformation Doctrine of *Usus Legis*." *Mercer Law Review* 31 (1980) 509–529.
Althaus, Paul. *The Divine Command*. Translated by Franklin Sherman. Philadelphia: Fortress, 1966.
Alwast, Jendris. *Dialektik und Rechtstheologie. Eine Grundlagenuntersuchung zu Ansatz und Methode der rechtstheologischen Konstruktion "Christokratie und Bruderschaft" von Erik Wolf*. Köln: Böhlau, 1984.
Aristotle. *Nicomachean Ethics*. Translated by J. A. K. Thomson. London: Penguin, 1953.
Aulen, Gustav. *Law, Church, and Society*. New York: Scribner's, 1947.
Aultman, Mark. "Technology and the End of Law." *American Journal of Jurisprudence* 17 (1972) 46–79.
Aus Der Au, Christina. "Being Christian in the World: The *Tertius Usus Legis* as the Starting Point of a Reformed Ethic." *Studies in Christian Ethics* 28 (2015) 130–41.
Barnett, Victoria. *For the Soul of the People: The Protestant Resistance to Hitler*. Oxford: Oxford University Press, 1992.
Barth, Karl. "The Christian Community and the Civil Community." In *Community, State, Church*, translated by G. Howe, et al., 149–89. Garden City, NY: Doubleday, 1960.
———. "Church and State." In *Community, State, Church*, translated by G. Howe, et al., 101–148. Garden City, NY: Doubleday, 1960.
———. *Church Dogmatics*. 13 vols. Translated by G. T. Thompson, et al. Edinburgh: T&T Clark, 1936–77.
———. "Die christliche Gemeinde und die bürgerliche Gemeinde." *Theologische Studien* 104 (1970) 49–81.
———. *Eine Schweizerische Stimme. 1938–45*. Zurich: Theologischer, 1945.
———. *Ethics*. Edited by Dieter Braun. Translated by Geoffrey Bromiley. New York: Seabury, 1981.
———. *Ethik I 1928*. Edited by Dieter Braun. Zurich: Theologischer, 1973.
———. *Ethik II 1928/30*. Edited by Dieter Braun. Zurich: Theologischer, 1978.

———. *Gespräche: 1963*. Edited by Eberhard Busch. Zurich: Theologischer, 2005.
———. *The Holy Spirit and The Christian Life*. Translated by R. Birch Hoyle. Louisville: Westminster, 1993.
———. *Kirchliche Dogmatik*. 15 vols. Zollikon-Zurich: Evangelischer, 1955–67.
———. "Rechtfertigung und Recht." *Theologische Studien* 104 (1970) 5–47.
———. *The Word of God and The Word of Man*. Translated by Douglas Horton. New York: Harper, 1957.
Bauer-Tornach, Günther. *Sozialgestalt und Recht der Kirche: Eine Untersuchung zum Verhältnis Karl Barth und Erik Wolf*. New York: Peter Lang, 1992.
Baxter, Hugh. "Niklas Luhmann's Theory of Autopoietic Legal Systems." *Annual Review of Law and Social Science* 9 (2013) 167–84.
Beaumont, Paul. *Christian Perspectives on the Limits of Law*. London: Paternoster, 2002.
Bedford-Strohm, Heinrich. "Public Theology and Political Ethics." *International Journal of Public Theology* 6 (2012) 273–91.
Bell, John. "Justice and the Law." In *Justice: Interdisciplinary Perspectives*, edited by Klaus Scherer, 114–42. Cambridge: Cambridge University Press, 1994.
Berman, Harold J. "Christian Sources of General Contract Law." In *Christianity and Law: An Introduction*, edited by John Witte Jr. and Frank Alexander, 125–42. Cambridge: Cambridge University Press, 2008.
———. *The Interaction of Law and Religion*. Nashville: Abingdon, 1974.
———. "Law and Logos." *DePaul Law Review* 44 (1994) 143–64.
Betz, Hans Dieter, et al., eds. *Religion Past and Present: Encyclopedia of Theology and Religion*. 14 vols. Leiden: Brill, 2007–2013.
Biggar, Nigel. "Barth's Trinitarian Ethics." In *The Cambridge Companion to Karl Barth*, edited by John Webster, 212–27. Cambridge: Cambridge University Press, 2000.
———. *The Hastening That Waits: Karl Barth's Ethics*. Oxford: Clarendon, 1993.
Black, Henry, ed. *Black's Law Dictionary*. 4th rev. ed. Minneapolis: West, 1968.
Borgmann, Albert. *Technology and the Character of Contemporary Life: A Philosophical Inquiry*. Chicago: University of Chicago Press, 1984.
Bromiley, Geoffrey. "Barth's Influence on Jacques Ellul." In *Jacques Ellul: Interpretive Essays*, edited by Clifford G. Christians and Jay M. Van Hook, 32–51. Urbana: University of Illinois Press, 1981.
Brunner, Emil. *Christianity and Civilization*. 2 vols. New York: Scribner's, 1948.
———. *The Divine Imperative: A Study in Christian Ethics*. Translated by Olive Wyon. Philadelphia: Westminster, 1947.
———. *Dogmatics I. The Christian Doctrine of God*. Translated by Olive Wyon. Philadelphia: Westminster, 1950.
———. *Dogmatics II. The Christian Doctrine of Creation and Redemption: The Christian Doctrine of God*. Translated by Olive Wyon. Philadelphia: Westminster, 1952.
———. *Dogmatics III. The Christian Doctrine of the Church, Faith, and the Consummation*. Translated by David Cairns. Philadelphia: Westminster, 1962.
———. *Justice and the Social Order*. Translated by Mary Hoettinger. New York: Harper, 1945.
———. *Man in Revolt: A Christian Anthropology*. Translated by Olive Wyon. Philadelphia: Westminster 1947.
Busch, Eberhard. *Karl Barth: His Life from Letters and Autobiographical Texts*. Translated by John Bowden. Philadelphia: Fortress, 1976.

———. *Unten dem Bogen des einen Bundes: Karl Barth und die Juden 1933–1945*. Neukirchen-Vluyn: Neukirchener, 1996.
Calavita, Kitty. *Invitation to Law and Society*. 2nd ed. Chicago Series in Law and Society. Chicago: University of Chicago Press, 2016.
Calo, Zachary. "Faithful Presence and Theological Jurisprudence: A Response to James Davison Hunter." *Pepperdine Law Review* 39 (2013) 1083–89.
Calvin, Jean. *Institutes of Christian Religion*. Translated by Henry Beveridge. 2 vols. Grand Rapids: Eerdmans, 1957.
Carney, Frederick. "Review of *The Theological Foundation of Law*, by Jacques Ellul." *Perkins Journal* (1962) 43–44.
Cassin, Barbara, ed. *Dictionary of Untranslatables: A Philosophical Lexicon*. Translated by Stephen Rendall, et al. Princeton: Princeton University Press, 2014.
Center for the Study of Law and Religion, Emory University. "Christian Jurisprudence II." http://cslr.law.emory.edu/research-programs/law-and-christianity/christian-jurisprudence-ii.html.
Charles, Daryl. *Retrieving the Natural Law: A Return to First Things*. Grand Rapids: Eerdmans, 2008.
Chase, Edward, "Law and Theology." In *A Companion to the Philosophy of Law and Legal Theory*, edited by Dennis Patterson, 421–35. Oxford: Blackwell, 1996.
Cobb, Daniel. "Review of *The Theological Foundation of Law*, by Jacques Ellul." *Encounter* 31 (1970) 286–87.
Cochran, Robert, Jr. "Christian Traditions, Culture and Law." In *Christian Perspectives on Legal Thought*, edited by Michael McConnell, et al., 242–52. New Haven: Yale University Press, 2001.
Cole, David. *Engines of Liberty: The Power of Citizen Activists to Make Constitutional Law*. New York: Basic, 2016.
"The Competing Claims of Law and Religion." *Pepperdine Law Review* 39.5 (2013).
Cotterell, Roger. "Comparative Law and Legal Culture." In *The Oxford Handbook of Comparative Law*, edited by Mathias Reimann and Reinhard Zimmermann, 710–33. Oxford: Oxford University Press, 2006.
Couvenhoven, Jesse. "Karl Barth's Eschatological Rejection of Natural Law: An Eschatological Natural Law Theory of Divine Demand." In *Natural Law and Evangelical Political Thought*, edited by Bryan T. McGraw, et al., 35–55. Lanham, MD: Lexington, 2013.
Cover, Robert. "Violence and the Word." *Yale Law Journal* 95 (1985) 1601–629.
Dabrock, Peter. "Helmut Thielicke." *Zeitschrift für evangelische Ethik* 63 (2018) 154–58.
Dallmayr, Frederick. "Faith and Communicative Freedom: A Tribute to Wolfgang Huber." In *Freedom and Solidarity: Toward New Beginnings*, by Frederick Dallmayr, 135–52. Lexington: University of Kentucky Press, 2016.
Dombois, Hans. *Recht und Institution*. Zweite Folge. Stuttgart: Ernst Klett, 1969.
Dreier, Ralf. "Hans Dombois." In *RPP* 4:156.
———. "Justice-Law." In *RPP* 6:113–14.
———. "Recht." In vol. 3 of *Evangelisches Kirchenlexikon*, edited by Erwin Fahlbusch et al., 1445–55. Stuttgart: Kohlhammer, 2006.
Dujancourt, Sylvain. "Law and Ethics in Ellul's Theology." Translated by Charles L. Creegan. *The Ellul Studies Forum* 5 (1990) 10–11.

Durham, Cole. "Religion and Criminal Law" In *The Weightier Matters of the Law: Essays on Law and Religion*, edited by John Witte Jr. and Frank S. Alexander, 193–228. Atlanta: Scholars, 1988.

Durham, Cole, et al. "Editorial." *Oxford Journal of Law and Religion* 1 (2012) 1–4.

Dworkin, Ronald. *Law's Empire*. Cambridge, MA: Harvard University Press, 1986.

———. *Taking Rights Seriously*. Cambridge, MA: Harvard University Press, 1977.

Eagleton, Terry. *Reason, Faith & Revolution: Reflections on the God Debate*. New Haven: Yale University Press, 2010.

Ellul, Jacques. *In Season, Out of Season: An Introduction to the Thought of Jacques Ellul; Based on Interviews by Madeleine Garrigou-Lagrange*. Translated by Lani Niles. San Francisco: Harper & Row, 1982.

———. *The Presence of the Kingdom*. Translated by Olive Wyon. Colorado Springs: Helmers & Howard, 1989.

———. *The Technological Society*. Translated by John Wilkinson. New York: Knopf, 1964.

———. *The Theological Foundation of Law*. Translated by Marguerite Wieser. New York: Doubleday, 1969.

———. *To Will & To Do: An Ethical Research for Christians*. Translated by C. Edward Hopkins. Philadelphia: Pilgrim, 1969.

———. *What I Believe*. Translated by Geoffrey W. Bromiley. Grand Rapids: Eerdmans, 1989.

Ericksen, Robert. *Theologians under Hitler*. New Haven: Yale University Press, 2010.

Faye, Emmanuel. *Heidegger: The Introduction of Nazism into Philosophy in Light of the Unpublished Seminars of 1933–1935*. Translated by Michael Smith. New Haven: Yale University Press, 2009.

Fazakas, Sandor. "Karl Barth." *Zeitschrift für evangelische Ethik* 62 (2018) 213–17.

Foljanty, Lena. *Recht oder Gesetz: Juristische Identität und Authorität in den Naturrechtsdebatten der Nachkriegszeit*. Tübingen: Mohr-Siebeck, 2013.

Fort, Timothy. *Law and Religion*. Jefferson, NC: McFarland, 1987.

Frei, Norbert. *Adenauer's Germany and the Nazi Past: The Politics of Amnesty and Integration*. Translated by Joel Golb. New York: Columbia University Press, 2002.

Fuller, Lon. *The Morality of the Law*. New Haven: Yale University Press, 1964.

Gäfgen, Kerstin. *Das Recht in der Korrelation von Dogmatik und Ethik*. Berlin: de Gruyter, 1991.

Garcia, Ruben. "A Democratic Theory of Amicus Advocacy." *Florida State Law Review* 35 (2008) 315–57.

Gascoigne, Robert. *The Public Form and Christian Ethics*. Cambridge: Cambridge University Press, 2001.

Gessler, Philipp. *Wolfgang Huber: Ein Leben für Protestantismus und Politik*. Freiburg: Herder, 2017.

Goddard, Andrew. "Law, Rights and Technology." *The Ellul Studies Forum* 23 (1999) 5–8.

———. *Living the Word, Resisting the World: The Life and Thought of Jacques Ellul*. Carlisle: Paternoster, 2002.

Goodrich, Peter. "Law and Religion: Law, Religion, and Critical Theory." In vol. 8 of *Encyclopedia of Religion*, edited by Lindsay Jones, et al., 5358–61. 2nd ed. Detroit: Thomson Gale, 2005.

Gordon, Bruce. *Calvin*. New Haven: Yale University Press, 2009.

Grabill, Stephen. *Rediscovering Natural Law in Reformed Theological Ethics*. Grand Rapids: Eerdmans, 2006.

Greenawalt, Kent. "Reflections on Christian Jurisprudence." In vol. 1 of *The Teachings of Modern Christianity on Law, Politics, and Government*, edited by John Witte Jr. and Frank S. Alexander, 715–51. New York: Columbia University Press, 2006.

Greenman, Jeffrey P., et al. *Understanding Jacques Ellul*. Eugene, OR: Cascade, 2012.

Grenz, Stanley. *Reason for Hope: The Systematic Theology of Wolfgang Pannenberg*. 2nd ed. Grand Rapids: Eerdmans, 2005.

Guardini, Romano. *Welt und Person: Versuche zur christliche Lehre vom Menschen*. Würzburg: Werkbund, 1939.

Gundlach, Thies. "Theologische Ethik unter modern Bedingungen: Zu den politischen Implikationen der Ethik Karl Barths 1928/29." *Kerygma und Dogma* 37 (1991) 209–226.

Habermas, Jürgen. "Religion in the Public Square." *European Journal of Philosophy* 14 (2006) 1–25.

———. "Secularization as a Twofold and Complementary Learning Process." In *The Dialectics of Secularization: On Reason and Religion*, edited by Florian Schuller, 43–48. Translated by Brian McNeil. San Francisco: Ignatius, 2006.

Haddorff, David. *Ethics as Witness: Barth's Ethics for a World at Risk*. Eugene, OR: Cascade, 2010.

———. Introduction to *Community, State, Church*, by Karl Barth. 1960. Reprint, Eugene, OR: Wipf & Stock, 2004.

Hammond, Jeffrey. "Protestant Legal Theory? Apology and Objections." *Journal of Law and Religion* 32 (2017) 86–92.

Hart, John. *Karl Barth vs. Emil Brunner: The Formation and Dissolution of a Theological Alliance*. New York: Peter Lang, 2001.

Hatzel, Eveline. "Nationalsozialistisches Rechtsdenken." *Jura* 11 (1997) 575–81.

Heinig, Hans Michael. "Gerechtigkeit im demokratisch legitimierten Recht. Eine verfassungstheoretische Perspektive auf Karl Barths 'Christengemeinde und Bürgergemeinde.'" *Zeitschrift für dialektische Theologie* 28 (2012) 87–103.

Herget, James E. *Contemporary German Legal Philosophy*. Philadelphia: University of Pennsylvania Press, 1996.

Herms, Eilert. *Politik und Recht im Pluralismus*. Tübingen: Mohr-Siebeck, 2008.

Herr, Theodor. *Zur Frage nach dem Naturrecht im deutschen Protestantismus der Gegenwart*. München: Schöningh, 1972.

Hesselink, I. John. *Calvin's Concept of Law*. Allison Park, PA: Pickwick, 1992.

Höffe, Ottfried. "Justice–Philosophy." In *RPP* 6:108–111.

Hollerbach, Alexander. "Erik Wolf." In *RPP* 13:523–24.

———. "Erik Wolf (1902–1977): Zur Erinnerung an einem bedeutenden Freiburger Rechtsgelehrten." In *Jurisprudenz in Freiburg: Beiträge zur Geschichte der Rechtswissenschaftlichen Fakultät der Albert-Ludwigs-Universität*, by Alexander Hollerbach, 331–44. Tübingen: Mohr-Siebeck, 2007

———. "Erik Wolfs Wirken für Kirche und Recht." In vol. 2 of *Jahrbuch für badische Kirchen und Religionsgeschichte*, edited by Albrecht Ernst, et al., 47–68. Stuttgart: Kohlhammer 2008.

———. "Zum Verhältnis von Erik Wolk und Martin Heidegger: Ein nicht abgeschickter Brief Erik Wolfs an Karl Barth." In *Heidegger-Jahrbuch 4*, edited by Holger Zaborowski and Alfred Denker, 284–347. München: Alber, 2009.

Honecker, Martin. *Auf der Suche nach Orientierung im Labyrinth der Ethik.* Stuttgart: Kohlhammer, 2017.

———. *Einführung in die theologische Ethik.* Berlin: de Gruyter, 2002.

———. *Grundriß der Sozialethik.* Berlin: de Gruyter, 1995.

———. "Kirchenrecht II." *TRE* 18:724–749.

———. "Recht, Ethos, Glaube." *Zeitschrift für evangelisches Kirchenrecht* 25 (1988) 383–404.

Huber, Wolfgang. "Barmen Theological Declaration." In *Lutheran Churches, Salt or Mirror of Society? Case Studies on the Theory and Practice of the Two Kingdom Doctrine*, edited by Ulrich Duchrow in collaboration with Dorothea Millwood, 28–48. Geneva: Lutheran World Federation, 1977.

———. "Das ethische Stichwort: Menschenwürde." *Zeitschrift für evangelische Ethik* 57 (2003) 62–65.

———. *Ethics: The Fundamental Questions of Our Lives.* Translated by Brian McNeil. Washington, DC: Georgetown University Press, 2015.

———. "Freiheit und Institution: Sozialethik als Ethik kommunikative Freiheit." In *Folgen christlicher Freiheit: Ethik und Theorie der Kirche im Horizont der Barmer Theologischen Erklärung*, by Wolfgang Huber, 113–27. 2nd ed. Neukirchen-Vluyn: Neukirchener, 1985 [English translation in *Christian Responsibility and Communicative Freedom: A Challenge for the Future Pluralistic Societies; Collected essays*, edited by Willem Fourie, 41–54. Berlin: LIT, 2012].

———. *Gerechtigkeit und Recht: Grundlinien christlicher Rechtsethik.* Gütersloh: Chr. Kaiser, 1996.

———. "Law and Jurisprudence: Ethics of Law." *RPP* 7:366–67.

———. "Legitimes Recht und legitime Rechtsgewalt in theologischer Perspektive." In *Gewalt und Gewalten. Zur Ausübung, Legitimität und Ambivilanz rechtserhaltender Gewalt*, edited by Torsten Meireis, 225–31 Tübingen: Mohr-Siebeck, 2012.

———. "Menschenwürde." In *TRE* 22:577–60.

———. "Parteiliches Rezenzion?" *Archiv für Rechts- und Sozialanthropologie* 85 (1991) 434–40.

———. "Recht als Beruf–Verantwortung für das Recht im Horizont der Gerechtigkeit." In *Ist der Rechtsstaat auch ein Gerechtigkeitsstaat?: Interdisziplinäre Referatsreihe an der Universität Basel im Wintersemester 1998/1999*, edited by Denise Buser, et al., 31–59. Interdisziplinäre Referatsreihe an der Universität Basel. Basel: Helbing & Lichtenhahn, 2000.

———. "Recht im Horizont der Liebe—Eine theologische Skizze." In *Ein Richter, ein Bürger, ein Christ. Festschrift für Helmut Simon*, edited by Willy Brandt, et al., 1045–58. Baden-Baden: Nomos, 1987.

———. "Rechtsethik." In *Handbuch der Evangelischer Ethik*, edited by Wolfgang Huber, et al., 127–93. München: C. H. Beck, 2014.

———. *Violence: The Unrelenting Assault on Human Dignity.* Translated by Ruth C. L. Gritch. Minneapolis: Fortress, 1996.

Hunsinger, George. *How to Read Karl Barth.* New York: Oxford University Press, 1991.

Hunter, James D. "Law, Religion, and the Common Good." *Pepperdine Law Review* 39 (2013) 1065–82.

———. *To Change the World.* New York: Oxford University Press, 2012.

Inazu, John. "Stanley Hauerwas and the Law: Is There Anything to Say?" *Law and Contemporary Problems* 75 (2012) i–xiii.

Jacob, Herbert. "Courts and Politics in the United States." In *Courts, Law & Politics in Comparative Perspective*, edited by Herbert Jacob, et al., 16–80. New Haven: Yale University Press, 1996.

Jamal, Arif. "Addressing Religious Plurality: A Consideration of Four Models." *Oxford Journal of Law and Religion* 2 (2013) 330–53.

Janssen, Albert. "Fragwürdige Abschied vom *usus politicus legis* als Grundlage evangelischen Rechts- und Staatsdenken." *Zeitschrift für evangelisches Kirchenrecht* 54 (2009) 1–33.

Jehle, Frank. *Against the Stream: The Politics of Karl Barth's Theology, 1906-1968*. Translated by David and Mary Barrett. Grand Rapids: Eerdmans, 2002.

———. *Emil Brunner: Theologe im 20. Jahrhundert*. Zurich: Theologischer, 2006.

Jüngel, E. *Christ, Justice, and Peace: Toward a Theology of the State in Dialogue with the Barmen Declaration*. Translated by D. Bruce Hamill and Alan J. Torrance. Edinburgh: T&T Clark, 1992.

Kelsen, Hans. "What Is Justice?" In *Essays in Legal and Moral Philosophy*, by Hans Kelsen, 1–26. Translated by Peter Heath. Dordrecht: Riedel, 1973.

Kistner, Peter. *Rechtstheologie: Ein Problemdurchgang*. Münster: LIT, 2017.

Kommers, Donald, and Russell Miller. *The Constitutional Jurisprudence of the Federal Republic of Germany*. 3rd ed. Durham: Duke University Press, 2012.

Kreβ, Hartmut. *Ethik der Rechtsordnung: Staat, Grundrechte und Religionen im Licht der Rechtsordnung*. Stuttgart: Kohlhammer, 2012.

———. "Review of *Gerechtigkeit und Recht*, by Wolfgang Huber." *Zeitschrift für evangelische Ethik* 41 (1997) 235–38.

———. *Staat und Person: Politische Ethik im Umbruch des modernen Staats*. Stuttgart: Kohlhammer, 2018.

Küng, Hans. *Global Responsibility: In Search of a New World Ethic*. Translated by John Bowden. New York: Crossroad, 1991.

Lampe, Ernst-Joachim. "Rechtsanthropologie Heute." *Archiv für Rechts- und Sozialanthropologie* 44 (1991) 222–32.

Landau, Peter. "Canon Law-Protestantism." In *RPP* 2:357–71.

Lange, Dietz. *Ethik in evangelischer Perspektive*. Göttingen: Vandenhoeck & Ruprecht, 1992.

Laubscher, Martin. "A Search for Karl Barth's Public Theology: Looking into Some Defining Areas of His Work in the Post-World War II Years." *Journal of Reformed Theology* 1 (2007) 231–46.

Lienemann, Wolfgang. "Gewalt, Macht, Recht: Gewaltprävention und Rechtsentwicklung nach Karl Barth." *Zeitschrift für Dialektische Theologie* 17 (2001) 153–69.

Lindbeck, George. *The Nature of Doctrine*. Philadelphia: Westminster, 1984.

Lindenlauf, Herbert. *Karl Barth und die Lehre von der "Königsherrschaft Christi."* Spardorf: Wilfer, 1988.

Lippman, Matthew. "The Prosecution of Joseph Alstoetter, et al.: Law, Lawyers, and Justice in the Third Reich." *Dickinson Journal of International Law* 16 (1998) 343–433.

Little, David. *Religion, Law, and Order: A Study in Pre-Revolutionary England*. New York: Harper, 1969.

Lohmann, Friedrich. "Göttliches und menschliches Recht bei Jacques Ellul." *Zeitschrift für evangelische Theologie* 42 (1998) 122–39.

Lovekin, David. *Technique, Discourse, and Consciousness: An Introduction to the Philosophy of Jacques Ellul*. Bethlehem, PA: Lehigh University Press, 1991.

Lovin, Robin. *Christian Faith and Public Choices*. Philadelphia: Fortress, 1984.

Macquarrie, John. *An Existentialist Theology*. London: SCM, 1960.

Maihold, Harald. *Recht durch Liebe—Zur Rechtstheologie Wolfhart Pannenbergs aus der Perspektive des Kantischen Rechtsbegriffes*. München: GRIN, 2008.

Marmor, Andrei. *The Philosophy of Law*. Princeton: Princeton University Press, 2011.

Marsch, Wolf-Dieter. "Christliche Begründung des Rechts? Karl Barths Theologie des Rechts und die Theorie der Institutionen I." *Evangelische Theologie* 4 (1957) 145–70.

———. "Christliche Begründung des Rechts? Karl Barths Theologie des Rechts und die Theorie der Institutionen II." *Evangelische Theologie* 5 (1957) 193–218.

———. "Evangelische Theologie vor der Frage nach dem Recht." *Evangelische Theologie* 11 (1960) 481–510.

Marty, Martin E. "The Religious Foundations of Law." *Emory Law Journal* 54 (2005) 291–322.

Mathewes, Charles T. *A Theology of Public Life*. Cambridge: Cambridge University Press, 2008.

McCauliff, C. M. A. "A Historical Perspective on Anglo-American Contract Law." In *Christian Perspectives on Legal Thought*, edited by Michael McConnell, et al., 470–85. New Haven: Yale University Press, 2001.

McGrath, Alister. *Emil Brunner: A Reappraisal*. Chichester: Wiley Blackwell 2016

McIlroy, David. "Theology & Legal Theory." In *Theology, University, Humanities*, edited by Christopher Craig Brittain and Francesca Aran Murphy, 127–49. Eugene, OR: Cascade, 2011.

———. *A Trinitarian Theology of Law*. Milton Keynes: Paternoster, 2009.

Monsma, Stephen V., and J. Christopher Soper. *The Challenge of Pluralism: Church and State in Six Democracies*. Lanham, MD: Rowman & Littlefield 1997.

Morrison, Wayne. *Jurisprudence: From the Greeks to Post-Modernism*. London: Cavendish, 1997.

Moxter, Michael. "Der Mensch im Recht." *Zeitschrift für Theologie und Kirche* 105 (2008) 307–326.

———. "Recht und kommunitative Freiheit: Überlegungen zur Rechtsethik Wolfgang Hubers." In *Kommunikative Freiheit: Interdisziplinärische Diskurse mit Wolfgang Huber*, edited by Heinrich Bedford-Strohm and Paul Nolte, 109–125. Leipzig: Evangelische, 2014.

Müller, Gerhard, et al., eds. *Theologische Realenzyklopädie*. 36 vols. Berlin: de Gruyter, 1977–2004.

Müller, Ingo. *Hitler's Justice*. Translated by Deborah Lucas Schneider. Cambridge, MA: Harvard University Press, 1991.

Neville, David. "Dialectic as Method in Public Theology: Recalling Jacques Ellul." *International Journal of Public Theology* 2 (2008) 163–81.

Niebuhr, H. R. *The Responsible Self: An Essay in Christian Moral Philosophy*. New York: Harper & Row, 1963.

Niebuhr, Reinhold. "The Concept of the 'Order of Creation' in Emil Brunner's Social Ethics." In *The Theology of Emil Brunner*, edited by Charles Kegley, 265–74. New York: Macmillan, 1962.

———. *Does Civilization Need Religion?* New York: Macmillan, 1928.

———. *An Interpretation of Christian Ethics*. Cleveland: Meridian, 1963.

Nimmo, Paul. "The Orders of Creation in the Theological Ethics of Karl Barth." *Scottish Journal of Theology* 60 (2007) 24–35.

Nolte, Paul. "Theologen, Intellektuellen und soziale Bewegungen: Wolfgang Huber in der Geschichte der Bundesrepublik Deutschland bis 1989." In *Kommunikative Freiheit: Interdisziplinärische Diskurse mit Wolfgang Huber*, edited by Heinrich Bedford-Strohm and Paul Nolte, 17–38. Leipzig: Evangelische, 2014.

Nordsieck, Reinhard. *Recht und Gesetz*. Frankfurt am Main: Peter Lang, 1991.

Novak, David. "Law and Religion in Judaism." In *Christianity and Law: An Introduction*, edited by John Witte Jr. and Frank S. Alexander, 33–52. Cambridge: Cambridge University Press, 2008.

Olson, Roger. "Pannenberg's Theological Anthropology." *Perspectives in Religious Studies* 13 (1986) 161–69.

Outka, Gene. "Discontinuity in the Ethics of Jacques Ellul." In *Jacques Ellul: Interpretive Essays*, edited by Clifford G. Christians and Jay M. Van Hook, 177–228. Urbana: University of Illinois Press, 1981.

Pannenberg, Wolfhart. *Anthropology in Theological Perspective*. Translated by Matthew O'Connell. Philadelphia: Westminster, 1994.

———. *Basic Questions in Theology*. Translated by George Kehm. 2 vols. Philadelphia: Westminster, 1970–71.

———. *Beiträge zur systematischen Theologie*. 3 vols. Göttingen: Vandenhoeck & Ruprecht, 1999–2000.

———. *Christianity in a Secularized World*. Translated by John Bowden. New York: Crossroad, 1989.

———. "Christliche Rechtsbegründung." In vol. 2 of *Handbuch der christlichen Ethik*, edited by Anselm Hertz et al., 323–38. Freiburg: Herder, 1978.

———. "Christliche Rechtsüberzeugungen in einer pluralistischer Gesellschaft." *Zeitschrift für evangelische Ethik* 23 (1993) 256–66.

———. *Grundlagen der Ethik*. 2nd ed. Göttingen: Vandenhoeck & Ruprecht, 2002.

———. "An Intellectual Pilgrimage." *Kerygma & Dogma* 54 (2008) 149–58.

———. "Luther's Doctrine of the Two Kingdoms." In *Ethics*, by Wolfhart Pannenberg, 112–31. Translated by Keith Crim. Philadelphia: Westminster, 1981.

———. "On the Theology of Law." In *Ethics*, by Wolfhart Pannenberg, 23–56. Translated by Keith Crim. Philadelphia: Westminster, 1981.

———. "Recht und Religion." In *Beiträge zur Ethik*, by Wolfhart Pannenberg, 159–72. Göttingen: Vandenhoeck & Ruprecht, 2004.

———. "Religion als Ursprung des Rechtsgedanke (Diskussion)." In *Menschenrechte und kulturelle Indentität*, edited by Walter Kerber, 77–82. München: Kindt, 1991.

———. "Review of *Recht des Nächstens*, by Erik Wolf." *Archiv für Rechts- und Sozialphilosophie* 48(1962) 439–41.

———. *Systematic Theology*. Translated by Geoffrey Bromiley. 3 vols. Grand Rapids: Eerdmans, 1988–94.

———. *What Is Man?* Translated by Duane Priebe. Philadelphia: Fortress, 1970.

———. "What Is Truth?" In vol. 2 of *Basic Questions in Theology*, by Wolfhart Pannenberg, 1–28. Translated by George Kehm. Philadelphia: Westminster, 1970–71.

Pforten, Dietmar von der. "Rechtsethik." In *Angewandte Ethik*, edited by Julian Nida-Rumelin, 202–288. Stuttgart: Kröner, 2010.

Plathow, Michael. *Liebe und Recht: Zur Theologie der Liebe*. Leipzig: Evangelische Verlagsanstalt, 2018.

Pöhl, Ivar. *Das Problem des Naturrechts bei Emil Brunner*. Zurich: Zwingli, 1963.
Radbruch, Gustav. "Gesetzliches Unrecht und übergesetzliches Recht." *Süddeutsche Juristenzeitung* 1 (1946) 105–8.
Rae, Simon. "Gospel, Law and Freedom in the Ethics of Karl Barth." *Scottish Journal of Theology* 25 (1972) 412–22.
Ramsey, Paul. "Paul Tillich and Emil Brunner: Christ Transforming Natural Justice." In *Nine Modern Moralists*, by Paul Ramsey, 224–58. New York: New American, 1962.
Rawls, John. *Political Liberalism*. New York: Columbia University Press, 1993.
———. *A Theory of Justice*. Cambridge, MA: Belknap Press of Harvard University Press, 1971.
Reed, Esther. *Theology for International Law*. Edinburgh: T&T Clark, 2013.
Remy, Steven P. *The Malmedy Massacre: The War Crimes Trial Controversy*. Cambridge, MA: Harvard University Press, 2017.
Rendtorff, Trutz. *Ethics*. Translated by Keith Crim. 2 vols. Philadelphia: Fortress, 1986–89.
Reuter, Hans-Richard. "Das Recht in der Auslegung des Glaubens: Über Rechtsbegriffe in der neueren systematische Theologie." In *Rechtsethik in theologischer Perspektive*, 93–120. Gütersloh: Kaiser, 1996.
———. "Emil Brunner." *Zeitschrift für evangelische Ethik* 62 (2018) 313–16.
———. "'Fiat iustitia!' Zum Verständnis der Gerechtigkeitslehre in der Versöhnungsethik Karl Barths." In *Rechtsethik in theologischer Perspektive*, by Hans-Richard Reuter, 44–70. Gütersloh: Kaiser, 1996.
———. "Rechtsethik in der Neuzeit." In *TRE* 28:223–45.
Richardson, James. "Religion and the Law: An Interactionist View." In *The Oxford Handbook of the Sociology of Religion*, edited by Peter B. Clark, 418–31. New York: Oxford University Press, 2011.
Robbers, Gerhard. "Grundsatzfragen der heutigen Rechtstheologie—ein Bericht." *Zeitschrift für evangelisches Kirchenrecht* 37 (1992) 230–40.
———. *Law and Religion in Germany*. Alphen aan den Rijn, Netherlands: Kluwer Wolters, 2010.
———. "Woran das Recht gebunden ist: Eine Skizze." In *Vom Rechte, das mit uns geboren ist. Aktuelle Probleme des Naturrechts*, edited by Wilfried Härle, et al., 33–41. Freiburg: Herder, 2007.
Rosenau, Hartmut. "Schöpfungsordnungen." In *TRE* 30:356–58.
Safranski, Rüdiger. *Martin Heidegger: Between Good and Evil*. Translated by Ewald Osers. Cambridge, MA: Harvard University Press, 1998.
Scharleman, Robert. "Christian Theology and Law." *Lutheran Quarterly* 23 (1971) 210–22.
Scholder, Klaus. *The Year of Disillusionment, 1934*. Vol. 2 of *The Churches and the Third Reich*. Translated by John Bowden. Philadelphia: Fortress, 1988.
Schüller, Bruno. *Die Herrschaft Christi und das weltliche Recht*. Analecta Gregoriana 128. Rome: Gregorian, 1963.
Shingleton, Bradley. "Law, Principle, and the Global Ethic." In *The Global Ethic and Law: Intersections and Interactions*, edited by Bradley Shingleton and Eberhard Stilz, 43–63. Baden-Baden: Nomos, 2015.
———. "Motifs in Contemporary German Protestant Theologies of Law." *Oxford Journal of Law and Religion* 2 (2013) 278–306.
———. "Recognition and Mutuality: Pannenberg's Theology of Law." *Journal of Law and Religion* 27 (2013) 225–52.

Shklar, Judith N. *Legalism: Law, Morals, and Political Trials.* Cambridge, MA: Harvard University Press, 1986.
Simon, Helmut. "Die kritische Frage Karl Barths an die moderne Rechtstheologie." In *Antwort: Karl Barth zum siebzigsten Geburtstag am 10. Mai 1956,* by Ernst Wolf, et al., 346–56. Zollikon-Zurich: Evangelischer, 1956.
Skeel, David. "The Unbearable Lightness of Christian Legal Scholarship." *Emory Law Journal* 57 (2008) 1471–525.
Søe, Niels. "The Three Uses of Law." In *Norm and Context in Christian Ethics,* edited by Gene Outka and Paul Ramsey, 297–323. New York: Scribner's, 1968.
Staff, Ilse. *Justiz im Dritten Reich: Ein Dokumentation.* Frankfurt: Fischer, 1978.
Starck, Christian. "Law and Legislation." In *RPP* 7:373–76.
Steinmüller, Wilhelm. *Evangelische Rechtstheologie: Zweireichelehre, Christokratie. Gnadenrecht.* 2 vols. Forschungen zur kirchkichen Rechtsgeschichte und Kirchenrecht 8. Köln: Bohlau, 1968.
Stout, Jeffrey. *Democracy & Tradition.* Princeton: Princeton University Press, 2004.
Stuntz, William. "Christian Legal Theory." *Harvard Law Review* 116 (2003) 1707–749.
Sturm, Douglas. "Jacques Ellul." In *A Handbook of Christian Theologians,* edited by Martin Marty, et al., 561–82. Enlarged ed. Nashville: Abingdon, 1984.
Sullivan, Winifred F., and Robert Yelle. "Law and Religion." In *Encyclopedia of Religion,* edited by Mircea Eliade, et al., 5325–31. 2nd ed. New York: Macmillan, 2005.
"Theological Argument in Law: Engaging with Stanley Hauerwas." *Law and Contemporary Problems* 75.4 (2012).
Thielicke, Helmut. *Being Human—Becoming Human: An Essay in Christian Anthropology.* Translated by Geoffrey W. Bromiley. New York: Doubleday, 1984.
———. *The Ethics of Sex.* Translated by John W. Doberstein. New York: Harper & Row, 1964.
———. *The Evangelical Faith.* Translated by Geoffrey W. Bromiley. 3 vols. Philadelphia: Fortress, 1974–77.
———. *Modern Faith and Thought.* Translated by Geoffrey W. Bromiley. Grand Rapids: Eerdmans, 1990.
———. *Nihilism.* Translated by John Doberstein. New York: Schocken, 1969.
———. *Notes from a Wayfarer: The Autobiography of Helmut Thielicke.* Translated by David Law. New York: Paragon, 1995.
———. *Theological Ethics.* Edited by William Lazareth. 2 vols. Philadelphia: Fortress, 1966–69.
———. *Theologische Ethik.* 4 vols. Tübingen: Mohr-Siebeck, 1951–64.
Tracy, David. *The Analogical Imagination.* New York: Crossroad, 1981.
vanDrunen, David. *Natural Law and the Two Kingdoms.* Grand Rapids: Eerdmans, 2014.
Walther, Christian. "Königherrschaft." In *TRE* 19:311–23.
Wannewetsch, Bernd. "The Kingly Reign of Christ-Ethics." In *RPP* 7:197–98.
Weber, Klaus, ed. *Creifelds Rechtswörterbuch.* 18th ed. 753. München: C. H. Beck, 2004.
Weber, Max. "Religious Rejection of the World and Their Directions." In *From Max Weber: Essays in Sociology,* edited by H. P. Gerth and C. Wright Mills, 323–59. New York: Oxford University Press, 1958.
Webster, John. *Barth.* London: Continuum, 2004.
———. *Barth's Moral Theology: Human Action in Barth's Thought.* Grand Rapids: Eerdmans, 1998.

Welker, Michael. "Moral, Recht und Ethos in evangelisch-theologischer Sicht." In *Ethik und Recht*, edited by Wilfried Härle and Reiner Preul, 67–82. Marburg: Elwert, 2002.

———."What Could Christian Theology Offer to the Disciplines of the Law?" *Journal of Law and Religion* 32 (2017) 46–52.

West, Robin. *Normative Jurisprudence: An Introduction*. New York: Cambridge University Press, 2011.

Witte, John, Jr. "A New Concordance of Discordant Canons." In *The Integrative Jurisprudence of Harold Berman*, edited by Howard O. Hunter, 523–60. Boulder: Westview, 1993.

———. "Protestantism, Law and Legal Thought." In *The Blackwell Companion to Protestantism*, edited by Alister McGrath and Darren C. Marks, 298–305. Malden, MA: Blackwell, 2013.

———. "The Study of Law and Religion in the United States: An Interim Report." *Ecclesiastical Law Journal* 14 (2012) 327–54.

Wolf, Erik. "Althusius." In vol. 1 of *An Encyclopedia of Philosophy*, edited by Donald M. Borchert, 134–36. 2nd ed. Detroit: Thomson Gale, 2006.

———. "Biblische Weisung als Richtschnur des Rechts." In *Rechtsgedanke und biblische Weisung*, 33–64. Tübingen: Furche, 1948.

———. *Recht des Nächsten. Ein rechtstheologische Entwurf*. Frankfurt am Main: Klostermann, 1958.

———. "Rechtsphilosophie." In *Rechtsphilosophischen Studien*, edited by Alexander Hollerbach, 69–82. Frankfurt am Main: Klostermann, 1972.

———. "Vom Wesen der Gerechtigkeit." In *Rechtsgedanke und biblische Weisung*, by Erik Wolf, 9–32. Tübingen: Furche, 1948.

———. "Zur Dialektik von menschlicher und göttlicher Ordnung." In *Rechtstheologischen Studien*, edited by Alexander Hollerbach, 212–26. Frankfurt am Main: Klostermann, 1972.

Wolf, Ernst. "Recht." In *Evangelisches Staatslexikon*, edited by Hermann Kunst, et al., 1954–63. 2nd ed. Stuttgart: Kohlhammer, 1957.

———. "Zum Protestantischen Rechtsdenken." In *Peregrinatio II*, by Ernst Wolf, 191–205. Gütersloh: Kaiser, 1954.

Wong, Kam Ming, "From Eschatology to Anthropology: The Development of Pannenberg's Thought Over Christian Ethics." *Studies in Christian Ethics* 21 (2008) 382–402.

Woon, B. Hoo. "Pannenberg's Understanding of the Natural Law." *Studies in Christian Ethics* 25 (2012) 346–66.

Wright, William J. *Martin Luther's Understanding of God's Two Kingdoms: A Response to the Challenge of Skepticism*. Grand Rapids: Baker Academic, 2010.

Zahrnt, Heinz. *The Question of God: Protestant Theology in the 20th Century*. Translated by R. A. Wilson. New York: Harcourt Brace, 1969.

Ziefel, Helmut. *A Dictionary of Modern Theological German*. 2nd ed. Grand Rapids: Eerdmans, 1992.

www.ingramcontent.com/pod-product-compliance
Lightning Source LLC
Chambersburg PA
CBHW071247230426
43668CB00011B/1624